Arms Control in Transition

Also of Interest

Arms Control and Defense Postures in the 1980s, edited by Richard Burt

Nuclear Deterrence in U.S.-Soviet Relations, Keith B. Payne

* *Dear Survivors: Postnuclear Holocaust Planning,* John Burton

* *Arms Control and Security: Current Issues,* edited by Wolfram F. Hanrieder

The Military Balance 1981-1982, International Institute for Strategic Studies

Verification and SALT: The Challenge of Strategic Deception, edited by William C. Potter

The Political Economy of Arms Reduction: Reversing Economic Decay, edited by Lloyd J. Dumas

* *Managing U.S.-Soviet Rivalry: Problems of Crisis Prevention,* Alexander L. George et al.

* *Arms and Politics, 1958-1978,* Robin Ranger

Limited War Revisited, Robert E. Osgood

* *War, Morality, and the Military Profession,* edited by Malham M. Wakin

The Future of European Alliance Systems: NATO and the Warsaw Pact, edited by Arlene Idol Broadhurst

The Evolution of U.S. Army Nuclear Doctrine, 1945-1980, John P. Rose

* Available in hardcover and paperback.

Westview Special Studies in National Security and Defense Policy

Arms Control in Transition: Proceedings of the Livermore Arms Control Conference
edited by Warren Heckrotte and George C. Smith

In addition to its efforts to provide the best in nuclear weapons technology, the Lawrence Livermore National Laboratory has devoted much attention to the question of how to provide effective control of nuclear weapons. One consequence of this concern was a conference held at the Laboratory to examine policies and negotiating goals in five major areas of arms control: strategic arms limitations talks (SALT), long-range theater nuclear forces (LRTNF) restraints in Europe, nuclear weapons test limitations, arms control in space, and non-proliferation policies.

The participants focused on desirable long-term goals and criteria for successful policies, realistic estimates of how closely such goals and policies can be achieved, and concrete steps that could be taken toward these goals in the immediate future. None of the conference speakers saw an easy time ahead: the complexities and difficulties of arms control measures, both technical and political, were emphasized more than once. There was general agreement that SALT and LRTNF negotiations should be pursued; there was also a sharp and clear division on the desirability of a comprehensive nuclear weapons test ban, although it was agreed that a ban at this time is not propitious. Despite differences of emphasis, particularly over the future role of nuclear energy, there was substantial agreement in the approach to the elements of future policy. In the closing round table discussion, a prescription emerged for the formulation of arms control policy within the government.

Warren Heckrotte and **George C. Smith** are staff physicists at the Lawrence Livermore National Laboratory. Since 1961 Dr. Heckrotte has served on U.S. delegations concerned with disarmament; in 1980 he was deputy head of the Comprehensive Nuclear Weapon Test Ban Negotiations in Geneva.

Arms Control in Transition

Proceedings of the Livermore Arms Control Conference

edited by Warren Heckrotte
and George C. Smith

Westview Press / Boulder, Colorado

Westview Special Studies in National Security and Defense Policy

Published in 1983 in the United States of America by
  Westview Press, Inc.
  5500 Central Avenue
  Boulder, Colorado 80301
  Frederick A. Praeger, President and Publisher

Library of Congress Cataloging in Publication Data
  Livermore Arms Control Conference (1981: Lawrence Livermore National Laboratory)
  Arms control in transition.
(Westview special studies in national security and defense policy)
  Includes index.
  1. Arms control—Congresses. I. Heckrotte, Warren. II. Smith, George C. III. Lawrence Livermore National Laboratory. IV. Title. V. Series.
JX1974.L583 1981   327.1'74   82-10960
ISBN 0-86531-496-9

Printed and bound in the United States of America

This book is dedicated to the memory of
Dr. Joseph K. Landauer, friend and colleague.

CONTENTS

Contents

PREFACE

The Lawrence Livermore National Laboratory (LLNL) is one of three national laboratories managed by the University of California for the U.S. Department of Energy. The other two are the Lawrence Berkeley Laboratory (LBL) and the Los Alamos National Laboratory (LANL) in New Mexico.

LLNL is administered under a contract between the regents of the University of California and the U.S. government. The contract states that the Laboratory's work should consist of "research, development, and educational activities related to the nuclear sciences and the use of energy in mutually selected military and peaceful applications." The purpose is "to encourage basic scientific progress—in the interest of the national defense and public welfare," with "the paramount objective of assuring the common defense and security of the United States."

Since its foundation, the Laboratory has done research and development (R&D) on nuclear weapons. LLNL and LANL are the only laboratories in the United States that perform this difficult and in many respects specialized R&D. The laboratories' work on nuclear weapons also includes detailed designing of nuclear warheads, stockpile surveillance, non-proliferation analysis, treaty verification technology, and allied matters.

The nuclear weapons work currently accounts for about 50 percent of LLNL's operating budget. Another 5 percent of the budget is applied to defense-related work in nonnuclear fields, and the balance—over 45 percent—goes mainly to research on energy and in biological and environmental sciences.

This book is a product of a conference on arms control held at the LLNL on 26–27 May 1981. Several factors prompted LLNL sponsorship of this conference. First, in addition to the Laboratory's efforts to provide the best in nuclear weapon technology, it has also devoted much effort to the question of how to provide effective control of nuclear weapons and nuclear weapon technology. Second, the conference reflects University of California President David Saxon's efforts to increase the university's contributions to scholarship on international security and arms control questions. Third, with a new administration developing its policies and preparing to negotiate key issues, it was felt to be a propitious time for thought and discussion in this area.

The purpose of the conference was to examine policies and negotiating goals in five major areas of arms control: strategic arms limitation talks (SALT), long-range theater nuclear forces (LRTNF) restraints in Europe, nuclear weapons test limitations, arms control in space, and non-proliferation policies. The participants were urged to focus on desirable long-term goals and criteria for successful policies, estimates of how closely such goals and policies can be achieved given the realities of the international situation, and concrete steps toward these goals in the immediate future.

The conference opened with an introductory survey of the issues as seen by the previous administration's director of the Arms Control and Disarmament Agency (ACDA). Then, in each of the five major areas of arms control selected for consideration, there were two speakers, chosen to represent different points of view. A three-person panel, also representing different points of view, commented on the presentations. This was followed by a general discussion in which the audience participated. The final session was a round table discussion among four of the participants.

It was our expectation that the purpose and approach adopted would avoid a sterile debate over the past and look instead to the future. In this we believe the conference succeeded. The past, however, was not ignored; the speakers drew upon past experiences to build their views of the possible future steps for these categories of arms control. The speakers were well suited for the task because each had wide experience in national security matters and many dealt directly at some time with the political, military, bureaucratic, and negotiating problems of arms control. They were attuned to the desirable and the possible, the contradictions and the limitations that confront the policymaker and negotiator.

In general, none of the speakers saw an easy path ahead for implementing arms control measures. The complexities and difficulties, both technical and political, were emphasized more than once. Many participants felt that arms control is but one element in the quest for security, an element that to be successful must be closely integrated with political and military policies.

In a brief span, one cannot summarize with justice the contents of the presentations and discussions. Nonetheless, a few points may be noted. There was general agreement that SALT and LRTNF negotiations should be pursued and that the latter should be in the context of SALT. The substantive issues of LRTNF appear formidable and the political issues are crucial to the solidarity of the NATO alliance. There was a sharp and clear division on the desirability of a comprehensive nuclear weapon test ban—the issues are squarely put in the presentations and discussions—although it was agreed that a ban at this time is not propitious. With regard to arms control in space, the task remains to define the approach to, as well as the utility of, such an agreement. A framework for such considerations was presented. For non-proliferation policy the basic continuity of policy over several decades was recognized: It is in the interest of the United States to limit nuclear weapons proliferation. Although there were some differences of emphasis, particularly over the future role of nuclear energy, there was substantial agreement on the approach to the elements of future policy. Finally, in the round table discussion, one finds a prescription for the formulation of arms control policy within the government.

The talk given by Herman Kahn on arms control in the year 2000 is not included in these proceedings. It will be published elsewhere.

As noted earlier, one factor in the decision to hold this conference was David Saxon's effort to increase the university's contribution to scholarship on international security and arms control. At the conference banquet President Saxon gave a speech presenting his views on the pursuit of international security and the role the university can play. His remarks conclude this volume.

The proceedings were tape recorded. In some cases, the speaker's text is reproduced as it was written before the conference. In other cases, the speaker has edited his or her remarks on the basis of the tape recording. Each panelist has had the opportunity to review and edit the tape recording of his or her commentary. The editors are solely responsible for the editing of the discussions. We have not retained all questions and responses, and some passages have been condensed. We hope we have not done injustice to the intended meaning of any discussant's remarks. Additionally, and unfortunately, there were several brief "gaps" in the tape during the discussion periods that led to some unintended editing.

The conference was organized by Michael May with the assistance of Warren Heckrotte and the late Joseph Landauer. The practical arrangements were under the direction of Wilma McGurn, and it is a pleasure to thank her and the many people at the Laboratory who made this conference a success. For the arduous task of transcribing the tapes and preparing the final manuscript, we wish to express our great thanks to the staff of the Word Processing Center of the Laboratory.

Warren Heckrotte
George C. Smith

ARMS CONTROL
AT THE END OF 1980

SPEAKER

Ralph Earle II

Director, Arms Control and Disarmament Agency, 1980–1981;
Member SALT Delegation, 1973–1979

Some months ago, when I was asked to make the introductory remarks at this conference, I was concerned that we might take part in a repetition of what has gone on before so often: a heated, if somewhat sterile, debate of past issues—SALT, theater deployments, and so on. But now enough time has passed and enough has happened, or not happened, to cause me to believe that we are indeed at a critical juncture for arms control and its future and that the group assembled here this week at Livermore can indeed make a valuable contribution in the form of recommendations to those now in positions of responsibility. In the time available to me, I would first like to review the pending issues, then make a few comments about methodology for the future, and finally, add some personal observations.

With respect to pending issues there is the question of long-range theater nuclear forces (LRTNF, or briefly, TNF). This issue is on the front burner, in large part, because of the concerns and political problems of our NATO allies. As you know, we conducted some "preliminary discussions" with the Soviets last fall, and it now appears that the talks may be renewed before the end of the year. (These intermediate-range nuclear force [INF] negotiations began 30 November 1981 in Geneva, Switzerland.) I think there is general agreement that at least the image of TNF negotiations is necessary to support the new deployment of ground launched cruise missiles (GLCMs) and *Pershing II*s in Western Europe. But there is little or no agreement on the arms control objectives for TNF or even whether we really want any sort of TNF agreement.

Beneath these general questions lie many more unanswered questions. What should be limited? Long-range missiles only? Aircraft? Which ones? Short-range systems? Sea-based systems? What geographical area should be covered? Should there be a nuclear-conventional distinction? If so, how? What should be done about the reload problem? What about verification? And so on. It is a very difficult and complex subject, and even that is to understate it. But we will have to come up with credible positions if we are ever to acquire and maintain TNF modernization. But however complex and difficult and intellectually challenging these issues may be, they cannot be dealt with in a vacuum, particularly one from which SALT is excluded.

I don't think anyone would suggest that TNF can be dealt with except in a SALT context. What benefit is there in limiting the SS-20 if the SS-16 can run free or in limiting the *Backfire* if there are no constraints on existing and new Soviet heavy bombers? What good would it do to limit relatively long-range theater systems if submarine launched ballistic missiles (SLBMs) were uncontained?

Like it or not, SALT must be addressed and addressed promptly if there is to be any hope for TNF. But how? My own solution is an easy one—ratify SALT II. We are presently living within its limitations, as are the Soviets. The only difference between our world today and one in which the treaty were ratified would be the fact that the Soviets would already have dismantled 150 systems and would now be in the process of dismantling an additional 150. But ratification is, apparently, not to be. So, where do we go from here? Obviously, we should think through our objectives and determine whether we should try again for substantial reductions, impose additional numerical caps, and so forth. I know Nitze and Slocombe will take this up next, and I shall look forward to hearing their and others' views on what I see as a problem almost without realistic solution.

Of course, any discussion of strategic arms leads us to the MX (missile experimental) and in turn to the ABM (Anti-Ballistic Missile) Treaty in the light of possible ballistic missile defense (BMD) deployment. Here again, we are faced with a situation fraught with difficult questions. The ABM Treaty's future turns, it seems to me, on the MX decision. If the MX is sea-based, there should be little pressure to change the treaty. If the present multiple protective shelters (MPS) route is followed, the alternative may be a few hundred ABM radars and interceptors. Finally, if MX is placed in existing silos, there will be pressures for hundreds of radars and thousands of interceptors. In any event, we need a careful weighing of the benefits of a limited deployment of a U.S. BMD against the benefits to the Soviet Union of some BMD and the questions this would raise regarding penetration capabilities of our own RVs (re-entry vehicles). Further complications arising from a renegotiation of the ABM Treaty include the possibility that the Soviets may not want equivalent rights and might instead want a different ICBM (intercontinental ballistic missile) defense or a limited area defense, for instance, against China. The Soviets so far have shown no interest in changing this treaty, which raises the question of U.S. abrogation and all the consequent political problems that would ensue. Obviously, all these issues require the most thoughtful consideration.

Let me turn now to a different subject—arms control in space. Here, I believe, there is a real opportunity for agreements that genuinely enhance our national security. I believe it to be unarguable that the integrity of our reconnaissance and communications satellites is desirable. I also believe that a good argument can be made that it is in the U.S. interest for Soviet satellites to enjoy a similar invulnerability. Isn't it to our benefit that in time of crisis the adversary is aware of our activities (e.g., a higher nuclear-powered strategic ballistic missile submarine [SSBN] alert state) and can maintain strict command and control of his own strategic forces? In any event, space weapons are in their infancy, and if they are to be limited, now is the best time. Again, there are difficult questions to be answered. What kind of environment do we want space to be in the long run? Is a sanctuary to our mutual advantage? How much of a military advantage could we have in space? And for how long? How much would a true offense-defense space capability cost in the 1990s? Do we want to pay this price? What would be the benefits? With respect to negotiations, we have real advantages and can come to the table from a position of real technological strength; but we also have much to lose if Soviet military space capability grows. There is, as you know, apparent Soviet interest in antisatellite (ASAT) discussions, but there is again a long series of hard questions to answer if we are to pursue such talks. Do we want a total ban on space weapons? Should there be limits on satellite activities as well as on antisatellite activities? What is verifiable? As I said, an opportunity exists, but it must be carefully considered—and soon.

Another pending issue is the question of nuclear testing and its limitations. As you know, trilateral negotiations on a comprehensive test ban (CTB) have been under way for four years. Others will take this up later in greater detail, so I will just raise a few questions. Is a comprehensive ban on all testing in our national interest? If so, for how long? If not, what are the alternatives? A threshold lower than 150 kilotons (kt)? Limits on the number of tests? A mixed number/yield limitation—e.g., so many tests at X yield, so many more tests at Y yield? What can and cannot be verified? Here again, we must pose to ourselves all the difficult and relevant questions and answer them before pushing forward.

Not all of these questions can be answered in a technical manner because there are also serious political repercussions from whatever we do regarding nuclear weapon testing, especially in the area of non-proliferation. As I learned—the hard way—at the Non-Proliferation Treaty (NPT) Review Conference last summer, most other nations see their attitudes toward non-proliferation and supply issues as being greatly affected by the activities of the nuclear weapon states with respect to their own nuclear arsenals and their testing practices and restraints. It may be that a CTB would have all the bad results that some have predicted, but it may also be that the failure to achieve such a ban would result in an otherwise avoidable proliferation scenario. Again—hard questions without easy answers.

Finally, I would just mention some other arms control areas that need attention and care: chemical and radiological weapons, bacteriological weapons and compliance with the existing treaty, and the forthcoming Special Session on Disarmament at the United Nations (UN), which will undoubtedly epitomize the difficulties of and pressures on arms control negotiations in our polarized world.

Now I'd like to say a few words about methodology—or how we should proceed in the future.

Before we negotiate arms control for the 1980s, we ought to decide what it is we really want. We ought to plan a strategy for carrying it out. We should learn from our experiences and past mistakes. What do we want from arms control? Our objective is to enhance our national security. We ought to be and feel safer with it than without it. More specifically, this means that an arms control agreement should

- Limit the Soviet threat to the United States and our forces;
- Improve the survivability of U.S. forces if possible. At a minimum, arms control should not prohibit or inhibit the United States from steps required to maintain a survivable strategic deterrent;
- Improve our ability to monitor Soviet forces. Our uncertainties about Soviet forces and programs should be reduced as a result of arms control.

The United States should emerge from negotiations as a successful competitor and negotiator. This means that an agreement

- Must be and be seen as equal;
- Must be clear and without loopholes.

How will this come about? We should first decide on the acceptable outcome. Then, the United States must develop a broad bipartisan consensus in favor of arms control. Our goals must be clear, understandable, and reasonable. This cannot be accomplished unless the administration develops and propagates its foreign policy objectives in a way that includes the role of arms control. This also means that the administration has to acknowledge that the centers of power and influence are many in the United States and make sure that it does what it can to keep various groups informed and part of the process.

We must not exaggerate our expectations. The Congress and the American people appreciate candor. For example, there is little that arms control can do to save *Minuteman*. We must not oversell arms control.

We must find a streamlined way to develop detailed negotiating positions based on our overall foreign policy and security goals. Past ways of developing positions and responses to negotiating have been slow and cumbersome and permitted relatively low-ranking civil servants to "diddle" with high level decisions. This leads to long internal negotiations in which positions are overtaken by events and, in the case of SALT II, those who started it were not responsible at the finish. In fact, so much time elapsed that those who sired SALT II were able to disinherit it without cost.

Finally, we should, in the development of substantive positions and tactics, take into account the perceptions—to the extent that we can judge them—of our negotiating partners. This criterion has often been neglected. In March of 1977, the so-called "comprehensive proposal" would have deemphasized land-based ICBMs and fostered a move to the sea—both consistent with U.S. views of how to achieve stability. But was it consistent with Soviet desiderata? I think not. Rather, I believe they saw it as a U.S. attempt to weaken them where they were strong—ICBMs—and emphasize an area in which they were less strong and more vulnerable. It need hardly be said that one must consider the attitudes of the party across the table, but we have often ignored this obvious rule of negotiation.

In short, we should improve our procedures by determining goals at the outset, asking and answering the hard questions early, and then deciding on the strategy and tactics to achieve those goals. At the same time, the effective constituencies should be encouraged to participate where appropriate and to maintain an informed status.

Finally, I want to make two personal comments. Contrary to what a number of informed and intelligent students of arms control have said over the last eighteen months, I do not believe that the arms control process has been shown to be a failure. The example always cited by the critics is SALT II. But SALT II did not fail to be ratified because of its own flaws—it failed, in my view, largely because of unrelated events, e.g., the Cuban brigade affair and Afghanistan. If your Cadillac fails to reach its objective because a bridge has washed out, you don't call for a reconstitution of the automobile industry. On the contrary, I think it has been shown to be on the right track and worthy of continued pursuit. And I believe that the potential of that process is excellent. I am, quite frankly, somewhat pessimistic about its prospects as opposed to its potential. The former are in the hands of the Reagan administration and I remain hopeful, if doubtful.

At the outset of my remarks, I said I did not want to rehash old arguments. But there is one issue that is old but remains current and will remain alive in the future—linkage. Personally, I believe in substantial linkage in dealing with the Soviet Union, but with one notable exception: that regarding arms control negotiations and agreements. If you believe that arms control is a zero-sum game that the Soviets will usually win, then you shouldn't have any agreements, regardless of how well they are behaving elsewhere in the world. But if you believe, as I do, that it's a nonzero-sum game, with potential benefits to both sides, then you should pursue sound, balanced, beneficial, and verifiable agreements, even if their behavior elsewhere is undesirable. If your neighbor's tree is growing and increasingly threatens to fall on your house, should you refuse to discuss it with him until you have satisfactorily resolved a sewer dispute at the other end of the property? I think not.

DISCUSSION*

Herman Kahn: I think linkages are important. With regard to the analogy used, if the tree is drawing from the sewer, so to speak, and the sewer is feeding the tree, it's connected, and it's exactly the connection you're ignoring when you use that analogy.

Ralph Earle: I was careful to point out that the sewer was at the other end of the property, and the tree was not being nurtured by that particular sewer. Let's not pursue the sewer analogy too far. Perhaps I overstated it when I said arms control agreements are an exception. If they are insignificant, or not terribly significant, then I think I would take your point. I was talking about major ones, where the national security of the United States can genuinely be enhanced by such an agreement and there I would maintain that I oppose linkage.

Herman Kahn: I think that we agree, and that the issue is degree.

*The affiliations of discussants are listed at the end of this book.

Paul Nitze: Just to pursue this point of linkage, it seemed to me your argument depended upon the proposition that there were nonzero-sum benefits in SALT II. I think that is the main issue. I felt that the Russians were not looking at SALT as being a nonzero-sum game. We devoted at least two years trying to persuade them that that was the way in which one should look at the negotiations, but they never did agree. And I think SALT II reflects that. It reflects a zero-sum outcome in large measure, but not entirely because they had to make some concessions to us. So it doesn't seem to me that your point is well founded.

Ralph Earle: You and I disagree about the substance of the agreement, and so your second point is well taken given that disagreement. The first point—that the Soviets never accepted our position or our arguments that it was a nonzero-sum game—is right in terms of rhetoric, but the proof of the pudding of any agreement is what is in the agreement, as to whether or not it's a nonzero-sum agreement or a zero-sum agreement.

Brent Scowcroft: I would like to pursue linkage a little bit further. It seems to me that U.S.-Soviet relations are a unitary whole and that intergovernment relations cover a wide variety of things, no one of which is unconnected, in the way of the tree and the sewer, from any other. Your argument is basically saying SALT II is in our interest. Therefore it shouldn't be subject to linkage. It seems to me that any kind of agreement that we have with the Soviet Union is going to be in our interest unless we negotiate even worse than some people here think that we do. Therefore, if you're going to apply linkage, it's got to hurt somewhere. And it seems to me that if you believe in linkage at all, you cannot exclude SALT from it.

Ralph Earle: I thought of exactly that argument when I was drafting my own, and what it comes down to is a matter of degree: At what point are you willing to punish yourself in order to punish them? If on balance the agreement is sufficiently beneficial to you, you shouldn't punish yourself in order to punish them.

Herman Kahn: It seems to me that we've left out the two most important parts of the discussion. The reason why many people want to establish linkage is they think they can get arms control that way. In other words, they think they can push the Soviets around. And I think that's a reasonably accurate estimate of the situation. On the other hand, I think the Soviets believe in linkage automatically. They look at everything as a unified whole. They have no concept that the arms race is so dangerous that you have to treat it differently from all other aspects of human life.

They are more concerned with us than with the arms race. That asymmetry in the psychological area is, I think, terribly important. I think that linkage is almost the only way to straighten it out; not arguments about the control of the arms race itself.

I would argue that until the Soviets themselves accept the concept that arms control is too important to be linked and therefore you have to sit in a separate arena, it's wrong for us to accept that concept. It leads to bad agreements.

Ralph Earle: I'm not sure I agree with your premise that the Soviets link everything. Bear in mind that in 1972 the SALT I Treaties were signed five or six days after the bombing of Hanoi in which Soviet ships were hit.

Herman Kahn: The point is that the biggest virtue of the treaty for them was that it recognized their eminence as a world power. That was very important to them. Second, it created a more detente-ish feeling in the United States. From my point of view, going to the Senate and trying to get an arms control agreement has this impact. You have to create a detente-ish mood. The biggest single defect of the treaty was that it created this detente-ish mood. It said in effect that things are going moderately well and we need not worry about the Soviets. I don't object to detente, which has the literal meaning of decreasing tensions. I object to the entente aspects of it.

Mark Schneider: You speak of building a national consensus for arms control. How can you possibly build a national consensus when you continue to advocate the ratification of SALT II, which is a thoroughly discredited agreement that could not possibly obtain the objectives outlined?

Ralph Earle: Well, obviously, I disagree with the premise. But let's assume what you said about the treaty is true. I'm no longer in office. I'm giving advice to the people who are in office, not to myself. It seems to me they have an opportunity, a burden, and an obligation to do the things that I suggested, and they may in the course of it come up with a SALT treaty that satisfies you. But whether or not that's the case, it still seems to me they should make an effort to educate the public and the Congress and to keep them informed, and demonstrate to them the importance of good arms control agreements.

Tom Comstock: How can you build a national consensus without linkage? How is the Senate going to pass a SALT treaty unless the Soviets are, for example, practicing moderation in the Third World?

Ralph Earle: It's very hard. There's no question that a strategic arms limitation agreement has a much better chance of ratification if Soviet-American relations appear to be good. Senators don't always read the treaty and vote on the merits of the treaty. They vote on perceptions of constituents, among other things. And if the constituents' perceptions are that the Soviets are SOBs and we shouldn't deal with them, you're going to find more votes against the treaty, the very same treaty that might be ratified if the constituency saw it differently. So the answer to your question is, it's a very hard thing to do. All I'm suggesting is that we ought to try to do it.

Charles McDonald: I have a basic problem with the premise that we have gotten something from arms control agreements in the sense that we have lessened the potential damage to the United States. You said we should get a consensus of the American public. I am genuinely concerned that what we're doing is pulling the wool over the public's eyes. It was some of your predecessors who said that *Minuteman* would never become vulnerable. Well, some of us knew it would then, and it has. I can see no evidence that any arrangements that we have made have done anything to impede the growth of the Soviet strategic arms weapons systems, and particularly the counterforce feature of them. We knew it then, and it has been demonstrated now. I don't understand why we keep kidding ourselves about this matter.

Ralph Earle: With respect to the increase of Soviet hard-target capability, this was one of the problems that arose from the length of the negotiations. We went seven years between the signature of SALT I and the signature of SALT II. In effect, the Soviets could run virtually unrestrained with the exception of building new fixed ICBM launchers and increasing the SLBM launchers beyond a certain number in the SALT II Agreement. I'll point out one thing in SALT that limits the counterforce feature: the RV limitation. It isn't the greatest thing since sliced bread to limit SS-18s to ten RVs, but it's a lot better than letting them have thirty or forty. This was a step in the right direction. It seems to me you almost agree with my point—don't expect too much. SALT II didn't solve the problem, but it was a step toward solving the problem. And you can't expect one single agreement, or even two or three agreements, to solve all problems. I'm sorry that anyone ever told you that SALT was going to save the *Minuteman.* It never occurred to me that it would.

Van Hudson: Would you elaborate on your comments on the ABM Treaty? You suggested that the United States might have no choice except to abrogate the ABM Treaty.

Ralph Earle: I didn't mean to say that we would have no choice. I said there would be pressures. If SALT II is unratified or even if SALT II continues to be complied with in spite of lack of ratification, the threat to our ICBM launchers is going to increase. Therefore, there are going to be pressures to bring in a ballistic missile defense. Under the ABM Treaty, with the protocol of 1974, each side is entitled to one site. The Soviets have a site, around Moscow. We have a site at Grand Forks that is in moth balls. But if we were to defend multiple protection structures (MPS) in Utah and Nevada, it would need at least a renegotiation and an amendment of the ABM Treaty. When I spoke of abrogation, it was in the context that the Soviets have shown no interest in renegotiating or amending. If we go to them with a view toward amendment or termination, they can respond in one of three ways: "Fine, let's do it," which I think is unlikely; "We'll consider it but we want it a little differently than you want it," as I suggested; or, they might say "No, the treaty is fine." And that would put us in the politically difficult situation of abrogating the treaty.

Robert Coffin: You have reduced, perhaps even eliminated, traditional distinctions between tactical and strategic nuclear weapons. Specifically, you took everything from *Pershing II* through ICBMs, long-range bombers, perhaps even space weapons, and said they're all interrelated. That is a very broad spectrum of weapons. It seems that successful negotiations require negotiating things that are small enough that if negotiators have a problem they might come up with a manageable solution. My question is, how would you break into manageable packages this tremendous spectrum of weapons, which while interrelated, can't be negotiated as a whole.

Ralph Earle: If I knew the answer to that question, I think even this adminstration might hire me. You put your finger on exactly the problem that was faced in beginning the discussions of the so-called theater nuclear forces system last year. What was to be included? You can see a ratcheting down. If you begin with SS-20s and then go to *Pershing*s, and then you go to longer range aircraft, and then to shorter range aircraft, where do you stop? It's like the Art Buchwald column about the machine gun in Nevada that resulted in the full deployment of an ABM system to protect it. That was ratcheting up. SALT II was complicated but at least we had a limitation on what we talked about. Now, *Backfire* is an example of how hard it is to draw the line. We said SALT should deal with central systems—ICBM launchers, SLBM launchers and heavy bombers. Then *Backfire* comes in. We were prepared to exclude it, given Soviet assurances. But many people, including most of the new significant people in this administration, claim that *Backfire* is a heavy bomber. If you include *Backfire,* what do you do about FB-llls. If you include FB-llls, what do you do about F-llls? So, the question you ask is the hard one. I don't have the answer. All you can do is draw an arbitrary line. I just want to point out the difficulty of defining those systems that you want to deal with and those you don't.

Brent Scowcroft: You said that the first priority ought to be to decide what we want. Then you listed several criteria for what a SALT agreement ought to incorporate. It seems to me that you'd find little disagreement over your objectives. What worries me is that at that level of abstraction, we're not going to get anywhere. Ronald Reagan, during the campaign last fall, besides saying SALT II is fatally flawed, said its real problem was that it was not arms control. And I felt that unless we get below this level of ethereal abstraction that everybody can agree on, and decide in fact what we want arms control to achieve, that we're not going to get anywhere.

Ralph Earle: I can't argue with that. When I first went on the SALT delegation in 1973 I was terribly frustrated after three or four months because I felt that nobody knew where we really wanted to come out. I don't mean X number of launchers and Y number of heavy bombers, but what it was we were trying to do. And frankly I don't know that that was ever articulated through the Nixon, Ford, or Carter administrations. Maybe it's not a good thing to articulate it, because it would leak, and then everybody would know where you wanted to come out. But I feel that there ought to be a little more precision in terms of what's going on in the mind of the president and in the minds of the principal people as to what we are trying to achieve.

Michael Intriligator: I'd like to ask how you respond to the observation that the SALT process will inevitably cause a qualitative arms race and that a qualitative arms race tends to be more unstable than a quantitative arms race by its very nature. Kissinger once said that, as part of the SALT process, there was an acceleration of several weapons systems.

Ralph Earle: I think you put your finger on an important point. There's no question that there's a tendency to design around any agreement. Although the drive to improve things technologically exists even without an agreement, I think it is heightened by an agreement. It's a major problem. We tried in SALT II to get some so-called qualitative restraints. They were pretty insignificant ones. To get more is difficult because of the problems of verification.

George Schneiter: You alluded to verification a couple of times, and when you went through your list of criteria, you said "improve our ability to monitor Soviet forces." I'm sure that you feel that we need more than that. How do you see us grappling with the verification problem, not only in the qualitative areas that you alluded to, but also as we start to get down to the shorter range systems?

Ralph Earle: On the first point, I was talking about a secondary benefit of an arms control agreement. A noninterference provision, or a nonconcealment provision, obviously helps one's ability to monitor. We are better off with a limited ban on the encryption of telemetry than with no ban on encryption of telemetry. That's the point I was making there. The verification of TNF is about as difficult as the other aspects of TNF. I would use the conventional definition of adequately verifiable: the ability to catch them before they can get away with anything important.

Michael May: You've stated that the potential for arms control is excellent, and at the same time you've said that we shouldn't expect too much. And while those terms are not incompatible, they are, at least to some degree, opposite. Many people would expect quite a bit before they would call the potential excellent. The SALT II Treaty has been under fire from both the right and the left in this country because of the quantity of these weapons. You clearly have in mind some sort of process when you say the potential is excellent. Can you be more specific about where that process might go? If arms control is pursued with intelligence and vigor, what kind of improvements in the political process and relationships between ourselves and the Soviet Union do you see in the next few years?

Ralph Earle: As I said, the potential is there, but I don't think the prospects are, and that's simply because of the present political situation both internally and bilaterally, but particularly our own internal political situation at this time. In talking about the potential, rather than the prospects, there is no question in my mind that the Soviets are not interested in much greater reductions than they've already made in strategic systems until something is done about what they call forward-based systems—U.S. aircraft (and now missiles) in Europe. The potential lies in the possibility of going forward from SALT II into TNF, and then in conjunction with TNF coming to a SALT III, and perhaps a SALT IV, with the potential for reduction.

Pierre Lellouche: It's clearly my impression when I look at the TNF problem that no one has any idea of where you want to come out. I think the central issue we face is that the West is really not able to define a position and stick to it. This is the fundamental asymmetry with the Soviet Union. A SALT negotiation assumes such an enormous political importance for your own nation, for your allies, for the other side in terms of political and military value, that you have to make sure that you are going to stick to the line that you have. Instead we have seen oscillations throughout, which have had repercussions on public opinion and on the consensus for arms control in the United States. It has had enormous impact on Europe. There has been a fantastic shift from a Europe that was against arms control to a Europe that is fighting for it. The Soviet Union, on the other hand, clearly had objectives that it has achieved: recognition as a superpower and an increase in its defense program. Do you think, given those realities, that the United States is fit as a nation, or we are fit as a western world, to enter into sustained negotiations that last for seven or eight years in such a way that is not completely suicidal to our interests; or must we think of a really serious alternative, perhaps implicit agreements, and keeping the dialogue open in other ways.

Ralph Earle: I'm not sure I agree. With respect to delays, the delays were just as great for the Soviet Union with their monolithic continuum of government as they were for ours. We made a lot of deployments during that period also.

2

THE NEXT STEPS FOR SALT

SPEAKERS

Paul Nitze

Head, U.S. Delegation to the Intermediate-Range Nuclear Force Negotiations;
Former Chairman, Policy Studies, Committee on the Present Danger

I was asked to lay out what I think the United States should do about the strategic arms limitation talks with the Soviet Union, what should be the first steps, and what I think are the chances of success. I would like to preface my remarks by making three preliminary points.

The first point is that the SALT negotiations have two quite different but interrelated aspects. One aspect—I think of it as the substantive aspect—is the impact SALT agreements can be expected to have on the strategic nuclear capabilities of the United States and the Soviet Union, on the stability of the nuclear relationship between them in a potential crisis and thus on the management of potential conflicts between East and West, and finally on the expenditure of resources by the two sides on their nuclear forces. The other aspect is the impact made by the posture and statements of the United States and the Soviet Union—particularly with respect to disarmament, arms control, and SALT—upon the psychological and political outlook of people in the United States, in Europe, and in the world generally. This political-psychological aspect is almost as important as the substantive aspect.

The second point is that it is useful to bear in mind the distinction between the criteria for a desirable agreement (one that would, in fact, contribute to U.S. national security and reduce the risk of nuclear war) and a negotiable agreement (one that the Soviets will accept). This is a difficult line to draw. It is easy enough to outline arrangements that should contribute to the security of both sides; it is my view, however, that it is quite unlikely that the Soviet Union will agree to such terms under present circumstances. It is even more difficult to draw the line between an agreement that is one-sided in favor of the USSR but still on balance advantageous to the United States and one that is so one-sidedly unfavorable to the United States as not to merit U.S. ratification.

The third preliminary point is that the desirability or acceptability of an agreement from the U.S. viewpoint depends heavily upon the nature of the nuclear threat the Soviets are expected to develop under the agreement and whether the agreement permits the United States to have the programs it needs to offset and counter that threat. Here judgment presupposes an understanding of future Soviet capabilities and a view as to what strategic forces the United States will need to counter those capabilities.

With this introduction, let me turn to my charge: to outline what I think should be the first steps the administration takes in the arms control field. To date, attention appears to have been concentrated on resolving the issues of personnel appointments relevant to the issue in the State and Defense departments and the ACDA and on coordinating positions to be taken in discussions with our allies, primarily in NATO. I should think the next step would be to work out a basic framework of ideas that would then be used as a guide both to the treatment of the substantive aspects and to the political-psychological aspects of the problem.

The first issue is whether or not the United States should seek a renewal of serious arms control negotiations with the USSR. There is in my mind little doubt that the answer will and should be "yes." The political-psychological aspects call for a positive answer even if one can have little confidence that, under present circumstances, a concrete agreement meeting the substantive aspects of the problem can be negotiated. The timing of the initiation of negotiations is a separate issue. I should think they should be gotten underway reasonably soon, but not until there is a clear decision in the Executive Branch on a conceptual framework to guide the U.S. position during the negotiations. Obviously, we should be reasonably clear in our minds on what we wish to accomplish. Stated in another way, what are the criteria for a good agreement? That is, an agreement that would serve the security interests of the United States, one which we and other like-minded people in the world would consider fair to the reasonable security interest of the USSR, and above all, one which would reduce the risk of nuclear war in a world of continuing contest between the USSR and much of the rest of the world.

What are the criteria for such a SALT agreement? I would suggest that the first criterion be that of the duration of the agreement. The original aim of both sides in the SALT II negotiations was an agreement of indefinite duration limiting strategic offensive arms to parallel the

SALT I ABM Treaty. This was confirmed in the 1973 documents on "Basic Principles of Negotiations on the Further Limitation of Strategic Offensive Arms." Those documents refer to "a permanent agreement that is more complete in its limitations and which provides for subsequent reductions in strategic offensive arms."

It was expected that such a treaty would include a five-year review provision and each side's right to withdraw if extraordinary events related to the subject matter of the treaty were to jeopardize its supreme interests.

SALT II as signed at Vienna expires in 1985, and would now have less than five years to run. Hence, it is not worth much to either side. Four to five years is too short a time frame in relation to the time involved in developing new strategic weapons, which is typically ten to fifteen years or more. Its principal significance would be in its impact on the SALT III negotiations. On one hand, the weak provisions of SALT II would be urged by the Soviet side as setting a precedent for comparable provisions in any follow-on agreement. On the other hand, it is by no means certain that those provisions, which are of potential benefit to the United States, will be carried over into a successor agreement. Rather than cluttering up the SALT III problem with a highly debatable SALT II, it would appear to be much more sensible to go directly to the negotiation of SALT III. A desirable SALT III agreement should have duration, review, and withdrawal provisions similar to those in the ABM Treaty.

Let us now turn to what the principal substantive objectives of a desirable agreement might be. From the beginning of the SALT process, the U.S. position has been that a satisfactory and lasting agreement should favor neither side. We did not believe that the Soviet side would accept an agreement that favored the United States; i.e., that assured the United States greater strategic capabilities than the Soviet side. We saw no reason why the Soviet side should expect the United States to accept provisions that assured them of superiority in strategic capabilities.

The term equivalence was used to indicate that it was not necessary that the capabilities of each side be a mirror-image of those of the other. But advantages in certain capabilities of one side should be offset by advantages in other capabilities of the other side. Rough equivalence in the strategic nuclear capabilities of the two sides should continue to be a criterion of a desirable agreement.

A second substantive criterion should be the fostering of what used to be called "crisis stability." The words "stability" and "instability" have been so corrupted and abused in polemical debate, however, that it is perhaps better to use a precisely defined symbol.

Let us define "Q" as being a situation in which the strategic nuclear deployments and capabilities of the two sides are such that neither side can hope to gain in relative enduring capabilities by initiating a strike against the nuclear forces of the other side. The fostering of Situation Q should be considered to override most of the other criteria of an agreement. As long as the Soviet side is unwilling substantially to reduce the threat to the U.S. ICBM component of its nuclear forces, the United States must be free to do what is necessary to offset that threat through the proliferation of small missiles, the proliferation of MPSs, or the installation of a hard-site defense system or some combination of those measures.

New consideration should be given to the relation between limits on intercontinental systems—what used to be called "central systems"—and gray-area systems, including theater nuclear systems. The Soviet side has persistently argued that it is entitled to compensation in central systems for the presumed advantage of the United States and its allies in forward-based systems. The facts do not support that claim; in fact they support the reverse. A desirable agreement would equitably and constructively take into account the interface between central systems and gray-area systems.

It is important that the significant aspects of nuclear capabilities be precisely defined and usefully limited. It is not sufficient to limit the number of launchers if those launchers are either not necessary to the launch process, can be quickly deployed, or can be reloaded within a useful time period. The power of missiles can be as significant as their number or degree of MIRVing. The distinction between fixed ICBM launchers and mobile systems should be precisely and unambiguously defined, bearing in mind that mobile systems are apt to foster Situation Q while fixed are not. A desirable agreement should reasonably balance the criterion of verifiability with the criteria of significance and precision.

Technological advances can threaten Situation Q, but they can also be necessary to the maintenance or recovery of Situation Q. The degree to which modernization should be permitted or limited in a desirable agreement must be worked out on a case-by-case basis.

Reductions in a desirable agreement should be so designed as to (1) foster Situation Q, and (2) bring the limits closer to what is politically and economically practicable for both sides (in practice, particularly for the United States). Reductions in the number of missile launchers are apt to work against Situation Q, particularly if one side is permitted or is apt to have more and bigger RVs on the missiles the launchers are capable of launching. Reductions in the throw weight (or volume) of the force of fixed ICBM missiles and their launchers will serve to foster Situation Q. The United States has no missiles programmed or planned to replace its aging single RV missiles. Reductions that reduce the ceilings on single RV systems may support the objective of rough equivalence but not necessarily the objective of crisis stability.

A desirable agreement should be reasonably verifiable. The criterion of verifiability should take second position, however, to the criteria of substantive constructiveness.

It is not to be expected that a desirable agreement will become negotiable until the United States has demonstrated that it is determined to maintain an adequate and stable nuclear deterrent posture, whether it is made easier by a SALT agreement or not. It will take time for the United States to so demonstrate. The pace of negotiation should not therefore be rushed.

In any case, it is doubtful the Soviets will agree to any SALT agreement that would significantly reduce the hard-target counterforce capability of its nuclear forces. It is therefore essential to the restoration of crisis stability that the United States reduce the vulnerability of the land-based component of its deterrent forces and of its command, control, communications, and surveillance facilities. Its SALT position should be coordinated with the program that is determined to be essential to accomplishing that end.

George Kennan has proposed a more radical approach—a 50 percent across the board reduction in the forces of both sides. I would suggest one amendment to his proposal: that both sides reduce their largest missiles first—the ones that produce the greatest danger of a crisis degenerating into a nuclear war.

But again I seriously doubt the USSR will accept any such proposal. From the political and psychological standpoint, I should think it nevertheless wise to take a positive attitude toward such a proposal.

Walter Slocombe

Caplin and Drysdale, Washington, D.C.; Deputy Under Secretary of Defense (Policy Planning), 1977–1981

It is a pleasure to be able to begin by saying that I agree with a great deal of what Paul Nitze said. In particular, I agree with his implicit judgment that it is better now to talk about what we must do in the future than to rehash the rights and wrongs of the past. Nonetheless, it seems to me that it is important to try to draw some lessons from what we have gone through to date, and as an advocate of the process and of the SALT II agreement, it seems to me particularly appropriate to offer some suggestions as to what I think are some of the lessons of the SALT experience.

My thesis is that SALT has been a substantial technical success, but so far, a political failure. The task, therefore, is to preserve and to expand as much as possible the technical success, more or less in the ways that Nitze outlined, while meeting the problems that have caused the political failure. I say it's been a technical success because even though I recognize the continuing controversiality of the claim, it seems to me that SALT has been able to bring some limits to the strategic competition. These limits enhance the security of the United States and our allies, both in the specific military sense and in the broader sense of reducing the risk of nuclear war.

But I acknowledge that SALT has been a political failure. It has failed politically not merely in the immediate tactical legislative sense of the inability of the Carter administration, of which I was proud to be a part, to win Senate ratification for the SALT II Treaty, but in the broader sense of the failure to agree on the role of arms control in our continuing confrontation with the USSR.

With respect to the substance, I want to begin with a proposition that I recognize may be controversial. I believe the record of nearly fifteen years—counting the preliminary exchanges under the Johnson administration—of the strategic arms control process indicates that good agreements are, in fact, possible. Specifically, experience shows that the Soviet Union is prepared to accept limits on the degree to which it will add to its military power in ways that would be dangerous to us by exploiting capability that is clearly within its economic and technical capacity. This latter test is my criterion for a meaningful agreement. Examples of such limits agreed to by the USSR include the ban on ICBM fractionation, the limit on MIRVed ICBM levels, and the 1972 limits on ABMs. It is even true, and perhaps more surprising, that the Soviet Union has been prepared to concede some essentially political points; for example, the agreement that was reached at Vladivostok in 1974 on equal aggregate levels.

Therefore, I begin my analysis of what we have to do to build a political basis for the process on the proposition that SALT presents an opportunity for meaningful agreements. This is not self-evident in other areas of arms control, for example, mutual balanced force reduction (MBFR). And this proposition suggests that it would be a serious loss to retreat to a policy of implicit agreement or mutual restraint only, quite apart from the difficulties of that course on its own. And still more, the proposition suggests that there are serious potential costs, not only financially, but much more importantly, in terms of our national interests and the chances of avoiding war if we go to an unconstrained competition. I don't propose to discuss in detail today the technical agenda for the future. Nor do I propose to address the specifics of the task of finding a way to restart the process in ways consistent with the new administration's political commitments at home, its desire to lead the alliance, and its desire to define its own relationship with the Soviet Union. On those immediate and short-term tasks I would be glad to offer my advice, but I will restrain myself. However, with respect to the longer term, what we do after the process begins—what we do in SALT III, if you will—there are areas that require thought and planning, outside as well as inside the government. Even in the heady and analytic days of a new administration, a bureaucracy is not good at long-term planning and issues requiring longer term thinking rather than immediate negotiation and tactics ought to be addressed outside as well as inside the government.

These long-term questions begin, I think, with asking how arms control can cope with the vulnerability of ICBMs. I agree that it is entirely out of the question that arms control will solve the problem of ICBM vulnerability and that it is essential that the United States proceed to its own solutions. But it is also true that neither side has a perfect solution to the ICBM vulnerability problem, and that it is at least worth asking the question whether arms control can enhance the stability of the situation, whether it can contribute to Situation Q, if you will, with respect to whatever technical weapons system answers are finally decided on. If one or both sides regard mobiles as needed, should there be special rules, as some people say, to make the world safe for mobiles and make mobiles safe for the world? Should there be throw-weight reductions? Should we end the focus on launchers and shift to limits on RVs? Is there a feasible way to favor single RV systems? Is it possible to negotiate preferential reductions in the high throw-weight, high accuracy, high RV number ICBMs that are the core of the problem?

In focusing on the vulnerability of ICBMs as a topic for analysis of the potential of arms control, it is also important to think about how arms control may be able to help with longer term potential vulnerabilities of other parts of the force. For bombers, one must consider measures affecting both the pre-launch survivability aspect and the penetration aspect. With respect to submarines, putting the issue of antisubmarine warfare on the table is conceptually unassailable, although it is extremely difficult to foresee any useful agreement. Nonetheless, it seems clear that in any broadened negotiation, strategic antisubmarine warfare will be an issue high on the Soviet agenda, and for that reason, if for no other, we should prepare ourselves to deal with that issue. There are also questions of the vulnerability of command, control, communications, and intelligence, and here again it is worth raising the question of how arms control might help, even though we realize that to meet our requirements we must mostly look to our own resources.

From this substantive base and this program of questions to be raised for the future, I want to make a few propositions about the process itself. First of all, the technical complexity of the issues and their immense political sensitivity make the process inevitably slow. It's all very well to say the answer to that is to go faster, but in a sense that is merely to restate the problem rather than to offer a solution. Similarly, calling for simplicity is not much of an answer. Much of the technical detail in SALT II was rightly focused on issues of overwhelming concern to the United States, such as our desire for flexibility in cruise missile development and our insistence on tightness of a new types rule. There are palliatives to the delay problem such as agreements on concepts (on the order of the Vladivostok agreement) or recognition of the potential utility of external deadlines like party congresses and elections and summit meetings. But even with them we have to expect that any future talks will take time.

Moreover, patience in negotiating with the Soviet Union has many virtues. I think it is simply not the case that the United States was outnegotiated on the treaty. There is obvious ground for debate about whether the objectives set were correct ones and whether the result was an appropriate one. But I think that it is very, very difficult for anyone who will bother to read the publicly available record, much less the full record, to accept the commonly asserted proposition that the United States was simply outbargained. And the way to avoid being outbargained is, in large part, to be patient, to insist on positions, and to be prepared to go through long periods under pressure for "flexibility" without wavering on crucial points.

The second proposition is that "boundary condition" problems are becoming more and more acute, that what will be included is as much a critical issue in the negotiation as how to treat what is finally included. As we expand the subject matter and seek more fundamental agreements, that problem becomes more significant.

Third, I think the negotiating process itself, the maintenance of a dialogue, is not in fact terribly useful except in so far as it is directed at, to use Paul Nitze's terminology, achieving desirable, if not necessarily negotiable, agreements. Some people argue that we have learned a lot about Soviet perspectives from the negotiations. I don't find that to be true. I think that it is not clear that the exchange has added substantially to our understanding of Soviet views on the strategic issues. Rather, the process must seek a result. In my view, the temptation to hold talks only to prove that an agreement can't be reached is a very risky process, both politically and substantively. The West needs to have a position that can be publicly defended almost indefinitely, if need be, against pressures for flexibility—a publicly understandable position that, whatever its negotiability, would in fact produce a sound and equitable agreement if accepted. In short, playing propaganda games with gimmicky arms control proposals is not a competition in which the West has any comparative advantage. Advancing serious proposals is such a competition. Further, and relevant to both politics and substance, a basic lesson of the process is that there is no free lunch. Something for nothing is impossible. This is a caution for doves who unrealistically want arms control to substitute for needed programs. But it is also a caution for hawks who demand major improvements in negotiated agreements with no thought to what the United States will have to give in return. It seems to me absurd to criticize SALT for its failure to fix the ICBM vulnerability problem, and at the same time be prepared to let essentially local political pressures have a tremendous impact on how we go about fixing it unilaterally. Indeed, the test of the new administration's seriousness, not about arms control, but about maintaining strategic stability, will be whether or not the solution for the ICBM vulnerability problem it adopts is in fact a serious effort to deal with the survivability problem. Adequate military capability is a key determinant, both with and without an agreement, of our ability to lead the alliance and our ability to rally the U.S. public for the measures of both arms control and military funding that are necessary. Indeed, in a broader sense, it is critical to our overall relationship with the Soviets. We cannot avoid by arms control the need for adequate military programs.

What nonetheless makes arms control attractive is that it offers an almost unique opportunity to adjust what is required for adequacy. The proposition that arms control cannot substitute for adequate programs is now commonplace in the United States, but it is not in Europe. Historically, the idea was not accepted in the United States and perhaps it may not be again. The pressure for arms control negotiations is very strong in Europe, and I believe it could revive in this country as the costs of the unquestionably necessary but very expensive increases in our defense capability become clearer.

This brings me to the question of the political support for SALT in this country and to some degree in the alliance. In this country, political support for the SALT process has been undercut by the paradox of simultaneously overselling the agreements' actual accomplishments while not fully convincing people of the urgency of the need to do what can be done. Unrealistic expectations and standards are set up for SALT like "end the arms race" or, even less plausibly, "change the character of the Soviet regime." In fact, given the stakes of reducing the danger of nuclear war and the cost to U.S. military priorities and alliance leadership of an unconstrained strategic arms race, a modest but useful agreement is very desirable. There are in public life few enough things that are useful, even if modest, that those available should not be lightly cast aside.

Nonetheless, the fundamental political problem has been the failure, under both the Nixon-Ford administrations and the Carter administration, to put SALT effectively and acceptably in a context of U.S. foreign relations. Although that failure of public understanding is most dramatic in the case of SALT, it is not limited to SALT. This failure is, I think, a part of a broader failure to develop a publicly supportable policy for dealing with the Soviet Union over the long pull, without either war or appeasement. The term "linkage" summarizes the problem. It is a basic fact of international relations that we face a series of Soviet challenges, and yet we must develop a workable system for managing this profound and long-term—in all likelihood indefinite—competition. To that end, while competing effectively, we need to continue to seek agreements that shape and control that competition and particularly to shape and control the nuclear part of that competition to make it, if possible, less dangerous.

Broadly there are three possible statements of the relationship between SALT and U.S.-Soviet relations. The first is that SALT is possible and desirable because—or in the alternative formulation, only to the extent that—the Soviet leaders are, at least in their international behavior, responsible people. This is at once the extreme linkage view and the softest position. It is demonstrably false as a statement of fact, and it is a self-injuring, unattainable condition if it is permitted to be an obstacle to progress on agreements that would in fact serve our interests. It is also a not very significant criticism of agreements that are reached, that serve our security interests, to say the Soviet Union continues to be an irresponsible country.

The second view is that SALT is somehow a way to make the Soviets into more responsible people. This can be shorthanded as the "web of relationships" theory of SALT and U.S.-Soviet relations. This view, though more realistic than the first, is, I think, also sure to be disappointed if it is carried beyond the basic proposition that there is some level of restraint in Soviet international conduct, that if not followed makes SALT impossible—not merely in the tactical or domestic-political sense, but even impossible in principle. That is why it is certainly correct that whatever the prospects and potential of SALT and arms control, generally a Soviet invasion of Poland would effectively destroy those prospects for the indefinite future.

The third view is that SALT is part of a way to deal with an unpleasant world in which one of the superpowers is not a responsible actor by any reasonable definition of a term. Nonetheless, the USSR has vast power and is not going to go away, nor let itself be "arms raced" into oblivion. Moreover, although immensely aggressive in doctrine and highly opportunistic in practice, the Soviet Union is rationally self-interested in some things that are also consistent with our interest, such as avoiding nuclear war. This third view is one to which I subscribe, and it is a view that expects only modest accomplishments. It is also, I submit, the view of arms control that ought to commend itself to those with the most malevolent views of the Soviet Union's long-term objectives, because it offers the greatest focus on our specific security needs and on managing the long-term conflict.

In any event, until we get a resolution of these choices, or more realistically until we build broad political support for adopting the third approach, we cannot have much success in arms control. But given a willingness to deal realistically with the political facts, real accomplishments are, I think, possible. It is far too early to tell where the new administration will go. My own view is that they should be given time to do their homework and to let reality seep in as in one way or another it does seep in on administrations, and to hope for the best.

PANELISTS

Spurgeon Keeny, Jr.
Scholar in Residence, National Academy of Science;
Deputy Director, Arms Control and Disarmament Agency, 1977–1981

I find myself in general agreement with Walter Slocombe's comments, and in fact with most of Paul Nitze's comments about the outlines of a SALT III agreement. I feel, however, that the two speakers have avoided coming to grips with the most urgent arms control issue in the SALT area: What is to be done about the SALT II Agreement? This decision will clearly have a fundamental impact on whatever future actions we may decide to take in going forward with SALT III or abandoning the process. Although President Reagan and many of his close advisers strongly opposed SALT II and characterized it as fatally flawed, I think they will find the decision on how to proceed an extremely difficult one. Whatever one may believe about constitutional issues and international law, it's clear that SALT II has taken on a life of its own, and it is, in fact, a part of the strategic equation. Three presidents over a period of seven years were personally deeply engaged in the process, the heads of state signed the agreement, and I think in the eyes of the world it is a commitment on both sides, until one side or the other formally decides to disassociate itself from the arrangement.

In deciding how to proceed, I assume the new administration will give careful consideration to the security implications of their decision for the United States. With the rhetoric of the campaign behind them, I think they will have to weigh what things SALT II prohibits them from doing that they might want to do, and balance these against the various options that would be available to the Soviet Union in the absence of SALT II. With regard to the United States, unless the country decides to go for an all-out position of nuclear superiority, it's hard to see what SALT II would preclude except certain options for dealing with the *Minuteman* vulnerability problem, options I believe are not the most favorable ones and probably will not be chosen.

With regard to the Soviet Union, however, it's clear that in the absence of SALT II they can do lots of things. Given the momentum of their existing programs, these will be options directly at hand, ranging from the testing of more than one new missile, increasing the number of MIRVs on existing missile systems, failing to retire older *Yankee*-class submarines as they introduce new *Typhoons* or other ballistic missile systems, increasing the total number of land-based MIRVed ICBMs above the limit of 820 imposed in SALT II, and resuming testing, production, and deployment of the SS-16. In short, there are many things that the Soviets might choose to do.

The administration will also have to take into account the impact of their decision on the rest of the world. I have in mind particularly our NATO allies, but also general world opinion of the U.S. position toward the Soviet Union and toward security and peace.

What are the alternatives the administration has? The administration can seek to ratify SALT II as it stands; it can seek to have it ratified with minor cosmetic modifications; it can seek to modify it in a radical fashion; it can essentially do nothing and tacitly accept the restraints of SALT II; or finally, the administration can repudiate and withdraw from the treaty.

Addressing each of these, I think conventional wisdom finds ratification of the treaty without modification politically impossible. I personally continue to believe ratification would be the most desirable outcome for the United States, for the reasons outlined by Ralph Earle and Walter Slocombe. I also think that it should not be dismissed out of hand. Once the Reagan administration has locked in a substantial increase in the military budget, and made whatever military decisions in the strategic area that they deem necessary, assuming that these do not conflict with the SALT II provisions, it would be a very interesting and courageous political act to proceed with ratification. It's something that could be done easily by the Reagan administration. It goes without saying that this would be welcomed enthusiastically by all of our NATO allies, and would create a very positive attitude toward U.S. leadership throughout the world.

The second alternative is to accept the treaty with minor modifications, by which, I suppose, one means modifications that the Soviets might well be prepared to accept, directly or after a relatively brief negotiation. The effect would be strictly cosmetic. I think that there's little question that such a treaty could be easily ratified with the Reagan administration's support. The drawbacks are that it's always hard to know how minor is minor, and in any effort to reopen the treaty some points going beyond simple clarification might be advanced, in which case the Soviets themselves might come back with modifications that would either be unacceptable to the United States or have a net weakening effect on the desirability of the treaty. An extension of the protocol comes to mind as an obvious point that the Soviets could pursue.

The next alternative would be to come in with major modifications, including points to which Nitze has referred. I think it's clear that if these are really major modifications, it's tantamount to initiating the SALT III negotiations, which is not really a solution to the SALT II problem. If we reopen the negotiations with fundamental changes, it's clear it's going to be a very long and difficult negotiation. I think only an extreme optimist would say it would be completed and ready for Senate consideration during this term of the presidency.

The next alternative would be simply to do nothing and tacitly accept the constraints of the agreement. This, as I understand it, is essentially what the administration is doing. Secretary Haig made this clear when he issued a statement clarifying some of the comments previously made by Navy Secretary Lehman. There is adequate precedent for tacit acceptance of international agreements, certainly in the arms control area. I would predict that this situation will continue until someone takes a positive step to change it. This situation is essentially the same as a ratified treaty though clearly less stable. I think NATO would find this an acceptable procedure, and it probably would provide an adequate basis to proceed with the TNF negotiations on which NATO places great political importance.

Finally, the treaty could be renounced. One could argue that this would not require a formal action; one would just not abide by it when the time came. For the reasons that I've indicated, this would, in the eyes of the world, put us in the position of acting in violation of an agreement. If we want to operate outside of it, we must withdraw from the treaty and indicate that we are no longer bound by it. While the Soviets in reaction might not, in fact, pursue all the programs that I indicated previously, it's hard to imagine that they will not exercise some of those options, many of which are anathema to people concerned with the Soviet threat.

I think such a development would be extremely serious in regard to our NATO and world relations. I wouldn't go so far as to say that it would destroy the alliance, but I think it would put very serious pressure on NATO countries concerned about a policy of confrontation with the Soviet Union, and it seems hard to imagine how one could even pretend to pursue the TNF negotiations in the absence of any SALT framework, formal or informal. If SALT II were repudiated, I find it very hard to see how the SALT process could easily be resumed again, or how the United States would easily regain a leadership role in world eyes, in NATO eyes, in the search for world peace.

Gough Reinhardt
Staff Physicist, Lawrence Livermore National Laboratory

I'll try to soften some of the remarks I have to make by stating first that I am proud to be associated with people who have spent so much effort in trying to limit strategic arms by negotiation, and this despite the skepticism with which many people like myself have viewed these efforts. History has not been kind to arms control negotiations. We made an honest effort, we made it again and again, and it appears to me that this new administration is about to make one more attempt, one more experiment. But I believe it's time for an assessment. I believe the evidence is overwhelming that this experiment has failed. The United States is far less secure today than it was even a decade ago. What is today seen as a worrisome imbalance in one arm of the triad, is, in the views of many of us, fast approaching a very serious situation that could become critical in the next few years.

Is it fair to blame this deterioration of the U.S. strategic position on arms control in general, and SALT in particular? It may not be fair, but let me speak of two things I think the process has done. The two key words that come to my mind are "delusion" and "compromise." I think that the SALT process has deluded our nation and its leadership and led us to make serious mistakes in the maintenance of a viable strategic deterrent. We've been deluded into thinking that SALT would end the strategic arms race and the delusion blinded us to the ascendancy of strategic arms in the Soviet Union. We've been deluded into thinking that SALT would save us money, money that could be spent on various humanitarian purposes. Maybe we forget that the principal purpose of free government is to maintain freedom for its people and, if possible, freedom for its allies. We've been deluded by arguments that SALT would bind Brezhnev's successor, that SALT was ammunition for the doves in the Kremlin, in the Politburo. We've even been deluded that the Soviet race to build strategic forces was due to a bureaucratic inertia, which would simmer down as the SALT process developed. We've let these delusions encourage attitudes toward nuclear weapons that I feel are childish. We've been blackmailed by fear and innuendo. In short, the delusions of which I've spoken have blinded us to Soviet malevolence.

I said these delusions have led us to compromise. SALT has allowed us to compromise strategic planning in the name of arms control. Resolute and hard decisions have not been made because of the fantasy of control by negotiation. In constructing a strategic force the defense planner compromises with himself as to what the SALT process will allow. The Department of Defense then compromises with the Arms Control and Disarmament Agency, and again with the SALT process. At the end of all this, the Executive Branch takes a position that is compromised once more in dealing with Congress. The nation now has a position. The nation takes that position to the SALT table and again, perhaps, compromises.

In the end what little impetus for constructive change may have existed is blunted. It's blunted by forces that, unfortunately, rally around the cause of SALT and arms control; forces that, under any pretext, would deny money to the defense establishment; forces that prefer to appease, rather than to compete with, totalitarianism.

So I believe the experiment has failed. The unjustified hope that arms control would relieve us from hard, strategic choices has led us to a constellation of dangers. What do you do when an experiment fails? You write it up carefully in your notebook, put the notebook away, and then abandon the experiment.

Roman Kolkowitz

Director, Political Science/Center for International and Strategic Affairs, University of California, Los Angeles

I agree to a large extent with Mr. Slocombe and Mr. Nitze. I would, however, like to turn our attention to one aspect of the several presentations. That is, how SALT and the arms control process are related—both in the Soviet Union and the United States—to other policy processes and national objectives.

My point will be that, upon examination of the record, we will observe profound asymmetries between the Soviet and American situations. There is an absence of even rough equivalence in the way Soviet decision makers and American decision makers view the role and importance of the arms control process in the flow of policy.

Briefly, I suggest the following. In the United States, for better or worse, we have come to look on the arms control process as a holistic universal process; that is, to link it with a number of other American interests abroad. Our stance, therefore, has by and large been that either the Soviets perceive and understand the mutual interest, wisdom, and logic of such linkage or we will do something else. I suggest that the Soviets have a quite different way of going about arms control. The Soviets consider arms control issues as tactical problems subordinated to other larger, and possibly more pressing, Soviet national interests. One might say that in the Soviet Union, Clausewitz leads not only in strategy but also in arms control. That is, the political considerations that shape foreign policy and arms control policy in Soviet defense policy choices are at all times subordinated to a kind of political grand plan.

In the United States, one might say that Professor Parkinson leads. If in the Soviet Union there is a sense of national politics that determines where SALT and the arms control process leads, in the United States it is, as most of us know, bureaucratic politics. These are two very different kinds of politics, and therefore, one might say two different problems of linkage. One kind of linkage that we should be interested in is linkage at home—linkage between our arms control interests, processes, tactics, and our broader foreign and defense policy interests and objectives. I would suggest, while not trying to make the Soviets seem ten feet tall, that there seems to be a better integrating system at work in the Soviet Union. That kind of linkage is not a problem in the Soviet Union, in my opinion. One might also want to ask, in the context of SALT and arms control, what purpose does such linkage serve, how does it relate to defense, strategic, and other interests?

Well, in a simplistic fashion, one might summarize the asymmetry between Soviet and American attitudes to SALT as follows. The United States, by and large, remains a status quo power. Its interests are essentially those of a conservative, international system. It is not interested in destabilizing various parts of the world. It's not a revolutionary power. I would characterize the Soviet Union in the last number of years, and this is open to disagreement, as an expanding power. One that is quasi-revolutionary; that is, its foreign and defense policy interests are often best achieved by selective and controlled destabilization or instability in various parts of the world. Therefore one might suggest that the Soviet interests in arms control are different than American interests in arms control, because Soviet interests around the world are different. These Soviet aims might be roughly described as being of three different kinds: (1) vis-à-vis the West, stabilization and normalization; (2) vis-à-vis China, containment and partial isolation; and (3) in the Third World, selective destabilization and expansion. I am suggesting that arms control or SALT is, from the Soviet perspective, a highly desired negotiation process and a serious policy objective as long as it remains within that first sector of their global policy range. That is, as long as it doesn't interfere with those parts of their foreign and defense policies that support the expansionistic drive of the Soviet Union.

Let me summarize my remarks. The priorities and objectives of the two countries are intensely, profoundly asymmetrical. The tactical objectives that I've indicated are asymmetrical. The nations' respective perceptions of the other's interests are also asymmetrical. We, for example, have for many years thought we could use our arms control negotiations as a way of not only rewarding the Soviets, but also possibly compelling them, punishing them, or constraining them; even at times deluding ourselves into believing we could manipulate and fine-tune their domestic politics in such a way as to create certain desirable changes advantageous or preferable to us. All of this through the SALT/ arms control process. As a number of my colleagues have said, the record on all of this is rather gloomy, but this has nevertheless been part of our perception. Finally, to return to a point I made at the beginning, I would suggest that our expectations about the ability to use arms control as leverage, as an instrument to bring about both changes within the Soviet Union and changes in Soviet foreign policy interests, to essentially Americanize the Soviet foreign and defense process, is a delusion. In addition, the need for closer linkage at home between SALT and arms control interests and objectives, as well as other foreign political and strategic objectives, is clearly indicated. In other words, the record of SALT for the last ten years is a poor one, and the prospects, on the basis of those past ten years, are not very promising.

DISCUSSION

Brent Scowcroft: I think that an exercise in lessons learned from SALT can be very valuable if we maintain a sense of perspective. But Reinhardt bothered me by lumping on the back of SALT all of our problems and strategic planning over the last decade or so. In the current climate it's far too easy to overlook the mood of the country at the time we really began arms control, back in 1968 and 1969. There was Vietnam and a demand for reordering our national priorities. The ABM Treaty, for example—needed by the hawks for military purposes and by the doves for SALT—passed by one vote in the Congress. MBFR, undertaken to defuse the Mansfield Amendment, succeeded in large measure. Part of the reason for SALT I was that we were, in fact, not competing with the Soviet Union in strategic weapons, and one way to call a halt to the whole thing was by negotiation rather than by competing. In addition, we got things like *Trident* accepted by the Congress in part because of SALT I. So I think as we look over the record of SALT we need to keep some perspective and to relate it to the climate of the times in which the negotiations took place.

Ralph Goldman: I have two questions for Walter Slocombe. Most democratic political institutions assume that there is no final or total solution to human problems and thus a significant function of bureaucratic and legislative institutions is to keep the search and the communication going. Some of us hope this is what the SALT process is about. My question is how can the SALT process be converted into a permanent bureaucratic forum? A related question, and one that I think never receives the attention it deserves, is how can we make the SALT process a multilateral rather than a bilateral forum?

Walter Slocombe: To take the second part of the question first, I think it would be disfunctional to make the SALT process, which has enough problems of its own bilaterally, multilateral. There certainly is a place for multilateral arms control, and there is a relationship between what the United States and the Soviet Union do in their bilateral military and political relationships and what other countries do. But I think the threat to Situation Q from third countries is not a significant part of the problem and to introduce third countries into the negotiations would only complicate the situation for practically no benefit.

With respect to the permanent bureaucratic forum, I don't think that having ambassadors read prepared statements at each other does much for the human condition, except if there is some purpose to those statements. While I think the picture of SALT deluding us is grotesquely overdrawn, the process must be aimed at specific agreements to be useful, and to avoid the danger of expecting results when none are forthcoming. There may be some agreements that are negotiable but not desirable. The test is not to enter into a negotiation unless you have a sense of the result that you want, a result that would be in your interest and that you can publicly defend. What I see as the important permanent process is defining those steps that are in our interest and obtainable now, gradually building on that, and moving forward with a continuing expansion of limitations.

Charles Henkin: My first question is to both Nitze and Slocombe. Do they think it's feasible to develop a coherent strategic doctrine and do they believe that it's feasible to integrate such a doctrine with arms control planning? Next, Mr. Nitze mentioned a need to have an interface between TNF arms control and central system arms control. Would he comment on how this relates to extended deterrence?

Paul Nitze: I think it's possible, but extremely difficult, to develop a coherent strategic doctrine. People have worked on it, are working on it, and I know of no task requiring more objective and strenuous thought. It really is immensely difficult. But I don't believe that's any reason for not doing it, and I think it ought to be done. It's never going to be done perfectly, but let's do it as well as we possibly can. Next, can it be integrated with one's arms control policy? I think it must be integrated with arms control policy. That also is difficult because the pressures on the people dealing with arms control are somewhat different from pressures on those who are trying to deal with strategic doctrine.

Your last point had to do with extended deterrence and its relationship to TNF. I'm not sure that I see it that way. I see the problem of TNF modernization and negotiation as a very difficult problem arising largely from the political needs of our allies and their desires and their particular way of looking at things. What we can do in order to accommodate those needs and desires is not directly related to extended deterrence. To me extended deterrence comes as a by-product from having an adequate standoff with the Soviet Union in overall strategic offensive capabilities. It's somewhat separated from, but not totally separated from, the question of TNF modernization and the negotiations there.

Walter Slocombe: I think it's important to work on strategic doctrine. Strategic doctrine is sometimes used in the relatively narrow but important sense of what propositions about the use of nuclear weapons, if they had to be used, contribute to deterrence. I think the basic proposition about that part of the strategic doctrine is that there is not a contradiction between attention to the question of how you would use nuclear weapons, if necessary, and deterrence. Because deterrence, by definition, depends on shaping Soviet understanding of what would happen if a war started. More broadly, though, I think a consensus on the role of strategic weapons and strategic nuclear power in our overall security policy is critical to arms control policy. It sets the criterion for evaluating an arms control outcome, or an arms control proposal. One has to have a coherent sense of what one expects of nuclear weapons in terms of foreign policy. It is a reasonable test of arms control proposals that they should, at a minimum, make it easier, not harder, to get whatever results you want from nuclear weapons in terms of U.S. foreign policy.

I don't agree, of course, with the proposition that arms control has fundamentally shaped our doctrinal or program decisions over the past ten or fifteen years. There is, of course, a view that it's rather too much the other way around. But I do think that one ought to test arms control propositions by their relationship to an overall concept of the role of nuclear weapons. One of the advantages of that process is that it tends to introduce an element of realism in the demands that are placed on arms control policies. When one asks whether or not arms control policy solved all of these problems, one also has to ask whether there is anything else that will solve these problems. One must ask whether one is really prepared to pay the price, politically, economically, and in terms of stability, of trying to solve these problems entirely unilaterally. That is one of the things one learns in an effort to determine the role of nuclear weapons in our overall strategic policy.

Joseph Nye: I have a question for Nitze. I, as always, was impressed by the clarity of his presentation, and I was intrigued by the objective as rough equivalence or parity. How does that relate to the NATO doctrine established in Document MC-14/3* in 1967, which holds that Soviet conventional superiority requires an American nuclear superiority, first at the theater, and then at the strategic level, thus forming a rough equivalence overall. Yet that doctrine when played back through the Soviet Union leads them to increased defense spending, which is something that we need less of, not more. How would you relate your objective of rough equivalence to existing doctrine, and what sort of over-arching concept might alleviate that particular problem?

Paul Nitze: That problem arose very clearly in 1965 and 1969 when we surveyed seriously the problems of SALT negotiations with the Soviet Union. As I said in my prepared remarks, we came to the conclusion that we couldn't expect the Soviet Union to accept an agreement that gave us superiority in strategic nuclear arms. It was our thought that if there were balance in the overall strategic equation— essential equivalence—that would be enough to maintain the security of Europe if that were coupled with a sufficient effort to assure not too great a deficiency in conventional forces in Europe. This depended

---

*MC-14/3 is the NATO document of 1967 which established the defense doctrine for Western Europe. It mandated that Western Europe be defended by a conventional forward defense—a long thin line at the eastern frontier of West Germany. This approach was necessary because of German political conditions. A Soviet breakthrough would be defended by the ability to control escalation at the nuclear level either in the immediate theater capabilities or long-range theater, and then finally at the central strategic levels.

upon the idea that we would stick with a pretty rigorous approach to essential equivalence, and that bears upon Pierre Lellouche's question this morning. He asked whether a democracy can stick with its decisions for a long enough period of time. I still think that the decision in 1969 was correct. We should have sought, and stuck by, the idea of essential equivalence despite any impact upon European security. But we have, I think, let slip this insistence upon essential equivalence and we've got to worry about that.

Joseph Nye: If we follow your advice on parity at the central strategic level, does it still follow that we have to do something about revising 14/3? The escalation dominance that it implies is not there.

Paul Nitze: No, I don't think one ought to tinker with 14/3. We went through years of argument about 14/3 and finally got it approved. It is the best compromise with respect to that kind of document in NATO that one can arrive at. If one were to open that up now, I think the result would be bad, not constructive.

Michael May: You said we departed from the criteria of rough equivalence. Could you say in what way we have departed from the criteria of rough equivalence in SALT?

Paul Nitze: We departed from the criteria of rough equivalence when we agreed to the Soviet monopoly on the large ballistic missiles.

Michael May: Is that a meaningful departure? Do we need such missiles? Or is it mostly a symbolic departure?

Paul Nitze: It's a departure from essential equivalence. The question of whether or not we ourselves wanted such missiles is quite a separate problem, which just confuses the issue. We thought strongly that those large missiles, missiles larger than the SS-11s as we saw it at the time, were positively destabilizing, and would be disadvantageous to the search for Situation Q. They shouldn't be there. Anybody who takes seriously the idea of crisis stability should recognize that.

Charles Schwartz: It was said, I believe by Mr. Slocombe, that an important reason for SALT was the assumption of a rational self-interest on the part of the Soviet Union in avoiding nuclear war. I'd like to turn that around and pose the following question: Is there a rational self-interest on the part of the leadership of the United States in avoiding nuclear war? Now, I know that's very provocative, but I think the discussion so far has been extremely narrow. I don't mean to suggest that there is anything like malevolence in the intentions of the United States's leadership, as Reinhardt sees in the Soviet Union, but I think an objective look at the weapons, at the counterforce developments over the last decade and projected into the future, combined with the number of rather explicit statements that have come out of the present leadership in Washington, give a substantial basis for many people to worry about that question. I think people who are seriously concerned with arms control, or whatever is left of the concept of arms control, should seriously address themselves to that question. How can they push or provoke the present government in this country to convincing skeptics—a few like myself in this country, I think a substantial number in Europe, and perhaps crucially, a number of people of importance in the Soviet Union—that the United States, in fact, is not preparing primarily, though not overtly, for fighting nuclear war?

Walter Slocombe: I'm sure there are certain people in this room who have more confidence in the current administration than I. But not on this point. It is all very well for people who are concerned about avoiding nuclear war to say all the responsibility for the nuclear arms race does not rest exclusively with the Soviet Union. There is something to that. On the other hand, I think it is very hard to look at the record of arms control negotiations over the period since 1945 dealing with nuclear issues and not come away with the feeling that it has not been from a lack of American willingness to try more radical proposals that we haven't gotten farther. That's one proposition in terms of the history of arms control very broadly painted.

With respect to the question of preparation for nuclear war, unfortunately, until we come up with a better scheme, the only way we can avoid a nuclear war, given the realities of Soviet objectives and Soviet military power, is to deter it. As I said in response to Henkin's question, there is no contradiction between readiness to fight a nuclear war and deterrence of a nuclear war, because by definition deterrence depends on affecting Soviet predictions about how a war would be fought.

That is very different from saying that you believe that nuclear war can be an affirmative instrument of U.S. foreign policy, chosen deliberately. Right or wrong, the United States can choose deliberately to send troops into El Salvador, just as the Soviet Union can deliberately choose to send troops into Afghanistan. Those two decisions may or may not be good ideas, but they are available rational choices. It is quite different to say, on the one hand, that the United States adopts a military posture to prevent the Soviet union from getting any military advantage from fighting a nuclear war, compared to saying that we believe in war fighting in any sense as a deliberate instrument of policy.

Michael May: I'd like to follow up an aspect of Professor Schwartz's question that I think has not been sufficiently answered.

The buildup of thousands of nuclear weapons on both sides may not be an irrational thing, but certainly its rationality needs explaining in the minds of everyone. One of the underlying concerns in these questions, and I know in the minds of other people here, is what kind of policy framework can be given so as to make as sure as possible that one kind of irrationality may not lead to another, that an arms race will not lead to a war. In what way do the directions for arms control, in particular, take into account this feature of human affairs? I'd like to ask that of both Nitze and Slocombe.

Paul Nitze: What comes to mind is the debate I had last summer in Germany at the University of Freiburg with Ambassador Graver. Frankly, that was a dull debate because we agreed with each other. But the students disagreed with both of us. After the debate, some of the students came up to me and said that they thought the continued emphasis by Graver and me upon armaments in order to deter the Russians was nonsensical. Clearly a conventional war in Europe would be a disaster for Germany; a theater nuclear war would be a greater disaster; and an intercontinental nuclear war would be an unbelievable disaster; and, therefore, there was no sense in any part of this. And what did I have to answer to that?

My answer to them was, "What you're really asking is the question, isn't it better to be red than dead?" And they said, "Well, that is, indeed, the question bothering the youth of Germany today, and in particular is bothering us." I said, "Well, you don't want to be red, do you?" And they said, "My goodness, NO! The worse thing in the world that we can think of is to accept Soviet rule of Germany." I said, "The point is that all of Allied policy since World War II has been devoted to creating a situation in which the question of 'red' or 'dead' does not arise; where you don't have to be either 'red' or 'dead.' Certainly the policy that we have followed in your country and our country and the rest of Europe since World War II has been successful. That issue has not arisen, as to whether it's better to be 'red' or 'dead.' Do you think there's a better chance of avoiding that question if we work together, if we do the reasonable things in the various fields of armament, in the conventional and theater nuclear field, and in the intercontinental field, than if we just abandon the effort? If the latter, then the issue clearly will arise as to whether it's better to be 'red' or 'dead,' and is that what you want?" And they said, "Well, nobody's put it to us that way." For the moment, they were satisfied. Now, I don't know whether that bears upon your question, but I think it does.

Walter Slocombe: I agree with virtually all of that. If you look historically at why wars have started, you will find they have rarely started because a group of leaders sat down and decided that today the correlation of forces was just right in order to get away with it. Wars have arisen out of political conflicts in which countries have been driven to the use of military force on a large scale, not because they believed it was particularly likely to work, but because they believed it was necessary to avoid a worse result. It is important to bear in mind the dangers of an irrational decision. That's why I think it's important to continue to pursue what opportunities there are in arms control. It's also obviously important to continue to build up our defenses. But it is simply untrue to suggest that because of arms control we haven't built an ABM system that will ensure us all against nuclear war. No such system exists. None ever will exist. I assert there is no immediate prospect of any such system. Therefore, we need to continue to work in an immensely difficult world. One of the things that makes it difficult is nuclear weapons. But it is, unfortunately, not the only thing that makes the world difficult. My basic answer is that I do think that arms control, for all its problems, continues to have a role in reducing the danger of an irrational use of nuclear weapons.

Charles McDonald: These remarks are addressed to Nitze. As a technologist who has spent most of his life trying to make good the national premise that we have technological superiority over the Soviets, and therefore will always be in a position to outweigh the sheer numbers, weight advantages, or whatever, I have to say that there is a limit. Enough compromises have been made in these last several agreements, or proposed at the present time, to cause me to despair of our intellectual and technological ability to keep up with the serious and major desire for one more signature on one more treaty.

It is true that a good, big guy can beat a good, little guy any day in the week. I sincerely hope that people, yourselves included, appreciate that we aren't looking for a fight in the nuclear arena. However, one could occur, for rational or irrational reasons, and the position the United States must be in at that point is to be able to attend to it in a way that total shambles will, in fact, not occur.

I have always been appalled that the United States decided in SALT I that we would use our population as a shield for our strategic nuclear forces. I thought it should be the other way around. I would like to ask, do we still believe that ABM in all forms is morally unacceptable or are we going to go on believing that deterrence will somehow succeed and that war will never occur?

Paul Nitze: Let me start with SALT I. Preceding SALT I was the debate in the Senate on the ABM authorization, which was won by one vote, and, frankly, I think I was instrumental in getting that vote won. One of the arguments that I made during that debate was that President Nixon had asked for approval of this authorization with the intention of negotiating with the Soviet Union on an ABM treaty. And I thought one should support President Nixon because I couldn't see any way in which an ABM treaty could be negotiated unless we had an ABM program going forward with vigor. I think that was a correct judgment. The upshot was that we did negotiate an ABM treaty. But the reason we had really very little alternative was that the Congress was not about to support, for any period of time, an ABM deployment beyond one and possibly two sites; and one and possibly two sites weren't really going to give us much in the way of an ABM.

It seemed to me that the problem was not so much whether we ought to have the ABM Treaty, because I think we had no alternative, but whether we got enough from the Russians for signing the ABM Treaty. There are many Russians who say that it was a disaster from the standpoint of those people in the Soviet Union who believed in arms control. The Soviet military had taken the position they could get an ABM treaty on equal terms without giving up anything in the field of offensive weapons, and the people in the foreign office maintained that wasn't so. They believed the United States would insist on some payment on the offensive side. We didn't get it. That was, in part, due to many of the political problems that existed in 1972.

Your other questions dealt with technology and whether or not it is possible for us to assume that we will have technological superiority in the indefinite future. In a way, I differ with your viewpoint. I think if we work at it, we are in a better position in certain fields of technology than is the USSR and will continue to be in a better position. At the moment, the Soviets are putting three times the effort into it that we are, and our edge in technology is not the equivalent of three times the effort. So I think today we are falling back in the field of technology. One other point is that, certainly, twenty years ago everybody held the view that technology was increasing exponentially in its significance. Frankly, I didn't believe then that was true, and I believe we are at the other part of the "S curve" on technology, particularly with respect to its impact on defense. A third point is that you don't need exact equivalence. I think if we have rough equivalence, that can be a very effective deterrent because I'm sure the Russians don't want nuclear war either. If the difference between the capability of the two sides is too great, then I really don't think it's possible for the weaker side to long outsmart the strong side. But if it's close, I think then it is possible, but it's got to be pretty close, in my view.

3

THEATER NUCLEAR FORCE RESTRAINTS

SPEAKERS

John Woodworth
Office of the Assistant Secretary of Defense (International Security Policy)

It is a pleasure to be here. I know that Richard Perle* would like to have been here, especially with so many targets of opportunity gathered together in this audience. I do not propose to carry Richard's brief today. Rather, I prefer to address you as someone who has been involved in theater nuclear policy and other national security issues for a substantial period of time and, more recently, involved in the question of TNF arms control.

I think this kind of discussion is important. TNF arms control is an area where we need good ideas and new thought and imagination to apply to the problem. Very often we hear learned lamentations about the complexity of TNF arms control, and about the fact that we are engaged in a political charade, or about the fact that we cannot go forward with TNF arms control in the absence of SALT. All of these are lamentations I have made myself. But the fact remains that we are on the road to negotiations and we need to treat the subject with all the seriousness we can bring to bear.

When I reviewed the agenda that referred to TNF constraints—meaning arms control—it occurred to me that we do not operate in a vacuum in terms of restraints, especially in the area of TNF. There are several other kinds of restraints that I think are useful to bear in mind.

First, there is, as always, a resource constraint. Rarely are there times

---

*Richard Perle, Assistant Secretary of Defense for International Security Policy, was the scheduled speaker but was unable to attend.

when our defense planners and our weapons designers do not have good ideas on ways we can improve our TNF. Seldom, however, do we have the resources to be able to fully exploit those kinds of ideas even if we would like to do so. Second, I think it is fair to say, to borrow a phrase from another context, that for TNF, politically, there is no such thing as a free lunch. TNF by definition involves our allies and defense cooperation with them and requires the most astute and careful management. Third, there are military restraints we should be aware of. TNF involves the whole nexus of problems associated with how we would use nuclear weapons. It's not a simple problem because the other side, whom we are seeking to deter, possessing large inventories of nuclear weapons, faces us with all of the perennial problems that have been debated for years about how to effectively use nuclear weapons, how to develop an effective doctrine, and how to combine that doctrine with our weaponry. In short, we have to contend with all of these kinds of restraints; they are important to bear in mind when thinking about restraints in terms of arms control.

Let me turn now to the context, as I see it, in which TNF arms control now exists. We are in a situation of multiple pressures. Quite obviously, we are faced with a substantial growth in the threat in the TNF area. It's an across the board threat. Especially notable is that of the SS-20. I think it is worth noting that our estimates about the SS-20 that we made a couple of years ago appear to be wrong. That threat has been growing much more substantially than we thought it would. We do not know how far or how rapidly it will go but it is apparent that we face a major and growing build-up. We also face a threat that is growing in other areas. It involves other missiles that the Soviet Union is currently deploying—SS-21s, SS-22s, SS-23s. It involves a wholesale replacement of Soviet aircraft with new-generation aircraft. And it involves other battlefield systems, as well. We cannot ignore this.

An additional pressure is the public debate we face right now; in particular, the public debate in Europe. I have never seen the debate at such an extensive level before. Clearly, much of it centers around the 1979 decision to deploy new LRTNF. It is not surprising that we would have this kind of debate; it was anticipated. But I must confess that it has been even sharper than I thought it would be. Quite frankly, it is a debate that we must win, because in its more extreme forms, if we lose it will produce, I believe, very fundamental alterations in our security and our relationships with our allies.

An additional pressure is propaganda. Quite clearly, the Soviets will not lose opportunities for engaging in propaganda. This is especially true in the area of TNF and as it relates to TNF arms control or our modernization efforts. It is a very vulnerable area for propaganda, for reasons that most of you well know. In some ways the Soviets have been rather clumsy at it. Their recent moratorium proposal was not skilled in substance or in timing. But I think in the future we will see more sophisticated efforts. In any case, we will see very persistent efforts.

A number of you today have commented on the complexity of TNF arms control. I think it goes without saying that if nothing else we have discovered in our arms control experience over the past two decades that the issues are almost invariably more complex than we think they will be when we begin. TNF will not be an exception. The policy choices are hard. The analytical foundation for understanding TNF is, in fact, more complicated than it is for strategic forces. The technical problems related to an effective TNF arms control regime are very difficult. Coupled with this is the political dimension that makes it different from SALT. TNF inevitably involves our allies, whose political sensitivities we will have to manage with utmost care.

By and large, TNF arms control is a new issue. I have been struck, in attempting to keep up with the literature that is published outside of government, by the relative paucity of constructive literature on the subject. I think this contrasts, surprisingly, to the rather massive amount of literature that you find on arms control in general and especially on SALT. By and large, people in the government must look to their own resources in thinking about the problem of TNF arms control. Since it is a new subject, and one which will receive increased attention, I hope it will receive more emphasis in universities, research organizations, and elsewhere, producing ideas that we will need and a consensus and understanding about what we should be trying to do.

TNF was involved on the margins of SALT and in MBFR. The talks in Geneva last fall, however, represented the first time in which the United States and the Soviet Union sat down and focused on TNF arms control as a discrete issue. In that context, I agree with Nitze's remark that we need a concerted effort to make the Soviets understand that forward-based systems (FBS) are not somethng for which we should owe compensation in strategic terms. I would say, with the focus on TNF in Geneva, we spent a lot of effort hammering home that very point. Now, negotiating that kind of point with the Soviets is not something that after a half-hour's debate, they say, "You win." Obviously, it is going to take a lot of time. In this vein, those talks did give us some indication of the road ahead. Not surprisingly, the major lesson we got is that the road will not be easy, and it will not be short.

Finally, in terms of the context, a number of people this morning have talked about the lessons from the past decade of arms control.

We are going to have to be realistic. Arms control, especially as it relates to SALT, but in other areas as well, has had a checkered history. A consensus has not emerged and we cannot ignore this. There is heightened skepticism about what arms control can achieve. We are going to have to be quite candid with our publics. This is true in this country and I think it is going to have to be true in Europe. There must be explanations by responsible officials at all levels to make clear what we can and cannot expect arms control to do. If we fail to do that, I think we are going to have serious difficulties. I would like to think that there is a new sense of realism in the United States. I am afraid that it is less true in Europe in the current debate that is going on there. My own feeling is that in that debate there are unjustified expectations about arms control that are emotionally and ideologically based. The need to bring about a greater sense of realism is more serious in Europe than in this country.

Let me turn now to some goals and criteria. I do not want to get into specific goals, which will have to be developed over time. At the highest level of generalization, however, we need limitations that are genuinely stabilizing, equitable, and verifiable. We need to ensure that limitations we entertain do not give only the illusion of these qualities and not the reality. In TNF arms control there is a great risk of moving toward agreements, or features of agreements, that can produce such illusions of beneficial effects for our own security. It will take a good deal of self-discipline to ensure we do not make those mistakes. We need a sober and uncompromising fix on basic defense objectives. We must be clear with the Soviets, with our publics, and with ourselves, that with or without TNF arms control, we will meet our security objectives. Fundamentally, this means that we must look to our defense efforts and that we must not rely on arms control to solve our problems. It has been said many times, and I think correctly, that it is possible for the momentum of negotiations to take on its own logic. Our decision-making system must instill its own self-discipline to ensure that we keep our eyes on security objectives.

Let me suggest a few criteria relating to TNF arms control and the future. As a general proposition, I think our defense programs and objectives should drive our arms control positions. The limitations we seek should achieve genuine results. We need, for example, to reduce in a manifestly clear way threats to the survivability of our TNF and to supporting elements like command and control. Our positions must support the defense programs we deem essential. At the same time we must pay careful attention to future options.

Second, limitations we develop and propose must support our strategy. In the case of the United States and NATO, that strategy is flexible response. I foresee no basic change to that strategy. In that context, TNF is a critical linkage between conventional and strategic forces. We have required, and we will require in the future, a full range of options. We can afford no gaps in the spectrum of TNF, no levels at which the Soviets could achieve a substantial escalation dominance. Furthermore, I think we must bear in mind that TNF requirements are not simply a function of Soviet TNF; they are a function of conventional threats as well. In that sense, and this is important, much of our TNF, in terms of its military purposes, is not related to countering the other side's TNF. It is related to countering conventional capabilities of the other side and a variety of other targets that are nonnuclear in character.

Finally, with regard to criteria for TNF arms control, our positions, our approach, and the process we follow should support coupling. Historically, the United States has assumed major responsibility for the nuclear defense of our allies and we have done that in full cooperation with them. I realize that there have been long debates on the issue of coupling, whether it's good, bad, rising, lowering. I find most of that debate arid. Clearly the growth of Soviet strategic capabilities affects the perceptions of coupling and perhaps even its practice, at least in theoretical terms. Coupling has never been risk-free; that is clearly recognized. But I think, as a matter of fundamental political and military policy, it serves our interests and will be maintained. Coupling has specific military and political dimensions in planning and in policy. TNF arms control, as such, cannot produce coupling. By and large, we must rely on our programs, and our planning, and our declaratory policy to achieve that. Nonetheless, in the positions we develop and in the way in which we carry out negotiations, we need to be sensitive to how coupling is affected. At the same time, we need to recognize that Soviet motivation in this area is exactly the opposite. It has been a long-standing Soviet objective to decouple the United States from its allies. Their efforts will continue, and I think we will see it in spades once we are engaged in further and detailed negotiations on TNF.

I would like to talk about a few issues, call them design issues if you will, that are relevant to structuring a TNF arms control approach. Ralph Earle referred to some of these. They are not new and you are familiar with their complexities. I do not propose to offer any answers or positions right now; that would not be appropriate in an open forum from someone like myself. But I want to cite some examples for illustration.

First, and most obvious, is the question of systems. On both sides, U.S. and Soviet, there is a broad range of systems—missiles of long range, missiles of shorter range down into battlefield levels, a variety of aircraft, and other systems as well. The problem in TNF arms control is where to draw the line. In any sensible approach to TNF arms control you cannot encompass all systems on both sides. But when you are considering where to draw the line, you must consider the interrelation between them. In doing this, we need to guard against the perverse effect that could arise in terms of addressing certain systems and excluding others. We face geographical asymmetries with the Soviets. To limit some systems that have, for example, a substantial reach, let's say a capability to reach from Soviet territory to Western Europe, leaves the question of other systems that may be deployed forward and still be able to cover the same targets in Western Europe. These are difficult problems that need to be thought about very carefully.

Counting—how do we count systems that might be limited? The systems of each side are different in varying respects. With regard to missiles, the Soviets have a MIRV system, the SS-20. Insofar as U.S. systems are concerned—those in the field or those we plan to deploy— the GLCM and *Pershing* carry only one warhead. They have different capabilities, different qualities. Now the more pedestrian examples of ways to count systems are through launchers, warheads, and missiles. There can be combinations of these. A critical area we need to be concerned about is how to deal with the problem of reloads. I would suggest that we simply cannot afford to ignore this problem. For one thing, the systems we are talking about, in almost every case, are built for the purpose of facilitating reloads. To ignore this capability would mean ignoring a major factor that affects the military equation between the sides.

Geography—I am sure most of you who have read the various press stories on TNF arms control have seen the usual reference to negotiations on limitations in Europe. Indeed, there seems to be a mind-set focusing on Europe. We are dealing with mobile systems. I question whether regional restrictions for such systems are in fact practical. In addition, there is the question of the range of the systems involved. At a minimum, the SS-20 has a range that can reach Western Europe from areas far outside Soviet Europe. An additional factor is U.S. worldwide interests. However important our interests in Europe are, we have worldwide interests that cannot be ignored. I offer these few comments to suggest that I believe that a regional focus is not enough, either from a political standpoint or from a practical standpoint.

Let me touch briefly on verification. Verification will pose exceptional challenges in this area. The systems are new. In some cases, we do not have much experience, in particular in SALT, on which to formulate a verification regime for the kinds of systems that may be involved in TNF arms control. Most importantly, there is the problem of mobile systems, but there are other problems as well. There is going to be a need for great precision in how we design a verification regime. We cannot overlook the fact that there are asymmetries between the Soviet Union and the United States with regard to access to information. Verification is more of a problem for us than it is for them. This suggests to me that the ways in which verification should be applied may need to vary for each side. At a minimum, we need to take into account our own absolute requirements. I would suggest, especially in the area of TNF arms control, that national technical means (NTM) are not going to suffice, and that we are going to have to go beyond that. I am not in a position to suggest how far, but I think that it will require some fairly intrusive measures. Surely, the more significant the limitations we get, as a general proposition, the more intrusive the requirements for verification may be.

It seems to me that a part of any verification regime has to be a manifest determination to enforce that regime. We must be clear in advance that, should limitations be violated in any sense, there exists the determination to take appropriate steps. This kind of determination, which must be clear in terms of what we say and what we do, would be a very important part of a verification regime.

Finally, I have a few observations on the forum. Several people in this conference have questioned whether TNF arms control can go forward in any sensible way in the absence of SALT. That is a very serious question that I do not propose to try to answer now. But let me note that we currently anticipate negotiating TNF in the SALT framework. At a minimum that has two meanings. First, it implies that the negotiation will be bilateral; and second, it recognizes the obvious fact that there is a close relationship between TNF and strategic forces. Right now, we cannot and need not define that specific relationship. That will be a challenging problem, but for the moment I think it is sufficient to say that at some point in the future we foresee TNF and SALT coming together in some fashion.

To wrap up, let me very briefly review the status of our planning for the future. As I think most of you know, the United States has indicated its intention to enter into TNF negotiation with the Soviets by the end of the year. We have started and have in train a program of preparations—preparations that I think will be necessary if we are to negotiate successfully. Fundamentally, they involve concentration on the threat, and by that I mean not simply numbers, but understanding in more detail the implications of the threat, and in addition a review of our TNF requirements. These activities are being undertaken within the U.S. government and in consultations with our allies. This latter dimension will be extremely important because of the solid support we need from our allies and the common alliance view critical to the successful pursuit of negotiations.

This is a demanding agenda and a serious challenge for the people working on the issue in the government. We look to benefit from any thoughtful ideas that people such as you may have.

David Aaron

Oppenheimer & Co., Inc., New York;
Deputy Assistant to the President, National Security, 1977–1981

When I was asked to speak, I asked if the program could read a little differently. It would not only say, "Theater Nuclear Forces Restraints," but it would also have a subtitle, "An Insurmountable Opportunity."

Let me try to do two things briefly this afternoon. First, talk about the background to past decisions that brought us to the current circumstance; and second, talk about the arms control implications and perhaps offer a few ideas that may be helpful in overcoming this particular opportunity.

I think the most important thing to recognize is that the basic purposes of the long-range theater nuclear forces deployment program are political. This is not to take away the strategic importance of LRTNF or their military utility. But unless that basic fact of the political character of LRTNF is taken into account I do not think we will be able to come to grips effectively with the arms control aspects of the issue.

The military requirements for long-range nuclear forces have existed for some time; indeed, I would say from the outset of the NATO alliance. In the 1950s, there was SACEUR's requirement for a mobile, medium-range ballistic missile. It proved not to be acceptable politically and it had other drawbacks. Nonetheless, the requirement was laid down. In the 1960s the alliance grappled with the concept of a multilateral nuclear force (MLF), but did so quite ineffectively. The MLF debate and the ensuing crisis involved the credibility of the extended U.S. deterrence. It also, of course, was a debate about non-proliferation, particularly as it might apply to Germany and its future nuclear status. And the debate, at least from the European side, also involved the sense of the maturing power of our European allies in nuclear decisions.

The MLF crisis produced a consensus that lasted, I would say, up until Chancellor Schmidt's speech to the International Institute of Strategic Studies in 1978. The elements of that consensus were several-fold. First, the United States would commit itself to cover European targets on an equal basis with targets of interest to the United States.

Second, the United States would assign strategic submarines to SACEUR. Third, as a demonstration of our good intentions, NATO officers would be assigned to Omaha to participate in the planning of the use of our own forces. Fourth, a nuclear planning group would be created at the level of defense ministers, a select group that would discuss targeting policy and nuclear doctrine, a group that would share intelligence of the most sensitive character. Finally, and somewhat out of sequence to these developments, there was the agreement on the Athens guidelines, on how NATO was to go to war and how NATO was to consult in that circumstance.

Underlying these agreements was a strategic concept of sorts—MC-14/3, which provided for a spectrum of deterrence, but which also underscored and supported the concept that external U.S. forces were credible in deterring war above the threshold of battlefield nuclear weapons. This concept was difficult to work out with the allies, but nonetheless it ended up being the consensus position.

There were some implied negative dimensions to that consensus. First, there would be no force structures or policies that would tend to decouple the U.S. strategic deterrent from nuclear forces in Europe. No incentives would be created, more than exist in reality, for confining a nuclear war to Europe. The Federal Republic of Germany (FRG) would not have a finger on the trigger nor on the safety catch of systems capable of reaching the Soviet Union. Finally, there would be no more debilitating debates on how NATO goes to war. The United States would decide but the United States would also consult.

There were very important changes in the 1970s which opened up all these questions again. I'll mention them briefly: The Vietnam War led to questioning both our credibility and our wisdom; the Soviet military build-up across the board brought about strategic parity and raised questions about the consequences of gaps in the spectrum of deterrence; the problem of *Minuteman* vulnerability raised concerns about crisis stability; the relative success, particularly for the Germans, of Ostpolitik and detente, created a new political atmosphere in Europe; the negotiations with the Soviets on strategic nuclear arms slowly but inevitably crawled toward systems that the Europeans tended to regard as theirs; and finally, the emergence of the European community and, in particular, the German-French entente within the European community, gave certain European leaders a sense of political strength and maturity that led them to want to make policy in this area in a very direct way.

By the late 1970s we had a situation in which the Europeans wanted no negotiations over their heads on nuclear systems that they felt would be of central importance to their security. On the question of decoupling, they felt more worried about the Soviet threat to their security than any U.S. propensity to decouple. A convoluted strategic debate then took place. Some argued that decoupling would be enhanced if there were no long-range theater nuclear forces, the theory being that a firebreak in this area was more likely to deter escalation to strategic forces instead of "requiring" the United States to do so. Others argued LRTNF would make strategic nuclear war confined to Europe more feasible.

Some thought this approach would increase deterrence of Soviet aggression; others, the contrary. Still others argued that decoupling was inevitable anyway and therefore we should deploy LRTNF into Europe for its effect upon the Soviet Union. The main point, I think, is that the strategic rationale for the deployment of long-range nuclear forces was often confused and often contradictory, even among its proponents.

The military purposes, however, were quite clear and straightforward. First, to increase capabilities for selective use of long-range nuclear weapons against the Soviet Union. Second, to add to the resources that would be available to SACEUR's scheduled program. And finally, to relieve to some extent the burden on quick reaction alert aircraft and perhaps ultimately do away with quick reaction alert and make those forces available for a conventional role.

But the political arguments for LRTNF were the most compelling for the members of the alliance. First of all, there was a very deep desire to act with resolve following the neutron bomb fiasco. Allied leaders wanted to take a step in the nuclear field that would prove the alliance could make a decision in this area and stick to it. Perhaps even more important, I believe it was the policy of the Federal Republic of Germany to use LRTNF developments as an anchor in the West in order to give them more freedom to pursue their Ostpolitik. By making the FRG a base for nuclear attack on the Soviet Union the NATO allies would be given the most powerful assurance possible that the FRG would remain permanently fastened to the West no matter how broad their relations with the East. In this sense the West German decision to pursue the long-range theater nuclear force program was not so much pro-NATO as it was pro-detente and a token to NATO and to the United States that Germany's Ostpolitik would not carry them too far. This was clearly a very delicate operation for the Germans, both with the East and with the SPD itself because there are elements in the SPD who would be against this program even if the Soviets were not. There has been an irony, which is slowly evaporating, that the antinuclear forces in West Germany have focused on nuclear reactors and not on nuclear weapons. Unfortunately, that situation is changing as the prospect of the deployment of long-range theater nuclear forces pushes the issue of nuclear weapons to the fore.

For these reasons, there were three important constraints on the decision to go forward with long-range theater nuclear forces. First of all, there would be no "two-key" systems in the Federal Republic. Many other countries discussed the possibility of two-key systems with us because they wanted the implied veto of such arrangements. We were prepared to go along with the idea, but the interested countries could not pay for the purchase of the missiles and we weren't about to subsidize them. The current Secretary of State wanted to press the Federal Republic to purchase *Pershing* and cruise missiles, but it was our judgment that this was simply more than the political traffic would bear.

The second major constraint is that there must be, in addition to Germany, one other continental country in which long-range theater nuclear systems would be deployed. NATO's compliance with the condition is, at best, a shaky one. The Belgians have given us a definite "maybe." The Italians, I think, have been very courageous, but one never knows. And in the Federal Republic, I think it is fair to say that an increasingly articulate cadre against the deployment decision has emerged and will continue its efforts.

The third major constraint on the decision is the requirement for a parallel arms control effort. Let me then turn to that parallel effort and make a few suggestions and observations about it.

I think that it's important to take as a point of departure the fact that if the principal security objectives of long-range theater nuclear force developments are political, our arms control objectives ought to be openly and clearly political as well. I'm not denigrating the importance of an agreement that is equal, that contributes to stability, that is technically sound, that is verifiable, and all the rest. I am assuming that any agreement could meet such tests. But I think that it is extremely important to be explicit about the political objectives that we should seek. These objectives should be, first of all, allied solidarity; second, some level of NATO LRTNF deployment; and third, the establishment of a new framework both for SALT and for its integration into the allied concept of nuclear deterrence.

Let me start with the latter point first. Many people have commented today that the long-range theater nuclear force arms control problem is so complicated as to be a hopeless thing. However, it is possible that this complexity may be an opportunity. I don't think we should be deterred by the asymmetry of forces. I've been struck by many of the comments today suggesting that the asymmetry of interests, the asymmetry of strategy, and the asymmetry of political attitudes between the Soviet Union and the United States are so great that one cannot negotiate an agreement. That may be so, but my experience, reinforced by my new experience working in Wall Street, is that asymmetries and differences make a deal possible. If both sides have the same interests, if both have precisely the same goals, it's very difficult to make a deal. That is the definition of a zero-sum game. You can only make a deal when the sides have different interests and are therefore prepared to agree that each walked away from the table having gained something.

I view LRTNF negotiations as capable of several things. One is rectifying some of the conceptual deficiencies of SALT. On this matter I would say my views coincide to a great degree with what Nitze said this morning. We have had a very difficult time getting limits on those aspects of Soviet strategic forces that are of most military concern to us. They have had a similar problem in getting at those aspects of our nuclear force deployments and those of our allies, such as FBS, of concern to them. Moreover, SALT has been, I think, increasingly putting us in a position of being at odds with our allies. This is inevitable as SALT slides into the gray-area systems, the intermediate-range systems, and begins talking about whose threat is being limited more, whose options are being limited most. At the same time, I think it's fair to say that our allies are getting something of a free ride. If SALT is to be at all successful, and particularly if more sweeping reductions are to be achieved, the allies (the United Kingdom and France) will be building up while we and the Soviets will be tearing down.

There are, of course, a number of very concrete problems in long-range theater nuclear force arms control. Some of them were mentioned earlier—the asymmetry in missile launchers, other weapons platforms, trying to define what's included, what to do about the allies, the whole question of global versus regional ceilings, and the question of linkage to SALT. I would like to make a few suggestions in this regard.

First I'd like to suggest that the long-range theater nuclear force discussions should be used as a lead-in to a broader and deeper SALT negotiation. In my judgment, if we can't get SALT II ratified soon, perhaps with minor changes, we ought to simply leave it on the table and go back and start negotiating deeper arms control agreements, and we ought to start that process by focusing first on the issue that will inevitably come up first, and has come up first every time we've talked to the Soviets—that is the issue of U.S. forward-based systems and the issue of allied systems.

I think that this would be very helpful in strengthening the relationship between LRTNF and SALT negotiations. I believe there must be a strong link between the two because I am concerned that an independent or even quasi-independent LRTNF negotiation will simply reinforce the propensity for a Euro-detente, the notion that detente in Europe can somehow be separated from overall relationships with the Soviet Union. Strengthening this link provides an opportunity to do some of the things that Nitze suggested earlier, to start focusing our criteria, our yardsticks, on the things that bother us. The LRTNF measure of merit, warheads on launchers, is a far better yardstick than the ones that we've used in SALT to this time. I think the question of mobility and the restraints that should be placed upon it, the question of range limits, and the question of geographic and regional limitations are all extremely important questions for SALT that must first be resolved in the context of LRTNF.

I would, however, caution the administration that if they are looking for on-site inspection in the LRTNF talks to think very seriously, very early on, about the implications for the Federal Republic and that country's legal and political requirements. We've run into that problem many times before with the Federal Republic. Our negotiators may find that the allies have more problems with on-site inspections than the Soviets do.

The second thing I would like to suggest is that we find a way to include British and French forces in the negotiations. I think that we have an opportunity with the election of President Mitterrand to end France's nuclear isolation within the alliance and France's absence from the table at serious arms control negotiations. I believe that the British would go along with this. They have been deeply ambivalent about not being at the top table for some time, and I think they would be prepared to accept a role. I think the participation of the British and French forces would give us a broader strategic framework within which to deal both with the negotiations and with the whole question of the NATO deterrent. It would put more cards in our hand at the negotiating table. It would help avoid European fear of decoupling the U.S. deterrent or a U.S. "sellout." Moreover, it would increase the coupling between the British and French deterrents within NATO.

I think that such a consolidation of the Western nuclear positions would also have the advantage of making clear that British and French expenditures for strategic forces are part of the allied burden-sharing effort—a point that is very often missed within the alliance. And since the whole issue of burden-sharing is likely to become an intense one over the next few years as our own programs go forward and European conventional programs don't keep pace, it is important to try to keep some focus on the fact that those forces do make a direct contribution to the security of the alliance.

I think that the inclusion of allied forces in the negotiations will give our public a better sense of both the scope and depth of our strategic defenses. With the addition of six *Poseidon*-class French submarines and their associated missiles to the Western deterrent, the open acceptance of the British force, including their acquisition of the *Trident* system, should enhance the sense of allied security if they see their own forces as part of an overall allied nuclear deterrent.

The concept of including these systems is based upon the assumption that the price of SALT is going up, that in the new administration the United States is going to ask for more severe restrictions, limitations, reductions of various kinds, in SALT. My suggestion is based upon the notion that if we are raising the stakes we'd better get all our chips on the table.

Third, and I think this logically follows, it is important to multilateralize the LRTNF negotiations. I say that with some trepidation, having had unfortunate experiences in that regard. I also think there have to be some important caveats to fuller allied participation in the talks. There has to be a place for U.S.-Soviet private discussions. There must be an opportunity for just the nuclear powers to talk. But generally speaking, there also ought to be a forum in which all those involved in the LRTNF program have an opportunity to participate in some fashion in the discussions.

The advantages of such an approach include putting maximum political pressure on the Soviet Union, but perhaps the most important advantage would be to minimize the capacity of the Soviet Union to divide us from our allies. I think that a bad pattern is already emerging over LRTNF in which we have a private LRTNF discussion in Geneva with the Soviets and the Soviets discuss this with Schmidt and Thatcher and the French behind our backs. We really have no idea what they are saying to each other, and that is very dangerous. I think it would become an increasingly dangerous circumstance unless we can find a way to integrate our allies' discussions with our own.

There is a second major political objective to the negotiations. That is to make it clear that there is going to be some LRTNF deployment. We have to get past this notion that maybe zero is a theoretically acceptable outcome. It is not, in my judgment, an acceptable outcome. Reference has already been made to the SS-12s, the SS-22s, the SS-23s, and others. There is no question in my own mind that it is fully justifiable to have some level of LRTNF deployment and if we don't get this false note out of the way we will continually be subject to pressures that will come from false proposals such as the Soviet proposal for a moratorium.

But our overriding objective in all of this, it seems to me, has to be the solidarity of the alliance. The fact that the president has been a reluctant dragon on this issue has been alright up to now. I think it's actually helped him in his discussions with the Europeans and with the Soviets. But at some point, he's going to have to be ready to make a deal. The stakes are enormous.

Over lunch, Pierre Lellouche, who will speak in a few moments, and I were discussing the nightmare Europe faces in the next several years. It consists of increasing polarization in Germany, great struggles in France as the Mitterrand government seeks to reform that society, and continued weakness in Great Britain. And with U.S. policy becoming the object of dispute and the program of TNF deployments becoming the focus for opposition, we could have a real mess on our hands in NATO. So I think it's extremely important that the whole program and the whole negotiation be handled with that in mind. To do so, the LRTNF effort cannot be window dressing. I believe the president and the administration will have to prove their willingness to deal with the nuclear threat with more than simply weapons programs. They will have to show some earnest of their intent to deal with it on the basis of reason and negotiation. Otherwise the effect on Europe will not be to galvanize the alliance in support of our policies. The Europeans have become too proud, and quite frankly they are too scared, to react in that fashion. I think the much more likely reaction will be further disorder and demoralization, especially when it comes to U.S. leadership.

There are many similarities between LRTNF arms control problems and MBFR. In some sense, we are trying to redress a military balance with arms control, always a very questionable proposition. But there is one very big difference. We have an LRTNF program to redress the balance. We want to see it go forward and yet there is intense public concern, even if it's a minority, about the program.

A lack of a sense of sincere effort on the arms control front could lead to an effective grass roots opposition to the program and, in my judgment, could lead to a circumstance that could fundamentally alter the pattern of security cooperation in the alliance. I think it's extremely important not to treat our allies' concern for arms control with condescension. The Europeans believe, not surprisingly, that the arms race is dangerous to them, and they want to regulate it, or at least see that its regulation is being discussed.

Those who have talked here today at some length about the limits to arms control, its drawbacks, should think very seriously what the world would be like without the discussions that have taken place and without the modest agreements that have been achieved. Consider the Middle East crisis of 1973, or the strains that would exist if the Germans were trying to conduct Ostpolitik in the atmosphere of an arms race.

Let me conclude by saying that if the dialogue that takes place on LRTNF arms control is not entered into seriously I think it will become evident. And if it becomes evident, then none of the very important political and security objectives, above all alliance solidarity, will be achieved.

PANELISTS

Pierre Lellouche
Institute Francais des Relations Internationales, Paris

I'm very pleased to be here because, as you know, the TNF issue is primarily a European issue. But I am the wrong one to be here to the extent that I am French and, so far, the French government has done whatever it could to not get involved in this mess. Despite what Aaron just said, I frankly doubt that Mitterrand, being a good tactician, would decide to join any TNF negotiations tomorrow. What could happen in the future, however, is a more active involvement and at least a French position on this subject.

I will make three sets of remarks. The first is an overview of TNF, the second is on the current state of negotiations, and the third is where do we go from here?

On the TNF problem as a whole, I think there are two aspects that are incredibly intertwined because of the very nature of the issue. One side is a political problem, the other side is a military problem. My own view is that the NATO decision of 1979 on the deployment of a TNF system is militarily useful for the alliance, although far from solving all the military problems of NATO's deterrence doctrine. Although it is useful militarily, I think it is a complete political disaster. That is the problem we have to live with in the future.

Militarily, it's useful because it solves part of the problem of today, which is, how does the United States extend deterrence to Europe in an era of strategic parity? The situation is completely different from that of the 1950s and 1960s, for today we are dealing with strategic parity. We are also dealing with increased conventional superiority of the Soviet Union, and this situation pushes the Europeans into a corner in which they become more and more dependent on nuclear first-use by the Americans. At the same time, nuclear first-use becomes more and more improbable because of theater superiority by the Soviets and central parity. So, to the extent that you can fix that by weapons that can reach the Soviet Union from Europe, I think you do recouple, when you force the Soviet Union to contemplate the risk of a strategic exchange with the Americans, quasi-automatically, in case they have aggressive intentions on Europe. Now, I don't know whether the

American planners actually contemplated this when they devised the modernization plan. But that is what it does and the Soviet Union and Soviet analysts are very clear about this. It won't make any difference to them when they receive a nuclear warhead whether it's a *Pershing* warhead or a *Trident* warhead. For them it is a strategic strike. To that extent it is recoupling and that's why, as a European, I am in favor of that decision. I must add, though, that it doesn't fix all the problems on the military level. The deployment of TNF deters the use of SS-20s by the Soviet Union. No more. It doesn't fix a conventional imbalance. It doesn't fix whatever problem the United States has with the vulnerability of its own ICBMs.

This being said, it is a political disaster, even though I recall that the Carter administration in 1979 hailed the decision as a great victory. It was a disaster, it is a disaster, and it's probably going to grow in that direction more and more.

The TNF case is very interesting because it is a test case. It is an accurate reflection of where the alliance stands today and what has happened to the Europeans and to the Americans over the last ten to fifteen years. I won't go back over the origins of the problem and the neutron bomb incident, but for me the roots of the problem come from the mishandling of the whole business: the inability to present the case, to argue the case. I think the worst, the criminal part, if you allow me to use this term, was the mistake made by the Americans in asking the Europeans to stand up and say, "I want TNF," especially asking the West Germans to do this. This shows a complete misunderstanding of what Germany is today. Germany cannot make a nuclear decision for the alliance. It has never been able to do this since it was created as a Federal Republic and it will never do so when its nonnuclear status is a basis of its Ostpolitik. From the moment that you ask the Germans to make a decision, to stand up and say publicly, "I do want those weapons and I want to be able to target the Soviet Union," you have got a problem.

The other result was the so-called dual-track approach in which every weapon decision made by the alliance has to get the indirect approval of the Soviet Union by way of negotiation. I just wish the Soviet Union had the same approach. When they deploy the SS-20, I wish they would come to us and say, "Do you mind if we put in SS-20? Do you think we should open negotiations about this?" Unfortunately, it doesn't work that way. This is the kind of asymmetry you have. It becomes very dangerous because this dual-track approach does a number of things.

- It gives the Soviet Union fantastic leverage every day on European public opinion. I could cite hundreds of examples.

- It forces the United States to conduct dual negotiations—one with the Soviet Union, one with the allies. It has already started. I don't see how you are going to solve that issue.
- It accelerates the revival of certain neutralist trends in Europe. The ban-the-bomb movement is having a second life in Britain and elsewhere. And, of course, TNF is a special animal that is used by all these movements, whether it's in Britain or Germany or Holland or elsewhere.

So this is the context: political disaster, militarily useful.

What is the state of the negotiations? I would characterize them in two ways: one, absolute confusion; two, intense political exercise. There is confusion at every level, even if you look at the title of the negotiations: for the USSR, "the talks are related to nuclear arms in Europe"; for the Americans, "these are discussions on questions related to the limitation of certain U.S. and Soviet forces." What does this mean? It means that for the Soviet Union, TNF means all weapons that are able to reach the Soviet Union, including FBS. For the Americans, it means certain land-based systems.

There is also confusion as to an appropriate forum, bilateral or multilateral. You say it's going to be bilateral. The Soviets say it's bilateral now; tomorrow it's going to be multi-lateral. So it's unclear.

There is also confusion as to the basis and the objectives for those negotiations. The Soviets say there is parity—that's why they propose a moratorium. We say there is no parity. Can you start negotiations on this basis?

There is also absolute confusion on the types of weapons you're dealing with. Some weapons are conventional, some weapons are nuclear, some are dual capable, some are strategic, some are tactical. In essence, TNF is a case in point where all the nice categories that you had in previous arms control talks are nonexistent. The problem is extremely complex.

It is a fundamental strategic problem, because if you don't link it with SALT, you accept the concept of a separate Euro-strategic balance, which militarily doesn't mean anything, but politically means a lot. The notion of a separate European theater decoupled from the central strategic relationship between superpowers is a completely different political game. This is really the stake of the negotiation.

And this is why it is an intensely political exercise. Where are we now? We are seeing the Americans being pushed toward the TNF negotiation in order to save the cohesion of the alliance and in order to save the decision of 1979. This is the only reason why the Carter administration got into the negotiation in October and this is why, very reluctantly, the Reagan administration is going to have to do the same.

For the Soviet Union, they are pushing for the TNF negotiation to delay the deployment. They want to formalize the concept of a separate European theater. They want to get FBS, which is a long-term objective they have had since 1969. They also want to negotiate from a position of strength, which they can do.

In this context it is not arms control. What it is, really, is Cold War diplomacy. In the past, it is true that some arms control talk did help restore the political climate between East and West. For example, the test ban negotiation, after the Cuban crisis, or even SALT I helped restore some kind of political climate between East and West. At the same time, the experience of SALT II during the 1970s has shown that when you have a long drawn-out negotiation that's stuck, technically and politically, it hurts detente rather than the contrary. So I fear that this negotiation is not going to help detente and is going to damage the entire SALT process.

Given these realities, the question we have to face is where do we go from here? I don't think we can escape the fact that those negotiations are going to be needed both politically and psychologically. It's unfortunate that we have to start this negotiation at a time when there is so much discrepancy in the force relationship, especially when the new American administration has not made up its mind on its weapon programs and on its general attitude on SALT, and when there is so much going on in Europe politically. But despite all this, we have to negotiate.

What should be the guidelines? I will propose a few. First of all, I think it can be demonstrated that genuine arms control can only be based on an already stable or quasi-stable balance of forces. I don't believe you can start on the basis of the TNF force structure you have now in Europe and arrive at a genuine and balanced agreement. That underlines the need for deployment.

Second, the negotiations have to be bilateral. Here again, I disagree with Aaron. I don't believe that the French and British systems have a TNF role and they have nothing to do with the negotiations. These are strategic systems and I can argue the point at length that they have absolutely no TNF function.

Third, I insist that these negotiations have to be conducted in the context of SALT. The worst thing would be to have TNF discussions conducted in a separate forum as if a so-called Euro-strategic balance existed.

If you look at all the negotiating options, there are two serious options that could be used. The first is to let the deployment go, use the negotiations to stall, and wait for some kind of parity to come out after the NATO deployment has been achieved.

The other option is to take the offensive and propose deep cuts. I believe that both the Americans and the Soviets could live without TNF in Europe. I think we could live without TNF in Europe. So why not look for an offensive policy. Why not catch the Soviets at their own game? They're proposing a moratorium. Why not put a moratorium on its head, and say, O.K., we will give up the NATO plan provided that you dismantle existing missiles. This is a type of offensive move that is needed now. It is politically needed in the alliance and I think it makes sense militarily.

Barry Blechman
Carnegie Endowment for International Peace;
Assistant Director, Arms Control and Disarmament Agency, 1977–1979

If you noticed, there was quite a difference between Woodworth's and Aaron's presentations. And the difference had nothing, in fact, to do with different administrations. But I think it had a great deal to do with the different institutions with which they have been affiliated and the different perspectives that those institutions bring to the problem of preventing nuclear war. In the United States our decision making in this area tends to be dominated by military and technical considerations, as in the Defense Department. The alternative would be to have decision making about nuclear forces and nuclear strategy more heavily dominated by political considerations, as would be uppermost in the minds of those who serve in the White House. This distinction among American institutions is duplicated in differences between the American perspective on how to prevent nuclear war and the European perspective.

Let me hasten to say that I am speaking only of differences in emphasis and priorities, not a stark black-and-white distinction. In the United States, we essentially take a rationalistic approach. For the most part, we believe that war begins as a result of deliberate calculation in a particular circumstance, a calculation of relative advantages and disadvantages. And the emphasis there should be on the word relative. That is, even if it is understood that the likely absolute cost of a conflict would be quite high and that the possible absolute cost of that conflict could be extraordinary, as Americans perceive the problem, if there is a distinction in the relative gain and loss of the two sides, then a deliberate decision to go to war is quite plausible. The side that calculates that it has an advantage, even if its own cost also would be great, under certain circumstances might be tempted to act. As a result, we conclude that to prevent war, we must maintain a military capability at each potential level of conflict that is sufficient to deter the other side from making a calculation of relative advantage.

Many Europeans, on the other hand, see war and the decision to go to war as fundamentally an irrational act. They see it beginning not as a result of a calculation of relative advantage and disadvantage, but as the result of events and emotions simply getting out of control. It is sometimes difficult to foresee such a process unfolding, particularly in contexts in which the stakes are high and the present situation relatively stable. But international developments tend to create new realities with each step, so that the next incremental step appears not so significant as it did several steps before. At step five, for example, step six of an escalatory process may seem far less awesome than it did at step one. To illustrate, one simply has to think of the 1973 crisis in the Middle East in which there was a progressive escalation that, if continued, conceivably could have led first to conventional and then to nuclear conflict between the United States and the Soviet Union.

From this European perspective, the way to avoid war is, first of all, to avoid the development of situations in which such an escalatory process can begin. That is why the Europeans place such great emphasis on detente, on the development of extensive and intensive economic and human exchanges, the creation of a range of negotiations, and visits by government officials. I would add that this emphasis on detente is not strictly a concessional strategy because a part of the process is to define clearly which actions carry with them a risk of precipitating a situation that can lead to war; that is, there is line drawing as well as development of exchanges.

The second part of the European strategy is to maintain military forces and deployments designed to create the perception that if war begins, it would quickly escalate to the highest levels, involving U.S. and Soviet central nuclear forces, and that this escalation would be facilitated by the military strategy pursued by the alliance. Foreknowledge of this likelihood that any war in Europe would result in the highest absolute cost, the Europeans believe, may prevent even lower level conflicts from beginning in even the most extreme situations.

The deployment of long-range theater nuclear forces in Europe, by facilitating strikes on Soviet territory, would virtually guarantee strikes on American territory and therefore the engagement of American central nuclear forces. Foreknowledge of this likely escalation strengthens deterrence by making clear that the highest absolute cost of a conflict would be borne. With that as background, Europeans see TNF arms control talks as accomplishing two things. First, they make possible the deployment of long-range theater forces because of very real domestic political pressures that otherwise would oppose them, and second, they help to prevent war by contributing to the network of exchanges that help to avoid the development of those situations in which war might become a real possibility. In short, the TNF talks are seen by the Europeans, as attested to by Lellouche, as a political instrument in a strictly political context. The question is whether the United States understands this. Woodworth's presentation, which I assume reflects the thinking within the Defense Department, was very much concerned with the real substantive problems of the negotiations. But I don't think that those are the most salient problems we face. We are entering a process with exceptional dangers for U.S.-European relations. Over the next several years, there will be numerous points at which there will be opportunities for European parliaments to take actions delaying the TNF deployments. There will be considerable pressure to make the TNF negotiations, as a political process, a credible instrument. Both phenomena could result in great tensions within the alliance, made manifest in pressures to slow or defer or moderate the deployments themselves or to "make progress" in the talks. And the results of such developments could be extremely troublesome.

As a result, I support Aaron's point that the talks have to be understood overridingly as political, as a means to avoid difficulties in the alliance, and possibly as an opening for a wider and broader arms control process at some future point. To do that requires the existence of an overall SALT framework. In a situation in which the SALT II Treaty is no longer operable, either because it had been renounced explicitly or because de facto steps had been taken that violated basic provisions, the basic condition of political credibility of the TNF talks would not be present.

Avis Bohlen
European Bureau, Department of State

I would like to touch on one aspect of an issue that has been covered extensively by the previous speakers, that has to do with the mainly political nature of TNF arms control. A very novel feature is the extent of European involvement and the roles that the Europeans have played in the TNF decision to date and will play in TNF arms control in times to come.

They, of course, played a role in SALT II on certain issues where they had a keen interest, specifically on the cruise missile issues, and on noncircumvention and nontransfer. They are extensively involved in MBFR but with one very important difference from their role in TNF arms control. In MBFR we were the ones who were pushing the negotiations and it was the Europeans who were, to a large extent, hanging back. With TNF it has been exactly the reverse, starting with the December 1979 decision. Europeans were mainly responsible for including the arms control track in that decision. Whether this action has set a precedent that modernization must be accompanied by a parallel arms control track is debatable. I hope it is not the case.

Since that decision, Europe has also been the main force impelling us, in particular the new administration, toward negotiations. The background to this includes some very wide differences in outlook, not only politically, but also specifically on the value of arms control. In this country there is now great skepticism about arms control, as we have heard this morning. In Europe, in contrast, the pro-arms control sentiment, which very often goes hand in hand with antinuclear sentiment, is really at a peak and, as Woodworth mentioned earlier, the debate is sharper than ever. Why is this?

There are many different elements. One can look at the political configurations in certain countries, the dependence on coalition governments where strong antinuclear forces can sometimes have a disproportionate role. I think it goes much deeper than that. One has to go back to the controversy over enhanced radiation warheads, to the sensitization on nuclear questions that has taken place over the last few years for reasons mentioned by Aaron. The Europeans have a perception, which they find very uncomfortable, that the United States and the Soviet Union are both moving toward war fighting capabilities, the upshot of which could be a nuclear war fought on European territory. In this respect I am not sure that the coupling implications of the TNF decision really have a great deal of application.

The other side of the political aspect of TNF arms control is the way in which the Soviets have played this issue. It has given them opportunities that they have sought to exploit, but I think that it has not been as easy as they perhaps thought in December 1979. Immediately thereafter they sought to undo the decision by refusing to negotiate. The fact that they came to the negotiating table last October was proof that they had to disabuse themselves of that notion. One other point about the negotiations is that the Soviets have stated publicly what they see as the scope of the negotiations. They have offered as a counter for U.S. forward-based systems not Soviet central systems, but have put their own TNF on the table. This is in contrast to the way they raised the FBS issue in SALT I and SALT II where it was treated in the strategic context. This is novel—perhaps not unexpected, but it is a departure from the past.

Finally, with regard to what has been said about the inclusion of allied systems, I must say that I agree entirely with Lellouche that that does not seem a very likely prospect in the near future. But I would also ask Lellouche how he would justify Soviet reductions in their SS-20s without touching the allied systems?

DISCUSSION

Pierre Lellouche: If I had to handle this problem I would simply argue two things. If you take the land-based systems, the only thing we have to worry about for both France and Britain are the 18 French land-based missiles. Eighteen land-based missiles versus 450 SS-4s and -5s plus 220 SS-20s—that's about 1,100 warheads against 18. I don't think it's a serious problem. If the two superpowers were to agree to eliminate completely the TNF systems from Europe, they would still have on each side some 10 to 12 thousand strategic warheads. On the other hand, if we were in that negotiation what would we have left? It's not at all a debating point that French and British systems do not fulfill a TNF function. I've had this discussion with the Soviets and they perfectly understand the point.

Mark Schneider: I'd like to address a couple of questions to David Aaron. In your presentation you indicated that any LRTNF agreement would be balanced and verifiable. Could you outline in general terms the type of agreement you would regard as balanced and verifiable? The other question I would like to ask has to do with your proposal to include British and French forces in these negotiations. Are you talking about that in the context of a negotiation that would only involve long-range theater nuclear missiles or are you talking about that in the context of negotiations that would involve other strategic systems like the medium bombers and the cruise missiles?

David Aaron: On the first point, the position of the NATO allies is that the agreement has to be equal and must be verifiable. All I'm saying is that I believe those are important criteria and I don't doubt that the problem of achieving them is extremely difficult. But I do believe that the problems that we've encountered both in SALT and in the LRTNF area will be clarified if we take a larger view of nuclear arms and strategic arms discussions. That's why I think the artificial breaking off of the LRTNF issue becomes really an exercise in great arbitrariness. I don't think that you're going to find a doctrinal solution that's going to somehow magically tell you, as perhaps Lellouche has, that there's a real difference between French submarines and LRTNF as far as strategic nuclear deterrence is concerned. They have different roles, and they make a different contribution in some ways; but I don't think that you're going to find a real solution to the problem without taking a larger view. I also don't think you're going to be able to get the kind of real controls that I've always supported unless you're prepared to get all the stuff on the table, for a change. We've been negotiating in bits and pieces. We would have a blind eye to what they had and they would have a blind eye to what we had. I may be corrected here in a moment, but it's my conviction that at Vladivostok what you got was basically a deal in which we accepted heavy missiles, and sort of set those to one side, while the Soviets accepted FBS and allied systems as compensation for them. Is that a good deal? We never debated that extensively.

Mark Schneider: I think you're missing the point I'm trying to ask, which is basically this: You propose putting essentially everything that the United States or allies have that could be reasonably classified as strategic weapons systems on the table, yet permanently excluding upwards of 1,500, perhaps even 2,000, Soviet weapons from this overall SALT framework as well as, of course, excluding all Soviet strategic defensive systems.

David Aaron: I think there are two different problems. One is how far down the spectrum and how far away from strategic systems you draw the line. That problem isn't made easier by just talking about LRTNF and just talking about missile systems, the SS-20 and the GLCMs and the *Pershing*. It's made more arbitrary, but not any easier. The problem exists no matter how you approach it. I happen to feel that we're more likely to get a sensible strategic agreement that involves central systems as well as theater systems if you look at them in the whole, rather than trying to break them into two arbitrary parts.

Ray Orbach: This question is for Lellouche. You said TNF was a political disaster. You also said it was unfortunate that we asked the Europeans to say that they wanted TNF. Would it have been less of a political disaster if we had forced the TNF on Europeans?

Pierre Lellouche: Well, it's funny because Aaron and I just had an exchange of notes on this. He didn't like the critique I made of the Carter administration for asking the Europeans to stand up and be counted on the issue. And I understand that it is very frustrating for Washington to have a European ally who wants to have the cake and to eat it. That is, he wants to be militarily coupled and politically decoupled; he wants to keep detente and at the same time his U.S. protection; and he hates to make any nuclear decision because he doesn't want to antagonize the Soviets. I understand it's horrible for you, it's psychologically very difficult, it's politically horrendous, but it's reality.

I continue to believe that the Carter administration was wrong. What have you gained by putting the problem in the public domain? It could have been handled directly in all kinds of ways but all of a sudden here comes the neutron bomb and the TNF, in a matter of six months in Europe, and the Europeans are supposed to accept this. There is no military or political rationale, and then you're surprised by the result. I think this is a difficult world and I don't have a miracle recipe. But I know there are political ways to deal with the problem when it comes. You cannot expect, and I'm serious about this, you cannot expect from a nonnuclear member of NATO a decision on nuclear matters of the alliance. Moreover, I would say that it is a mistake for the leaders of the nuclear alliance to ask the protégé to make these decisions. It is no longer an alliance.

David Aaron: I think I deserve equal time. That is the most remarkable description of an alliance that I've heard come from Europe in a long time. I always thought the whole idea was that we consult on each other's interests. It's unrealistic to expect that we could have consulted, and with quiet diplomacy made the decision, so that Helmut Schmidt and others could have said, in effect, "Who, me? We didn't participate in that, that wasn't our issue." That's just unrealistic, given the circumstances. Knowing Germany as I do, and as you do, the issue would have immediately become a big issue in German politics.

In fact, before we ever made any proposals and had lots of quiet diplomacy, this was already being debated in the Bundestag. I would only remind you that it was Germany that led the charge here, particularly Chancellor Schmidt in getting this issue out onto the table. I would say that his judgment about Germany's position and interests was the leading reason that the issue came about. Slocombe and I traveled around Europe for a year and a half trying to tell the Europeans that external forces were fully creditable in providing for extended deterrence in Europe. And it just didn't wash. You can make the argument as long as you like, but if the people you are trying to reassure, the people that you're trying to have an alliance with, don't feel reassured, then you have to go back to the drawing board.

Finally, let me just say it is extremely important that we not avoid certain contentious issues with the Europeans. I am fully in favor of trying to take their interests into account and proceeding as delicately as possible in trying to proceed with this very difficult negotiation as well as the deployment program. But we've got to be straight with them. If we avoid tough issues like nuclear decisions, all we will be doing is going along with the dry rot that can exist in the alliance and one moment, at a point of stress, we'll find that it's nothing but ashes.

Joseph Taylor: I have a question for Lellouche. You said that you could live without LRTNF in Europe. Does that mean you don't want to see deployment?

Pierre Lellouche: No. In the context of an agreement whereby the Soviet Union would eliminate all their land-based systems directed at Western Europe, I think every European could live perfectly happily without the American TNF. That's why I say we should make a credible diplomatic offensive on that, asking for their elimination, and turning the Soviet proposal on its head. Say to the Soviets: "You are worried about the American TNF, you think it is a strategic threat; we're Europe and we think yours is a strategic threat to us. Take yours out and we take ours out." See what they will say. At least you put the ball in their court, and diplomatically that's what you need at this junction. If they accept, both alliances could survive perfectly well. Deterrence would work without that middle level of thousands of highly accurate counterforce warheads in Europe.

Michael Higgins: We have an interesting contrast in Woodworth and Lellouche talking, for very different reasons, in terms of bilateral negotiation, and Aaron favoring multi-lateral negotiation, at least of the nuclear powers in Europe. I think this bears elaboration. We have heard of some of the political problems in trying to include the allies in such negotiations. However, it seems to me that you have equally difficult problems in trying to deal with them on the sidelines of the negotiations, since the issues being debated are central to their security. So I'd like to hear Woodworth elaborate a little on why he and the administration believe that these negotiations should be bilateral, and then Aaron elaborate on his arguments why they should be multi-lateral.

John Woodworth: It seems to me that, in the first instance, there is a matter of practicality. As has been pointed out, it is the view of our allies that they don't want to be directly involved in these negotiations. At a minimum, if one wanted to change that, one would have a major job of persuasion. That's a practical matter.

Next, we need to be very careful about agreements with the Soviet Union in which the military power of the United States vis-à-vis the Soviet Union is affected by that of our allies. The negotiation between the United States and the Soviets that has to do primarily with European interests is almost certain to create incredible stresses within the alliance if any of the Europeans don't happen to agree with the probable outcome. The fundamental objective is to maintain alliance cohesiveness. The single element most likely to bring the thing down around our ears is if Europeans can charge that the United States has set aside their interests for its own.

David Aaron: I don't underestimate the importance and difficulty of

the task and I'm not arguing that the next step in negotiation ought
to include everybody. I think we ought to continue the exploratory
discussions for awhile, even for a considerable period. All I'm trying
to suggest is that there is an opportunity here to really stand back and
say "Wait a minute, this is a much more seamless web of interests in
strategic systems than existed heretofore. Let's see if there really isn't
a different concept of how to structure an agreement, structure its
negotiation, and structure our relationship with our allies, who are now,
no matter how you slice it, deeply involved in any outcome and
negotiation."

Charles Henkin: An issue that has risen in the discussion is whether
to broaden the scope of the agreement into shorter range systems or
at least to seriously consider this in the face of a rather aggressive
modernization program on the part of the Soviets at the less-than-
LRTNF range. Could we give some consideration to how desirable that
is, and the extent to which that might establish a precedent that whenever
the alliance seeks to counter Soviet deployments in a new area it
requires an arms control track as well?

John Woodworth: First, I'm very skeptical of the notion that for
every military requirement we might define in the future we have to
have an arms control track. I would hope that kind of framework is
not rigidly established. Second, in considering the question of systems,
one can't avoid the question of whether the range of systems that might
be included in the limitation should be expanded or not expanded. I
don't propose to answer that question today, but I do think that whether
they are included or not, one needs to consider very carefully the
implications of whether other systems are in or out. I don't think we
can underestimate the political motivations that underlay what the
Europeans have wanted to do, or what indeed the United States has
done. But, recognizing that, you have got to regard very seriously the
implications of any limitations for your security; I don't think that you
can treat the negotiation merely as a kind of political game. You have
to pay great attention to the consequences of any limitations and I
think this bears on the question of what systems are included. Those
choices can't be made on purely political grounds.

Ludger Buerstedde: I represent a nation (Federal Republic of Germany)
that is deeply involved in these issues. I want to make a comment on
the two-track decision. I don't think, as Lellouche suggested, that we
now ask the Russians whether we are allowed to modernize.

We believe that a decision within NATO on nuclear matters had to
be taken. This decision has been carefully prepared. I don't remember
any decision in recent years, among allies, that has been so closely
consulted on as this one, and I think that was wise because we had

to muster political support for very ugly deployment decisions. Nobody likes these things in his backyard. I can tell you that we in Europe certainly are watching very carefully what you do on the basing of the MX system and whether some parochial arguments prevail over very important strategic issues. Certainly the recent antinuclear movements in my country have a little bit to do with the decision not to ratify SALT II. This is just one point.

I have another comment on the double-track decision. I don't think it's a very new situation. When we had to face the Mansfield Resolution, and started MBFR, we were in a rather bad situation, but we managed with a common effort. It was difficult, but I think we are now somewhat better off than in 1970 when we started those negotiations. And one could note the ABM Treaty as a rather successful arms control treaty, in which you started with nothing to negotiate away. I'm not so pessimistic about possible arms control measures in the TNF field when we consider these precedents. I think we should seize the opportunity to make a genuine effort, because this is essential for the continuing political support for a very difficult deployment decision.

4

NUCLEAR WEAPON TEST BANS

SPEAKERS

Herbert York

Professor of Physics, University of California at San Diego;
U.S. Ambassador to Comprehensive Test Ban Negotiations, 1979–1981

I'd like to start by saying that it is a real personal pleasure for me to return to Livermore. I spent some of the best years of my life here, and my family did also. I made some of my oldest friends here. I take no little pride in this institution and its work, even though sometimes we seem to be working at cross purposes.

I find it necessary first to present my overall views on the questions before us in order to make sense of my detailed views on specific issues. And in this context I regard even the nuclear test ban as a detail. In brief, I believe that the basic purpose of the nuclear arms control and disarmament process is to provide the only sure means for avoiding a nuclear holocaust in the long run. I emphasize the word nuclear: I'm not talking about other kinds of arms control. I also emphasize the word disarmament: I'm not talking about nuclear arms control without considerations of nuclear disarmament. The purpose of nuclear arms control itself is to provide the necessary basis from which nuclear disarmament can proceed. I therefore regard nuclear arms control/disarmament as a separable and separate objective, and not simply as a means of achieving other objectives, however worthy they may be, such as international stability, national security, or saving money. International security, international stability, and national security are, of course, extremely important objectives, but there are other ways of obtaining them that are much more effective than by manipulating arms control and disarmament agreements. And I firmly believe that the process of nuclear arms control and disarmament should not be saddled with these other objectives. Of course the different objectives—nuclear arms control and disarmament on the one hand and international and national security on the other—have to be considered in a context that includes the others so that the means and the processes to achieve one do not gravely influence the others. But I emphasize that I regard nuclear arms control and disarmament as a separate objective and that plans and programs for achieving it should not be weighted down with other purposes. At the same time, I do support the various means by which these other purposes can be achieved, including military preparedness and the nuclear component of military preparedness (in the absence of agreements to the contrary), the formation and maintenance of alliances, and diplomacy.

The advocacy of nuclear disarmament is not, these days, particularly popular. I scarcely hear these words used. But it is a legitimate position, and one that has had many distinguished proponents, especially among those closest to nuclear development. My basic attitude toward nuclear arms and nuclear disarmament is the one Niels Bohr had in mind when he tried to persuade Franklin Roosevelt and Winston Churchill of the dangers of an impending nuclear arms race, even before it started. It was also, I believe, in Oppenheimer's mind and those of his colleagues when they joined together in inventing and promoting what later became known as the Baruch plan. In that connection, let me read from the introduction to the report of the Lilienthal Committee of which Oppenheimer was a member and which recommended the Baruch plan. The introduction to the report, which I believe was drafted by Oppenheimer, says,

> The program we propose will undoubtedly arouse skepticism when it is first considered. It did among us, but thought and discussion have converted us. It may seem too idealistic. It seems time we endeavored to bring some of our expressed ideals into being. It may seem too radical, too advanced, too much beyond human experience. All these terms apply with peculiar fitness to the atomic bomb. In considering the plan, inevitable doubts arise as to its acceptability. One should ask oneself, what are the alternatives. We have and we find no suitable alternative.

Revisionist historians in the years since then have suggested that the people who invented and proposed the Baruch plan could not have been serious. They say they must have known that it wouldn't be acceptable, and that it couldn't work. I do not believe that it was put forward in the spirit of insincerity; rather, it was put forward in a spirit of desperation, and the nuclear weapons situation is just as desperate today as it was then. I believe that the same kind of spirit motivates Andrei Sakharov, who knows more about the ugly nature of the Soviet leadership than anyone here, but who, just last year, from his exile in Gorki said, "despite all that happened, I believe that the questions of war and peace and disarmament are so crucial that they must be given absolute priority even in the most difficult circumstances. Most urgent of all are steps to avert a nuclear war which is the greatest peril confronting the modern world."

Why do I make these remarks in introducing a talk on a nuclear test ban? Because in confronting that particular narrow issue, one finds oneself faced with the problem of weighing the costs of a comprehensive test ban against the benefits. And there are, in my judgment, both costs and benefits to a nuclear comprehensive test ban, but these costs and benefits are incommensurate with each other, and one can only make a balance between them and arrive at the judgment of whether you're for or against it on the basis of how they fit into a greater scheme. The costs of a comprehensive test ban are short-term and they are specific, for example the matter of stockpile reliability and the question of foregone opportunities to design warheads specifically tailored to missiles that are already in the pipeline. The benefits of a comprehensive test ban are long-term and general. They are part of the whole process of trying to avoid and avert or delimit a nuclear war in all of its aspects, but at some unknown time far down the road. These benefits are general because a CTB is simply one more major act of nuclear moderation that, when added to all of the others, helps to promote, or sometimes to coerce, nuclear moderation in others as well.

One can only weigh these benefits and costs against each other in the context of some greater purpose. When I apply my purposes to the question of whether the CTB is a good thing or not, I conclude, and have so concluded for a long time, that it is a good thing and that it ought to be accomplished. I say that despite the fact that I'm as aware as anybody here that there's no hope of a comprehensive test ban at the present time, for bureaucratic reasons if for no others. If one looks at the present situation in Washington, at the top levels of the bureaucracy, there is essentially no one there who thinks a CTB is a good idea, and there are many people who think it's a very bad idea. The net result is foregone—there isn't going to be a comprehensive test ban negotiation in the foreseeable future and there isn't going to be a comprehensive test ban.

I need to add some qualifiers to my own position on a CTB. One is that I don't think that a comprehensive test ban is a good thing as an isolated act. A comprehensive test ban in a world in which all the other aspects of the nuclear arms race are going forward in full gear seems to me obviously unstable. It couldn't last, and therefore should not be put in place. The appropriate time for a comprehensive test ban is when things in general are moving away from a dependence on nuclear weapons, when the process is the reverse of what it is today and what it has been in recent years. Moreover, a comprehensive test ban is not my personal first priority in nuclear arms control and disarmament. SALT II, a beginning on SALT III (SALT II.1 and II.2 as Gelb described it), and doing something about the theater nuclear forces, for example, have a higher priority in my view than proceeding with the comprehensive test ban.

With that introduction, let me submit four recommendations to whatever people or group it might be that will resume CTB negotiations at some time down the road. These four recommendations do not constitute a complete set, but if they were all followed they would help to produce a useful result.

First of all, with regard to the substance of negotiation, I have only one particular recommendation. Generally speaking, I think that the U.S. positions on substance were pretty good, but there is one particular element that was very troublesome, both in the American position and in the Soviet position, and that concerns the duration of the treaty and, more important, what happens at the end of the first short period of duration of the treaty. Both the American and the Soviet positions were really very equivocal about that; they both carefully avoided making any real long-term commitment to continuity. I think that we should not be negotiating a comprehensive test ban if the purpose is not clearly a permanent treaty with, of course, the usual escape clause in the event of special circumstances, the kind of escape clause that exists in all such treaties. Unfortunately, the instructions both parties were working under did not contain the fundamental assumption that the treaty was forever.

My second point has to do with organization. There were, to simplify a very complex situation somewhat, four different bodies, each of which was involved in one way or another in determining policy and determining what instructions should be sent to the negotiators. One of these was a cabinet-level body, chaired by the president's National Security Adviser or his deputy and consisting of the members of the various cabinet departments concerned with a comprehensive test ban: State, Defense, the Joint Chiefs of Staff, Department of Energy, CIA. The second body was really a pair of bodies with basically the same and somewhat floating memberships, the so-called backstopping group and working group. These were made up of lower level assistants to the members of the first committee, and they met with greater frequency, considered the various issues that were raised as the negotiations proceeded, in theory made recommendations to the parent cabinet group, but in practice actually determined the policy and the instructions on a day to day basis.

The third group is the negotiating team itself, those who actually went off to Geneva and talked with the other delegations about these issues. The fourth body was not really actively involved at the time, but it was in everybody's mind, and that's the U.S. Senate. All of the people negotiating this treaty, or any other, cannot help but be constantly aware of the fact that what they're doing is of no purpose if it does not ultimately satisfy two-thirds of the Senators. Consequently, these Senators are there very much in spirit, and what they think about the CTB and related issues definitely has a bearing on what's going on all the time. Now, it's necessary in getting such a negotiation going that the president should consult with all of the principals and agencies involved—those who support the purposes of the negotiation as well as those who are against them. But once it is decided to proceed it seems to me that the only possible way to succeed in a negotiation is to turn the detail planning and negotiation over to people who actually believe in it, who believe the negotiation should be taking place, and even more, believe that it should achieve the stated result.

The members of the cabinet-level group will often have divergent views about these matters, including the basic purposes, but because of their positions and responsibilities it is right and reasonable that they should have an adequate opportunity to express them. However, in the cases of the working group and the backstopping group and the delegation itself, it does not make sense to me to fill their memberships with people more than half of whom were generally opposed to holding the negotiation at all and generally opposed to having a successful result. I could tell anecdotes about the way in which it was possible for these opponents to take every small issue and raise it to a cabinet-level issue so that it took several months to decide anything. And I could talk about the many other mechanisms by which it was possible for them to slow things down to the point where the negotiations couldn't move at all, which is what happened for the last two years that we were there. But I don't think there's any value in being personal about it in that regard. Let me just try to leave it as a general point and ask Batzel and Kerr how it would be to run this laboratory if more than half of the associate directors opposed the existence of the laboratory and opposed its purposes. It's not only wrong, it's stupid, yet that's the way the CTB negotiation was managed. That situation has somehow got to be changed. This was a special problem with respect to the test ban because the split within the government was deeper and wider than in other cases. For example, in the case of SALT, the agencies that were involved were not opposed to the process nor opposed to a successful result and neither were most of the people involved, with perhaps one or two exceptions. So it's a problem peculiar to the comprehensive test ban, although it could relate to others as well. In sum, do it differently next time. Don't set up a situation in which the majority of the people making day to day decisions with regard to all the little details is opposed to the process and opposed to a successful result.

Many of the people who were there on the delegation with me are here today, and I hasten to add that there's nothing personal in this, that in fact I'm referring primarily to the backstopping group and the working group. The people on the negotiation team all behaved in a perfectly delightful and proper way; and we did have overseas a team that worked together really quite smoothly. Part of the reason for that, of course, is that the negotiating team has so little authority. But the backstopping team and the working group are something else, and opponents of the goals of the CTB were able to slow things to a standstill, well before Afghanistan and Tehran. The latter were not the reasons that we didn't succeed.

The other two pieces of advice have to do with the process that the government goes through before it decides its overall policy on a particular treaty or issue. They have to do with what questions ought to be asked, what ought to be studied in connection with making the decision. There are a number of instances where I feel we asked and answered the wrong questions. I want to take just two of them to complete my remarks. One of the questions that was frequently asked was, "Does a comprehensive test ban interfere with the nuclear weapons stockpile reliability?" I think that's a wrong question. The answer to that question is both simple and trivial. The answer is, "Yes, it interferes with stockpile reliability." The question that should have been asked is, "Given that the comprehensive test ban does interfere with stockpile reliability, how does one cope with that problem and what can be done to maintain an adequate level of nuclear military preparedness in the face of that particular problem?" To illustrate the kind of issues I think would come up if one asked the question the way I suggest, consider those weapons systems that occur in very large numbers and that have the same warhead deployed on all launchers, such as the *Poseidon* system. Then the question of failing on a class basis means the entire system fails, and that's obviously something that is completely unacceptable. If one has to field large numbers of a particular type of launcher, there should be several different warheads employed and these should originate in at least two of the nuclear laboratories. Or, if the designs are marginal and finely tuned, one should back off. That might mean eight warheads instead of ten on a *Polaris;* it might mean only

80 percent of the range. Those, of course, are costs; they're certainly not benefits, but they are costs that can be analyzed and understood and weighed against possible benefits. I might add that the doves are at least as guilty as the hawks with regard to putting these questions in the wrong form, because many of the doves who were behind the comprehensive test ban were confident that the answer to the original (and wrong) question was either, "No, a test ban doesn't interfere with stockpile reliability," or if it does, it can be easily handled by stockpiling drawings, stockpiling knowledge or whatever. I think we would have been better off if we had started with the notion that, yes, indeed nuclear testing must be worth something, we've been doing so much of it, that eliminating it does have a cost—the issue is how to cope with that cost, rather than to deny it exists.

The matter of verification is another in which the key questions are incorrectly stated. In this case there were a great many discussions about verification in the context of the national seismic stations [special seismic stations within the territories of the parties; data recorded at the stations would be sent to the other parties for the purposes of verification] and on-site inspections only. The reason for that is plausible enough. Those were the particular verification systems that were under discussion in the negotiation itself. The questions that were asked about them centered around one issue: the threshold of the national seismic system and other seismic systems for detecting and identifying underground nuclear tests. Again, I think that's the wrong question. The answer to that question is not so simple but it's still trivial. The answer is that the threshold is somewhere within the region of special interest (whether it's at the low end or the high end can be argued forever, but there is a threshold and it's somewhere near the region of interest). However, that is not the right question. The right question is, given all of our intelligence resources, and the many synergisms between each of them and the purely seismic detection system, what can be said about verification, and what does it mean? That's a very different thing, because when one adds all of the other resources, one adds things nobody ever understands in full numerical detail and nobody ever talks about fully. That means that the other party doesn't know about or understand them all either. It's not beyond the possibilities of our overall intelligence system to detect tests that are fizzles, or even to detect a test a week before it happens, if we happen to have the right person in the right place. The issue is not the details of what we have, or whether we have a good spy in the program who can tell us things, but what the Russians think about the possibilities. The sort of person in the Soviet system who thinks that when a foreigner takes a picture of a bridge in Russia he is doing something that perils Soviet national security can also think that there are means of gathering intelligence that he is not aware of and that might trip him up.

The right questions must be asked when we again resume the effort to achieve a comprehensive test ban.

Donald Kerr
Director, Los Alamos National Laboratory

Bans or limitations on nuclear weapon tests are one of many types of arms control measures that have been attempted over the years. From the point of view of actually achieving treaties, they have been among the more successful. The first nuclear test agreement, the test moratorium, was made in 1958 and lasted until the Soviet Union unilaterally resumed testing in the atmosphere in 1961. It was followed by the Limited Test Ban Treaty of 1963, which prohibited nuclear tests in the atmosphere, in outer space, and underwater. In 1974 the Threshold Test Ban Treaty (TTBT) was signed. This treaty limited underground tests after March 1976 to a maximum yield of 150 kilotons. Although the Threshold Treaty was then followed by the treaty limiting peaceful nuclear explosions, neither of these treaties has yet been ratified by the U.S. Senate. Still, both the United States and the Soviet Union claim that the Threshold Treaty's provisions govern their nuclear testing. In the last few years an effort was made to replace the Threshold Treaty with a comprehensive (zero-yield) test ban. That effort has passed into limbo. The question I want to address is whether or not it should remain moribund for the time being.

At least one reason for the success of test limitations as opposed to other forms of arms control is that they have been isolated significantly from the numerous political and policy concerns that impinge upon most arms control negotiations. Test bans have been treated as a peripheral issue, primarily technical in content and largely independent from other arms control and national security considerations. However, nuclear tests and test bans are in fact important, integral parts of the nation's security and arms control posture. It is important, when evaluating and planning policy for nuclear testing and test bans, to take into account how they fit into this larger context.

First of all, what is the real danger that arms control historically has attempted to reduce, and how do bans on nuclear testing contribute to reducing that danger? The danger stems from the existence of thousands of nuclear weapons and megatons, ready to be unleashed swiftly and irrevocably following the decision of a handful of national leaders or by accident. The United States has attempted to reduce this danger with a combination of national defense and arms control programs.

The immediate object of all arms control approaches has been to reduce the danger posed by nuclear weapons, primarily by reducing their number. But several quite different aspirations have been implicit in these efforts. The most attractive and elevated, though most elusive, goal is for arms control to contribute to a new and better world order, in which all weapons or at least all nuclear weapons are absent. The details of this new world order, whether it would have to be enforced by an international police force, how it would be governed, and other essential issues are vague and disputed. But aspirations to move in this direction are visible in many of the more comprehensive arms control proposals.

A less elevated but more practical goal for arms control has been to shore up and stabilize the essential features of the existing world order, while reducing the risk of catastrophic conflict. Specific aims are to reduce the risk of nuclear war, reduce the nuclear arsenals of the major powers, and contain and control any conflicts that do arise between them. From the American point of view, these define the central purpose of most arms control negotiations.

A less noble objective for arms control might be to contribute to the unilateral interests of one of the countries involved: Arms control treaties could be sought that would strengthen one country and weaken its opponent.

As the world position of the United States has evolved over the past several years, our ability to pursue the highest, most disinterested aims has declined, and we have been forced to attend more narrowly to our own interests. So far we have not been impelled to compromise any deep national principles in our efforts to maintain ourselves. But it is worth remembering such compromises can result. When Churchill's England was against the wall in 1941, he gratefully accepted the help and alliance of Stalin's Soviet Union, although he had called that regime evil incarnate. But as he pointed out, he was prepared, in those dreadful times, "to make favorable references to the devil in the House of Commons" if the devil were willing to make common cause against Hitler.

Opinions differ about how much test bans can contribute to any of these arms control objectives, and hence about what effect test bans would have on national and international security. Some proponents of nuclear testing constraints believe that a complete test ban can be the key to a process that would eventually bring greater worldwide security and reduce the risks of nuclear war.

They argue, I think rightly, that the absence of nuclear tests would do much to cripple nuclear weapons. The weapons laboratories of the United States have maintained for years that testing is an essential element of the nuclear weapon capability of the nation. Without testing, the base of knowledge and experience needed for developing weapons would dissipate, and confidence even in the existing nuclear stockpile would decline. Thus, any nation scrupulously observing a total test ban would sooner or later lose confidence in its weapons and its willingness to rely on those weapons would decline.

So it could be argued that nuclear test bans provide a good way to achieve real arms control through the back door. And this route may seem especially attractive since the more direct approach, through quantitative and qualitative limitations on nuclear weapons and launchers, has proven to be so difficult.

Besides this rather grand end, test bans are often said to produce other, collateral benefits. They may reduce the prospect of accidental releases of radiation into the environment; they may eliminate or reduce the impulse of third countries to join the "nuclear club"; they may convince the public that nuclear weapons are being controlled; and they may improve the climate for negotiations to control other armaments.

Beginning from the same premise—that a test program is essential to the maintenance of a reliable nuclear weapon stockpile—I am forced to come to a very different conclusion. The United States must, at least for now, retain both nuclear weapons and nuclear testing. As a former Los Alamos director, Norris Bradbury, said, "The whole object of making the weapons is not to kill people but to find time for somebody to find other ways to solve these problems."

Since their inception, nuclear weapons have played a key role in the defense posture of the United States. Their role has become more critical with the passing of the years. The United States and our Western European allies largely demobilized after World War II. We expected to deter the large and growing Soviet conventional forces with our nuclear weapons. While this reliance has not changed in recent years, the Soviets have undertaken a general buildup of forces that has increased their conventional force advantage and given them parity or superiority in most parts of the strategic equation. Because of this imbalance of conventional and theater nuclear forces, any recognized weakening of our strategic nuclear deterrent, even if coupled with a known corresponding weakening of Soviet strategic nuclear forces, would be extremely serious for both the United States and NATO. The Soviet position would be correspondingly improved.

Our nuclear weapon test program is essential in designing, manufacturing, maintaining, and certifying weapons. Weapon certification is in effect a promise by the weapons complex to the Department of Defense that the weapons will perform within specifications if ever called to do so; that they will be safe under all operating conditions and resistant to unauthorized attempts to use them; and that they can be relied upon to meet these requirements for a predictably long time.

But weapons are affected by aging and obsolescence. Warheads, in particular, over an extended period will deteriorate physically. Their expected stockpile lifetime is typically between fifteen and twenty-five years, but some designs have required corrective measures much sooner. Both warheads and their delivery systems are subject to technological obsolescence. In the past, obsolescence led to stockpile turnover so that physical deterioration did not have time to develop. But under a test ban, the possible effects of physical deterioration would become increasingly important.

Maintenance of the nuclear stockpile depends on regularly scheduled random sampling. Irregularities that are found—as they are, from time to time—are referred to the experts at the weapons design laboratories for their judgment as to the severity of the problem and the necessary "fix." The solution often is one that can be validated on the basis of previous research and development tests related to the system in question or related systems so the fix can be made without a new nuclear test. In cases where such validation is not possible, a critical evaluation must be made that, occasionally, results in a decision that an additional test is required if the weapon is to be returned to the active inventory. In all such cases, without the test or tests required, certification of the weapon, at least as we have known it until now, would be impossible. There are sometimes administrative alternatives; for example, a weapon known or suspected not to conform to certain safety criteria could be removed from inventory. But for obvious reasons, solutions of this kind may carry heavy and often unacceptable penalties. I would be concerned, under a complete test ban, that given real life pressures and human fallibility, we might on occasion stockpile inadequately tested designs. Serious unreliability could result.

Besides increasing doubt about the existing stockpile, a complete test ban would preclude placing new weapons in the stockpile. Risk-free developments in the following desirable areas would be precluded.

- Enhanced warhead safety
- Increased weapon control to prevent unauthorized use
- Improved yield-to-weight ratios
- Reduced warhead cost and reduced usage of special nuclear material
- Tailored weapon outputs for specific military needs

• Understanding of long-term chemical and structural stability

In particular, enhanced safety and denial modifications could not be confidently made.

A frequently held notion should be specifically dispelled. The fact that we rarely conduct proof tests—that is, specific individual tests of a weapon pulled from the stockpile—is sometimes cited as evidence that testing is not necessary to maintain confidence in the reliability of the stockpile. This claim is false. We use the continuing testing program to confirm the design choices made in stockpile weapons. We reuse the tested technology of weapons in the stockpile in designing new weapon systems; if we encounter a stockpile problem, we may proof test its solution by adding an experiment to a test that is part of the continuing program. In effect, proof testing is built into the very philosophy on which our testing program is based.

Of course, demonstrating that testing is essential to continued confidence in our weapons, and arguing that nuclear weapons are central to the defense of the United States, does not imply that arms control measures will never make inroads into the threat posed by nuclear weapons without undermining the security of the United States. But so far the characteristic approach to arms control has failed both to reduce armaments and improve security.

Since the earliest overt attempt at arms control of which I am aware (by a pope who threatened to excommunicate anyone using the crossbow), our efforts have focused on constraining or reducing the technological implements of warfare. The Naval Treaties, the abortive World Disarmament Conference, and our numerous efforts to control nuclear weapons all have had as their theme constraints on the implements of war. These efforts have had lackluster results, and for a very good reason. The causes of war and enmity that are responsible for the acquisition of weapons are deep and political. Failing a resolution of these differences, efforts at controlling the military hardware that is but a symptom of that enmity have been failures. An analogy may be illustrative.

Handgun control in the United States is a controversial issue. Handguns, like weapons of war, may be viewed as means of self-defense, which all law-abiding people would like to be able to do without. But how and under what circumstances can handgun control be achieved? First it would require legislation and executive enforcement by the states or federal government. And for such controls to be effective, the American people would have to be convinced that the government would defend them as well as they could defend themselves with their handguns. Verification of compliance with the agreement would also be important.

Nations, unlike citizens, have no government to legislate or execute laws for them. They are accustomed to looking after their own security and to distrusting their neighbors. Until the political accommodations can be made that might mitigate this distrust, it is not reasonable to expect them to surrender their means of self-defense, however great the danger that might be implicit in retaining these weapons.

Seen from this perspective, the problems that have attended arms control negotiations, and in particular test bans, are not surprising. Verifying compliance with test bans is one such problem. It has been a long-time stumbling block and has given rise to additional questions in recent years. Verification of a nuclear weapons test ban involves complexities that have received much discussion, but no resolution. For example, one of the key components of treaty verification involves seismic monitoring. Any test carried out in violation of the treaty must be big enough to be detected against the ever-present background of natural seismic events and noise. It must also be located, and then it must be identified as an explosion rather than an earthquake. Under the best of circumstances—and by that I mean that no special techniques are used to hide an underground test—the Soviet Union could conduct low-yield tests that would not be detected by American monitors or, if detected, would not be distinguishable from earthquakes. They would have to be classified as "ambiguous events."

Some important verification issues have arisen in the past few years. First, large seismic signals have been observed accompanying Soviet experiments, even though the Soviets have announced that they would observe the 150 kiloton limitation of the Threshold Treaty. Since these observations, the relationship of yield to seismic signal has been revised downward. But the geophysical basis of this relationship is not well understood, and reliance on such data introduces uncertainty into treaty verification.

Second, on 22 September 1979 a *Vela* test detection satellite observed an "event" in the South Atlantic. After careful analysis of this data and other supporting data, some scientists concluded that the event was in fact a nuclear explosion. On the other hand, *Science* magazine reported, "lacking any clear physical proof that a blast had occurred, the White House assembled a panel of independent scientists—it was judged to have been caused by a natural event." I do not mean to argue whether or not the September 22 event was a nuclear explosion, but rather that there was strong disagreement in interpretation of the same data by presumably competent, trained people. Imagine the controversy that would surround seismic verification data in an open international forum.

The asymmetry that might be introduced by a treaty, given the above verification problems, could be very significant. A low-yield test program could be very useful in retaining a weapon program's infrastructure, and an occasional high-yield experiment could provide "proving" of warheads. Such a program surreptitiously carried out by the Soviets, while the United States abandoned an effective program, could be unverifiable. It could effectively allow them to maintain warhead confidence, while ours all but disappeared.

I have spoken thus far in the context of U.S.-NATO-Soviet considerations. The nonnuclear weapon states have, in recent years, been pressuring the nuclear weapon states for a complete test ban. Several argue that superpower testing provides stimulus for other states to build weapons, and they point out that in the preamble to the 1968 Nuclear Non-Proliferation Treaty, the nuclear weapon states recalled their determination to seek the cessation of all test explosions.

From a technical point of view a comprehensive test ban has only a marginal effect on the proliferation of nuclear weapons. Testing is not essential for designing and building the simple, first-generation fission devices that a would-be proliferator is likely to want at the beginning of a nuclear weapons program. He needs only the special nuclear material and the knowledge and skills to assemble the device. As you know, most, if not all, of the nations that have built nuclear explosives are believed to have detonated them on the first try. From this technical standpoint, it is my opinion that a proliferator would be sacrificing only one thing by signing a comprehensive test ban—the prestige or warning value he might see in carrying out a public explosion. He would not be depriving himself of the capability to develop nuclear weapons should he see these as essential to his national security or military ambitions.

On the policy side it is argued that a nondiscriminatory comprehensive test ban, adhered to by nuclear and nonnuclear weapon states alike, would inhibit the spread of nuclear weapons by making tests of nuclear explosives politically more costly. The improved climate, presumably created by the test ban, would allow the world to move in the direction of the highest aspiration of the Non-Proliferation Treaty, stated in Article VI: "Each of the Parties to the Treaty undertakes to pursue negotiations in good faith on effective measures relating to cessation of the nuclear arms race at an early date and to nuclear disarmament, and on a treaty on general and complete disarmament under strict and effective international control."

It is unlikely that the states interested in building nuclear weapons are driven primarily by the bad example of the major powers. They, like the nuclear powers, are assuredly driven by their own security requirements. It is very unlikely that a comprehensive test ban or even substantial nuclear disarmament by the major powers would materially effect their decision to build or not build nuclear weapons. For example, do we really suppose that Pakistan and India have been prompted in their actions by absence of a superpower comprehensive test ban?

I believe that a comprehensive test ban not only is unlikely to contribute to the goals of Article VI, but could do harm in other ways as well. A comprehensive test ban between the United States and the Soviet Union would not, for many years, eliminate nuclear weapons, so it would not end the distinction between nuclear and nonnuclear weapon states. Nor would it prevent the nuclear weapon states from developing new types of weapons equally out of reach of the nonnuclear weapon states. We should also be concerned that if we make a display of trying to accomplish the pious insincerities of Article VI and fail, we may give the nonnuclear weapon states a license to develop nuclear weapons. The approach suggested by some nonnuclear weapon states gives the false impression that our only choice is between non-proliferation and the degradation of our nuclear stockpile. It propagates the theory that we will not have to develop more appropriate weaponry in the future, and finally it pushes us toward making our weapons more suicidal and less credible. It obscures the real pressures for nuclear weapon proliferation, which are national, political, and genuine.

To conclude, I believe that pursuit of a comprehensive test ban is not an American priority. Its benefits would be modest; certainly modest enough to discourage as well various part-way measures such as a progression of Threshold Test Bans. The potential dangers are very great relative to the questionable gains.

PANELISTS

Paul Seabury

Political Science Department, University of California at Berkeley

My first reaction to these two presentations, radically different from each other, was to mold them together, like Roosevelt said, and get some kind of consensus, which is utterly impossible. My remarks, therefore, will in all honesty have to begin by saying that on balance Kerr's position is largely mine, as far as it goes. I would like, though, to point out several things.

One is the question that York raised in the beginning. Why can't one separate or depoliticize the arms control negotiations and set them aside in a special category? Now that the issue has been debated for years—fruitlessly I think—we ought to bear in mind the fact that the very act of setting the issues aside from the political realm would be a political act requiring enormous power and influence to carry off.

Another question that I would like to raise is the matter of what maintains the momentum of a nuclear arms race, seen as a process of proliferation? Again, I agree with Kerr that it isn't the bad example of the superpowers that causes the imitation, like a bad parent setting bad examples to little kids. Rather, one ought to look in other directions. It seems to me that one incentive for proliferation in the last ten years has been the diminishing credibility of certain kinds of security guarantees in the international community. One has only to look at the attitudes being taken by the Taiwanese, the South Koreans, the Israelis. In fact, one can argue in the case of the Israelis that this has been uppermost in their minds for a very long time. If you don't trust the outside guarantor, you make your private preparations. Fear as an incentive to proliferation is greater in a decentralized international community than when there is a sense of cohesion in collective security guaranteed, say, by a reliable American guarantor.

Another matter is the kind of stereotypical way in which we have come to speak of the arms race as some kind of monolithic thing that is intrinsically bad. As a student of international politics, I have never been very greatly convinced by the theory that somehow wars are the products of arms races. It simply doesn't follow logically; in fact, many of the worst twentieth-century wars have been ones that were not preceded by such an arms race but rather one side racing and the other side not. Another feature in this matter is that arms races seen as technological innovations do not necessarily destabilize the system. We have evidence of certain kinds of technological innovations that have made the relationship a good deal more stable than before. There are some who oppose the so-called nuclear arms race who, I think, teeter on the edge of being Luddites, in a sense that for them any kind of innovation is bad because it somehow threatens the balance. Well, the balance can be made safer by some innovations, and we should be able to recognize them.

Richard Wagner

Assistant to the Secretary of Defense for Atomic Energy; Former Associate Director for Nuclear Tests, Lawrence Livermore National Laboratory

York has set before us the ideal of disarmament, and that is an ideal that we should all keep before us. I suspect, though, that we can reasonably project that that kind of disarmament won't happen during the next ten or even thirty or forty years. The question then is whether we should try to live through that period without the advances in nuclear weapon technology that accrue from nuclear testing.

York and Kerr have laid out most parts of the argument, which by now have become pretty stylized. I'd like first to comment on the issue of stockpile reliability. York, I think, phrased the issue quite properly. He did not ask whether there will be a degradation in stockpile reliability, but rather what can one do to cope with the inevitable degradation. He laid out a couple of examples: One was to have more than one warhead for important systems, and the second was to relax the requirements so as to allow the designs to be more intrinsically reliable. The heart of the stockpile reliability issue goes deeper than those kinds of proposed solutions. The heart of it is that testing is so much a part of the science of weapon design that without doing those experiments the knowledge base here and at Los Alamos would fade away within a few years. The basis wouldn't exist from which to make judgments about which systems would need to have redundant warheads, which systems could be retrofitted, which systems should be retired. The people who know this technology would simply not be here to make those judgments.

I have been surprised, during the arguments about the CTB, at the lack of emphasis on three issues that seem to me to be more important than is reflected by the discussion we've heard. The first one is whether or not the characteristics of the weapons that have been put into stockpile during the last few decades of development, or might be put into stockpile during the next few decades, contribute to the maintenance of what Paul Nitze called Situation Q. Kerr mentioned safety and security. It seems obvious that improving safety and security helps the maintenance of Situation Q. Other features have been more controversial; for example, the enhanced radiation feature. I have not seen discussions of weapon features made in the context of the desirability or undesirability of a test ban, and that seems to me to be a deficiency in the debate.

A second deficiency seems to me to have been the almost total absence of discussion of weapons effects tests. Weapons effects are part and parcel of the issue of survivability. Survivability is really one of the pillars of maintaining Situation Q. We know very little about some key weapons effects that are involved in, for instance, the utility and survivability of command and control systems. It is difficult to pursue a better understanding of some of those effects with the limitations imposed by the Limited Test Ban Treaty, for many of the appropriate tests would need to be carried out in the atmosphere. We didn't know enough at the time, in 1963, to know whether we had done the right set of tests. In retrospect, I think we did not and are handicapped by that lack of knowledge today. To the extent that this lack of knowledge can continue to be gradually rectified by underground testing, we have another and considerably stronger argument for opposing the test ban.

The final argument that has been stated from time to time, but not pursued enough, is that we simply don't know what the Soviets can do with this technology. It's been about nineteen years since we last got good information on what the Soviets had done—nineteen years because the only really good information can come from the very fallout that it was the intent of the Limited Test Ban Treaty to preclude. We're in a situation now after nineteen years where we simply don't know where we stand with regard to our principal adversary in this technology. In particular, I think it is simply not true that a test ban would freeze a position of Soviet inferiority in this technology. I know of no evidence that would lead to that conclusion. In fact what fragmentary evidence there is indicates to me that there is some case to be made for the opposite conclusion. The Soviets appear to have been carrying out an imaginative program, and in that situation it strikes me that stopping the development of the technology has too much of an element of luck to it. I would rather retain some control of our position by being able to develop new weapons whose features fit the needs of maintaining Situation Q.

Jack Ruina

Center for International Studies, Massachusetts Institute of Technology

Listening to today's discussion reminds me of the subtitle to a short story by Rebecca West that went something like "there is no such thing as a dialogue, only interspersed monologues." At this meeting, one side is discussing all the costs of a particular arms control agreement, while the other discusses all the benefits.

Dr. York said that there's no hope for a comprehensive test ban. The sense of the conversations I have heard in the hallway is that the test ban was a bad idea whose time is past. But I think that the important thing to say about the CTB is that it's an issue that's not going to go away although many people here hope it will. It may recur during the next administration, and maybe some time afterwards. The reason for this is that a ban is easy to understand compared to, for example, setting upper limits on strategic weaponry. People readily identify nuclear testing with the interests that superpowers and others have in developing or improving their nuclear weapons. The association of nuclear testing with a preoccupation with nuclear weapons systems will keep the nuclear testing issue, and the possibility of a ban or other limits on nuclear testing, as an agenda item in arms control. The issue of a CTB is a bit of unfinished business that just won't go away.

Another reason interest in a CTB persists is its relevance to nuclear proliferation. Everybody agrees with the "sign" of the relevance—it helps in slowing proliferation. However, there is great disagreement about how much it helps. Agreement on the sign is encouraging because there are few issues where people agree even on the sign of the effect.

Next, nuclear test limits of some sort make an easy gap filler when other arms control possibilities are not making much progress. It's always easy to say, "Well, let's agree to lower the 150 kiloton testing threshold to 140 kilotons." Wasn't it lack of progress in other arms efforts that produced the TTBT to start with?

My own perspectives on the test ban are quite simple; they're not surprising and they're not new. Technically, the test ban is a more separable issue from SALT than, say, TNF limitations. You can deal with it on its own merits. It can come about at any time; that's why it could be a gap filler. Also, a ban on nuclear testing is symmetrical. If it's a ban, it's a ban for both parties. The kinds of concerns that Paul Nitze has about asymmetries and equivalence don't occur here. Only if you get into some deeper theologies on the test ban, do you see asymmetries. Some of these asymmetries are hard to understand. For example, I've heard speculation that the Soviets are behind us in nuclear technology, and therefore their weapons are cruder, but in that sense they're ahead of us because testing for reliability isn't as important to them. There is also the suggestion that the Soviets can keep scientists chained to their desks working on nuclear weapons technology so that they don't lose their competence even if there is a ban on testing, whereas people at Livermore and Los Alamos, if they can't test their designs, lose interest and go to Boeing or MIT or some other place. These are higher order asymmetries. Nothing as obvious as they have big missiles and we don't, or they have ten MIRVs and we only have three.

The national security issues in the test ban are not central; they don't bear directly on such questions as crisis stability or essential equivalence or possibilities of nuclear brinkmanship. Imposing testing limits does not mean limiting production or deployment or limiting undesirable or destabilizing weapons systems. A test ban will not *directly* affect the nuclear arms race. Both the qualitative and quantitative nuclear arms race can continue unimpeded—at least in the first order.

A test ban is easy to understand—it stops nuclear testing, and the public understands this as a stop in one component activity of the nuclear arms race. For the people in this audience and for most of us, the costs and benefits of a test ban are much less evident than for the other kinds of arms control agreements. You can't quantify any of the costs and benefits; you have to talk in qualitative terms indicating perhaps how speculative the consequences are. This is not to say that when one can produce numbers the consequences are less speculative, but at least they sound less speculative.

To repeat, the clearest benefit of a test ban would be some inhibiting effect on proliferation. It would also impose some limitations, however few, on new weapon systems development for the superpowers and this is beneficial from an arms control point of view.

Without a test ban there will be continued skepticism worldwide about the expressed interest of the superpowers in arms control. A CTB is so easy to negotiate and to write compared to SALT for example that if the big powers in all these years couldn't agree on one, how sincere are they about any nuclear arms control?

The costs of a test ban were described by Don Kerr. I couldn't make a better statement than he made. Herb York agrees with him. If they agree with each other, how can I disagree? I might say that I was not impressed with the risks of a CTB when they were stated twenty years ago, when people were worried about the Soviets cheating by testing behind the moon or making big holes in the earth to muffle seismic signals, and in that way developing new weapons such as neutron weapons that would change the nuclear balance. The arguments now are more sophisticated and more credible. The issues about stockpile reliability and the fact that the laboratories would have a very hard time maintaining the required competence are quite reasonable arguments, and these are indeed costs in a CTB. The important thing is to remember the benefits and weigh them against the costs. We must have some reasonable framework by which we can weigh one against the other. On balance I favor a CTB. This may well reflect prejudice rather than analysis as I'm sure everybody who has known me for years believes.

On the subject of the TTBT, it wasn't much as an arms control step, but now that we have signed it we shouldn't walk away from it. That would be more of a negative step than acceding to it was a positive one for arms control. Since we have the TTBT, why not ratify it, and get the extra gains from the information exchange called for in the TTBT? I would favor a reduction of the threshold to a lower number, to something like 10 or 20 kilotons, because it's a more honest number in the sense that it's closer to seismic verification thresholds. The reason there was so much cynicism about the TTBT was because the limit of 150 kilotons was so high; it was not based on any data or analyses about seismic detection or verification. I don't know what it was based on, but the limit didn't relate to detection capability. At least 10 or 20 kilotons has some resemblance to seismic detection capabilities.

I recognize that once you move to a low threshold TTBT, a CTB would be harder to get because of legitimate questions about seismic detection capability for low yields, say under 5 kilotons. But remember verification depends on more than seismic detection alone.

Finally, I urge you not to underestimate how dramatic it would be if the superpowers, hopefully followed by others, agreed to a comprehensive test ban. Although as a straight arms control measure it's hard to make a strong case for a CTB, it would be a clear signal to the world that the superpowers may finally be reducing their preoccupation with nuclear weapons and that would be an important and dramatic step. However, it's only important when the time is right. The time clearly isn't right now, so I don't propose that the CTB should be high on the agenda at this point in time.

DISCUSSION

Herbert York: It is sometimes said that arms controllers rely a lot on luck. That may be true, but those who rely on the deployment of tens of thousands of nuclear weapons for continuing a state of deterrence into the indefinite future are relying on luck and on the notion that there will never be an irrational act in that future. Wagner suggested that there are a number of developments that have taken place over the last few decades that add to stability, that is, Situation Q. However, the last twenty years saw the development of weapons that made MIRV possible and the development of high accuracies. The introduction of MIRV and high accuracies are at the root of the *Minuteman* survivability problem. The evidence is that it has no good solution. The efforts of the last administration and this administration to find a solution to that problem, the MX or others, I believe, are not going to work out. It has proved to be impossible to get a genuine consensus either in the public generally or in the defense establishment about what to do about *Minuteman* survivability, and I believe that situation will probably continue. So MIRV was a disaster and the developments that led to that have certainly not helped with regard to Situation Q, stability, or anything else you want to call it.

Francis Hoeber: I'm a little disturbed at the concept that one should have enthusiasts do the negotiating. If our elections mean anything, if a change of leadership means anything, we should recognize the political importance of enabling a president and his officials to appoint any kind of negotiating team they want. A particular outcome of the negotiation in question should not be prejudged by the selection of the team that we want. Another issue on which I would like to disagree is that I'm scared silly of the idea of relying on Soviet fears of being caught cheating to deter cheating. That has not really worked on previous agreements with them. We can argue the details, but I would cite some aspects of the ABM Treaty.

Herbert York: I did not say that the delegation should be composed of people who are enthusiastic about a particular result. I said it should not be made up of a majority of people who are opposed even to negotiations taking place. That's an entirely different thing. Furthermore, I agree that in deciding what to do, people of all points of view should be heard.

Michael Intriligator: I have two questions, one for York and the other for the entire panel. For York, I was interested in the idea of arms control as a mechanism to foster eventual disarmament. I for one believe that the three goals of arms control that Schelling talked about roughly twenty years ago still make a lot of sense today. The first was to limit the probability of nuclear war; second, to reduce the destruction if nuclear war does occur; and third, to reduce the cost of national defense. I think that's a very good way to organize one's arguments and discussion of the issues we've been talking about throughout the day. For example, with respect to SALT, one could argue that SALT might have the effect of slightly degrading the first goal but very much improving the second and third goals, and therefore establish some kind of a trade-off between the different goals that Tom Schelling talked about. In general, I would like York to respond to the usefulness of this alternative way of looking at the goals of arms control.

My second question is addressed to the entire panel. There is an element of all-or-nothingness about the kind of discussions we've heard. It seems that either we should go right away to the full CTB or we should go to the other extreme, if I understood the arguments, of going back to unlimited testing. I would like to ask Kerr, Seabury, and Wagner if they would favor revoking not only the TTBT, but the original Limited Test Ban Treaty?

Herbert York: With regard to the third goal—to save money—I don't agree with that as being a goal at all. In particular, nuclear arms control and disarmament, which is what I was talking about, are likely to cost money rather than save money. Any substantial nuclear disarmament in Europe would result in a situation that would probably call for increased expenditures on conventional arms that would more than balance the savings. Furthermore, the notion that nuclear arms are cheaper than other arms is one of the reasons that we have nuclear arms there and thus prepared the basis for this terrible situation. The fact that nuclear arms are in Europe is one of the things that provide the Europeans with an alibi for not doing much else, so that I reject out of hand the notion that the purpose of nuclear arms control is to save money.

With regard to the first two goals, that's more complicated. I would focus on the second goal, which is to limit the destruction if war should happen. I believe the only way that can be done with assurance in the long run is not to have more than some absolute minimum of nuclear weapons. With regard to the first goal, if there were no nuclear weapons there would be no nuclear war. I am willing to run somewhat more risk of conventional war in order to decrease the risk of nuclear war. Others may feel very differently about that question, which is clearly judgmental.

Donald Kerr: To take up the question that you posed to the middle three of us, with respect to possibly advocating abrogation of the Limited Test Ban Treaty, I would not expect to see that question come up out of context. There must be some other set of events that would motivate that consideration. Certainly, taken as an issue by itself, I would not advocate revoking that treaty or withdrawing from it in any way. As far as the all-or-nothing aspect of what some have called a stylized debate, I suspect one reason for that is that, in a formal sense, no new question has been asked. The only negotiation that has been on the table the last few years and still lies there, albeit in some limbo, is the question of a comprehensive or complete test ban. Earle made mention of other possibilities, like reduced thresholds or combinations of thresholds with numbers allowed above some limit. Those need to be addressed as specific cases before one could form opinions about them. They clearly would have to do with the numbers and types of military systems this country chooses to develop and deploy and maintain, and those issues would have to be properly structured and addressed.

To go back to the earlier question put by Hoeber about the makeup of the negotiating team, I believe that those who represent us in a negotiation should all be committed to the same end, and I don't see any other way to conduct a negotiation. The way you get that is for the president or others to pick the team in detail, rather than institutionally. And I think that's one of the defects of our methods in the past.

Paul Seabury: I am not in favor of going back to atmospheric testing. I don't take it as a particularly important question because that kind of retrogression in no way can contribute to anything but a more somber public. It's perfectly evident that the more visible these activities are, the more disturbing they are. It would make the international situation worse. For example, consider the political climate that followed

Khrushchev's announcement of the abrogation of the test moratorium in 1961. It had very severe implications and effects at that time.

Richard Wagner: I could imagine a situation in which a system might be proposed which could solve or reduce the problem of MX survivability. If that system depended for its functioning on knowing a nuclear effect that we didn't know, and which could only be resolved by a test in the atmosphere, I could imagine that that might be an attractive enough situation to do that test, but certainly not a return to unlimited testing in the atmosphere. Next, it's really not all-or-nothing, today. Both the labs, in the discussions leading to the Threshold Test Ban Treaty, were quite straightforward as to whether or not we could live with that threshold. The general tenor of the conclusions, and I won't phrase them as carefully as they were phrased at the time, was that there might be some doubts, but on the whole we probably could live with that threshold. That threshold is, in a sense, an experiment for which the data are not yet in, as to whether or not in the long term we can live with that threshold. If the next decade holds the necessity for deployment of systems that have new high-yield warheads, it may turn out to be difficult to live with that threshold. But today, it looks as if we can live with it, so it's not an all-or-nothing situation.

Jack Ruina: I would like to comment on what was just said. I think it is a perfect example. They were talking only about the cost to us, of what new system we might deprive ourselves of. Might we not have benefits from what the Soviets deprive themselves of under the Threshold Test Ban? We can't make that judgment very well, but why isn't it even in your equation?

Richard Wagner: It's certainly in my equation. I suspect that the Soviets face similar kinds of problems. I would hate to see the Soviets driven to some new deployment that might appear very threatening to us because they lack some piece of effects information.

Jack Ruina: I think that what was just said is representative of the main difficulty in all the arms control discussions. Some people here feel more secure in having freedom of action even though they acknowledge that if the Soviets have freedom of action it's bad for us. They say we know what's best for us and we'll keep ahead. That's a frame of mind that says arms control agreements basically have a problem because they restrain us, and the benefits we get from restraining the Soviets just aren't great enough for that cost. Others feel that restraint on both sides is terribly important. I think that's a clear point of view that marks differences about arms control agreements across the board, not only with nuclear testing.

Joseph Nye: I think it's true that we often hear the same arguments in this area, but it's not true that views don't change, at least on my part. They have somewhat since I spoke here two years ago in favor of the CTB. And I think that the basic view is the one that Ruina forwarded, which is that essentially it's marginal. It has small marginal benefits for proliferation. It has small marginal costs perhaps in stability areas. I want to ask York, is this the right way to go about arms control? I can imagine the political climate in which one would indeed want to go forward with some form of reduction of the threshold limits for the political effects that Jack Ruina mentioned. But if we wind up putting maximal claims for what are relatively marginal arms control issues, don't we wind up doing more damage to arms control than it's worth? In other words, if we think of arms control as dealing with major strategic security problems, it's hard to find what is the major strategic security issue to which the CTB is an answer. It is a part, but only a small part, of an answer to the problem of proliferation, and it may have some marginal negative effects in the other direction. It does, it seems to me, require a very different political climate before you get major gains from it. The concern I have is that if you promote this as a path to disarmament when the political climate is clearly the opposite, you wind up driving people away from a sensible approach to arms control, which is to ask it to contribute to the solution of real security problems.

Herbert York: I think I said, and I know I meant to say, that the CTB is not at the top of my priorities with regard to arms control. In fact most of the other topics, SALT, for example, I put at a higher priority. Furthermore, a CTB only makes good sense in a proper climate. A world in which the only act of nuclear moderation was a test ban, and which was otherwise characterized by nuclear exuberance, would not be a good situation, for reasons you, in fact, have discussed. In that circumstance, a CTB probably wouldn't be viable and entering a test ban that was doomed to fail or that had a high probability of failing would be worse than not doing anything at all in that regard. So I don't think I am very far from you in that respect. What I would like to see, then, is that the whole situation be changed in a way that nuclear moderation is the general mood, where the increasing dependence on nuclear weapons by us and by a growing number of countries is reversed, and in that environment I think that a nuclear test ban would be one more good element of a total program of nuclear moderation.

Michael May: I'd like to address this question to York. It concerns your general framework, not the conclusions you've drawn from it, regarding the nuclear test ban. I'd like to air a concern about nuclear disarmament that has troubled me and I'm now not talking about arms control, which I believe in and to which I've contributed. Intergovernmental crises with the kind of world system we have are a fact of life. And so, it seems to me, that if we go any significant way toward nuclear disarmament, far enough to affect the security feelings of various countries, whenever crises occur there are going to be powerful pressures to rearm. Now, high levels of nuclear weapons can be exceedingly dangerous. But I want to submit to you that very low levels of nuclear weapons could also be dangerous with the political international system that we have now. One of the features of current political life over the last decades is that even fairly major crises, such as the recent succession of crises in the Middle East, and Afghanistan, and others, have not provoked nuclear rearmament. One or two have. The Korean invasion did. But a number of major ones did not. I wonder what would happen if we drove the arms level below some number, which I can't possibly state, toward disarmament. This is not an argument that the numbers should be as high as possible. My question is, can you conceive of a world in which nuclear disarmament would be viable that did not, at the same time, have either world government or at least a much more tightly regulated organization of states than anything that we've experienced or are likely to experience soon?

Herbert York: My general response is that I don't believe that there is a safe future within reach, so the fact that there are certain dangers in connection with nuclear disarmament doesn't dissuade me, because there are dangers in connection with nuclear armament and there are dangers in connection with other things as well. I simply don't see a safe future ahead of any kind and the choice is one of various dangers; I stand by the choice that I named. I can imagine a world that has the same kind of anarchistic and chaotic relationships between states as the current one, but in which there are far fewer nuclear weapons. For example, I think that there are many classes of nuclear weapons for which there are nonnuclear substitutes that might not be quite so good technically, but which might be a lot better politically or practically. For example, weapons that might substitute for battlefield nuclear weapons might not be able to destroy three tanks at once, but they could destroy one. Since one would avoid the absolutely impossible chain of command required for permission to use a nuclear weapon, killing one is much better than the hypothetical possibility of killing three. There are whole classes of nuclear systems within which one could, in fact, go to zero. There are associated questions of verification, and possibilities of violation, but it's obviously impossible to get into those now.

With regard to strategic weapons, there is the problem of going to zero, and then having somebody cheat by one. This would give that country a very large advantage and I don't see any way around this problem at the present time. So, I don't see how one goes to zero on strategic weapons. But I think that one can go to figures that are far, far smaller than the 10 thousand or so we are at and still maintain the stability and the kind of deterrent situation that we have now. I think that one can have in our chaotic and anarchistic world far fewer weapons than today, and I'm not talking about reductions by half. I'm talking about the elimination of whole classes of nuclear weapons, and of very great reductions in others for which there is not substitute.

Ludger Buerstedde: I don't see much enthusiasm or optimism for a CTB during the next few years. One has to ask who should get the blame for stalling the negotiations? It seems that the Soviet Union did much more testing during recent years than the United States. Did they anticipate a CTB? Or is it just a different type of testing and what might be the motives behind it?

Herbert York: I've thought all along it was a mistake for the United States to cut back on its testing program just before a CTB. It really seemed to me like an upside down sort of thing to do, politically as well as from the point of view of testing and preparedness. With regard to your first question as to whose fault it was, that's a long story that I could not possibly go into now. I think the blame is certainly shared. Where the major blame lies, is something I don't really want to discuss at this time because it would involve more detail than I feel I can go into. But I said earlier, and will stand by that, that the process was dead in the water well before Iran or Afghanistan.

Charles McDonald: I'm glad to see that the panel seems universally in agreement. It's the first time I've ever seen that sort of thing. The gains to be achieved from a comprehensive test ban are marginal at best. Each for your own reasons is slightly in favor or slightly opposed to a CTB. I also am glad we don't have to argue whether or not a Comprehensive Test Ban would have an adverse effect on the confidence that we have in the nuclear stockpile. It appears that most people now generally accept that a CTB would have a detrimental effect on confidence. Some of you have even implied in other forums that that was an intent of the CTB, because nations would start to lose confidence in their nuclear weapons and therefore would be less inclined to use them. I'd like to ask York, in particular, how in the world can that be a stable arrangement, when you ask the country to base its whole deterrent posture on a set of weapons whose reliability is not assured?

Herbert York: Your first point was that we all agreed that the CTB is marginal. I did not agree that it was marginal. I said it's not the right time for it and furthermore I said it's not the highest priority, but that's not the same as saying it's marginal. With regard to your last point, I'm not sure who you are referring to up here. I have never said that the loss of reliability would be stabilizing. I recognize that a decrease in reliability is a problem, and it's a problem that has to be coped with. I think the decrease would be modest enough so that there are ways to cope with it.

Robert Buchheim: York made some eloquent remarks about the frequent failings of interagency working groups and backstopping committees in the government. I understand very well what he's talking about. I've lived with some of the worst. But the interagency group that worked on the Threshold Test Ban Treaty, in my opinion, was the finest I've ever worked with. That group was shot through with all kinds of diversity of opinion, but it worked, and it worked well. And it's not true, as was suggested, that the 150 kiloton figure was just plucked out of the air. That working group did a lot of work on the problems and factors associated with various levels of that threshold. Furthermore, the final figure was a result of negotiations participated in by both parties. As to the possible notion of lifting that threshold and allowing unlimited yields and tests, I would ask Wagner to characterize as well as he could in these circumstances what our opportunities are to go up in yield in Nevada, or anywhere else, and what Soviet opportunities are to go up in yield.

Richard Wagner: That is a subject of some uncertainty because the things that limit our ability to test at higher yield have something to do with the construction of the high-rise buildings in Las Vegas. Of course, we did do one underground test in Amchitka in the range of three to five megatons, and I suppose that Amchitka could be available again. My guess is that that may be roughly the limit. I don't know the Soviet limit. I would expect that they would be somewhat less limited than we in the ability to go up in yield.

5
ARMS CONTROL IN SPACE

SPEAKERS

Michael May

Associate Director, Lawrence Livermore National Laboratory; Member SALT Delegation, 1974–1976*

In this talk, I would like to review briefly what the defense objectives in space are, the space systems used to meet these objectives, and what kinds of weapons might be effective against these space systems. Then I will draw some limited conclusions about the utility and possible directions for arms control measures in space.

What we require from space is information. Perhaps the most critical information for defense purposes is warning information. One example is warning of a missile attack. The geosynchronous Defense Support Program (DSP) satellites provide the only practical means of observing missile launches from both land and sea starting within moments of the launch. Warning from these satellites can be confirmed by data from earth-based radar but only with a very substantial delay, a delay that might make a considered response impossible. The availability of this warning information, therefore, serves a major stabilizing purpose in the strategic standoff between the United States and the Soviet Union.

Of almost equal importance is the information from the reconnaissance satellites over areas in which hostile forces are deployed. The alternative sources of such information are impractical for most of the important regions of the world.

A third major defense space requirement is reliable, high-capacity, worldwide communications. These communications today go predominantly via geosynchronous satellites, as do civilian communications.

In addition, space systems provide, as we all know, meteorological

---

*This paper was co-authored by G. F. Bing.

information on a scale and with a promptness that cannot be equalled by any other method; and they can provide accurate navigation and guidance information under all weather conditions and in all areas of the world, in particular in remote areas where there are few conventional navigation aides.

Satellites could also be used as bases for weaponry of one kind or another. Such uses have not thus far been found interesting by either the United States or the Soviet Union, despite the absence of any arms control agreement against most space weapons, weapons of mass destruction being the exception. There are practical reasons for this lack of interest. The distances and time delays involved and the large amount of energy needed to boost mass up to orbit would make the storage of weapons in space a slow and expensive way to deploy munitions against earth targets. The situation may be different if the targets of the weapons were other satellites. We will discuss this possibility in a moment when we turn to the vulnerabilities of space systems. So far as earth battles are concerned, however, the most significant military uses of space are likely to be to provide warning, reconnaissance, communications, and other information.

Let us turn now to the vulnerabilities of space systems and the kinds of weapons that may be used against them. It is helpful to look at a few numbers that characterize the general scope of the deployments of space assets by the United States and the Soviet Union.

The United States has on the order of 100 active satellites of all types, civil and military, in orbit today and the Soviet Union about the same number. All other nations that own satellites have on the order of 10. There are altogether about 100 active satellites in geosynchronous orbits. Geosynchronous orbits are at a distance of about 36,000 kilometers (km), where satellites make one orbital rotation in 24 hours or the same time that the earth makes one rotation and therefore the satellites stay fixed over one point on the earth. About 15 of these geosynchronous satellites are Soviet satellites.

All these satellites must communicate with the earth and therefore all space systems require earth stations to send and receive radio signals between the earth and the satellites. There are all told about forty U.S. earth stations that track and command civilian and military satellites. There is an even larger number of stations that receive only the satellite-generated information.

Some argue that the space systems, that is, the satellites, the links and the ground facilities, are the weakest link in the chain of deterrence—that chain of known facts and surmises that must exist in the minds of any potential attacker, no matter what the crisis, and deter him from carrying out an attack. Buttressing that argument is the fact that

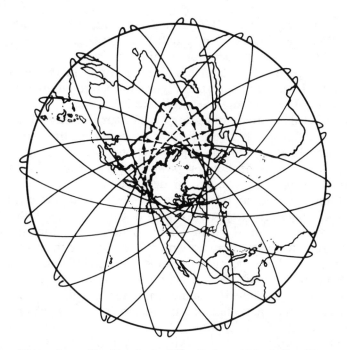

Figure 1.   One Day in the Life of a Low Altitude Satellite.
Low altitude satellites circle the earth about every ninety
minutes and this polar view shows the areas over which
a polar satellite would fly in a day. The dashed portions
of the orbit are over the Soviet Union.

many present ground stations are vulnerable targets that could be
destroyed more easily than the satellites they communicate with or the
weapons systems with which they are associated. To correct this weakness, ground stations must be either protected or proliferated in numbers,
or both. There is probably no more important or difficult task from
the point of view of preserving deterrence than preserving warning,
communication, and control capabilities.

Turning to the satellites themselves, three kinds of satellite systems
may be thought representative of a wide range of defense satellite
systems. We consider first a low-altitude satellite, for example, for
reconnaissance or verification of compliance with arms control agreements (Figure 1). The altitude range is between 150 and 1000 km. The
period, the time to make one revolution, is between 90 and 105 minutes.
In a day, our example satellite makes eleven passes over the Soviet
Union and spends about 1 hour there altogether, an average of 5½
minutes per pass. This is the altitude range at which detailed recon-

naissance can be effective. It is also the altitude range at which the Soviet ASAT has already been tested. On a straight-up intercept, the ASAT flight time would be 1 or 2 minutes. In this case, the target satellite must be over the launch site at the time. In the more usual case the ASAT makes at least one revolution before homing in on the target and the intercept time is more like 2 hours.

This is also the altitude range for which a ground-based laser might be effective, although after considerable development time and cost. A ground-based laser system can only function when the target satellite is nearly overhead. Depending on power and beamspread, most of the overflight time may be required for destruction.

ASAT missiles and lasers against a low-altitude satellite can also be based on airplanes or in space. An aircraft-based missile is the ASAT approach being developed by the United States. A small missile on an F-15 type aircraft is used. It appears more cost-effective than the ground-launched missile. It is also more versatile: The aircraft can be deployed to where the satellite will pass instead of having to wait for it to come overhead, the flight time is minutes, and the missile is smaller and cheaper. One concern is that, if this approach is truly better, it may be adopted by the Soviet Union.

Space-based missiles for attacking low-altitude satellites look, at present, like a more expensive variant of aircraft-based missiles without any major compensating benefit. A low- to moderate-altitude space-based laser, if and when it can be engineered, could reach out to perhaps several thousand kilometers and wipe out in a relatively short time most of the low-altitude satellites within its field of view. The laser satellite itself would be an attractive and vulnerable target as well as a very expensive one; certainly one or two billion dollars for each satellite, perhaps more. Further development in lasers could change this situation.

Next we look at an intermediate-altitude system (Figure 2). The Global Positioning System (GPS) is to be used for very accurate navigation and guidance anywhere in the world. It consists of sixteen to twenty-four satellites, at altitudes of about 20,000 km, whose period is 12 hours. A navigational fix requires four satellites and can give a three-dimensional accuracy of ten meters and very accurate velocity determination. Besides its usefulness for military navigation and guidance, it can also be used, with somewhat less accuracy, for navigation by civilian users of any nation.

A ground-launched ASAT effort would require at least sixteen to twenty-four launches of large missiles to destroy the system entirely, although destroying half of it or somewhat less might seriously degrade its guidance role. The minimum time to destroy one satellite would

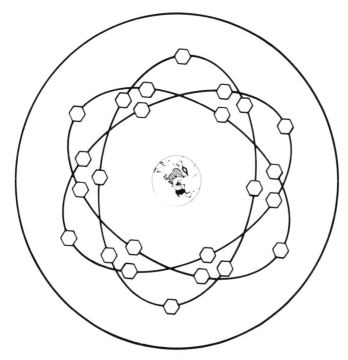

Figure 2. **NAVSTAR/GPS.** The Global Positioning System (GPS) is also called NAVSTAR and will consist of up to 24 satellites at altitudes of 20,000 kilometers where it takes 12 hours to circle the earth. With this many satellites there will always be enough of them in view from most locations on earth to obtain very accurate navigation fixes.

be about 1 hour. To inactivate the system from a few ground locations would take about one day. Because of the size and number of the missiles needed to reach the altitude, the attack would be quite expensive—perhaps a billion dollars or more.

It is not clear whether a practical ground-based laser can be built that could reach this altitude range with enough energy to destroy a satellite. Present technology is certainly inadequate to the task. Small missiles that could be launched from F-15 type aircraft cannot reach these altitudes. Large missiles launched from larger aircraft could be used but this would still be a very costly and time-consuming attack without compelling advantages.

Space-basing of either missiles or lasers near the target satellite orbits could cut down the time to negate the system, but at the cost of positioning a number of missiles or laser-firing space stations at 20,000 km. Again, we are looking at a very large effort, requiring much

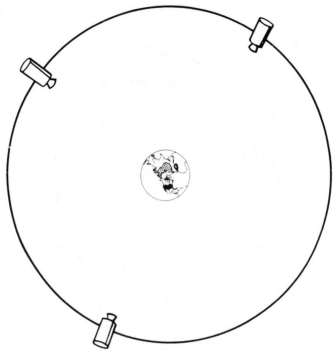

Figure 3.   Early Warning Satellites/DPS. Satellites at altitudes of 36,000 kilometers complete an orbit in 24 hours and thus stay over a fixed spot on earth. Early warning satellites of the Defense Support Program (DSP) have infrared (heat) sensors that can detect the launch of missiles from land or sea.

development and ten billion or more dollars (or rubles). We thus note that increasing both the altitude and the number of satellites in the system makes the time and money problems of the attacker much greater. It also makes covert preparations for attack much more difficult.

A third case of considerable interest is that of satellites in geosynchronous or stationary orbits (Figure 3). These satellites, at 36,000 km, stay fixed over a selected point of the earth near the equator. This is the altitude utilized for most communication and warning satellites. The warning satellite system in particular consists of three such satellites that can promptly warn us of missile launches from the Soviet Union and from the Atlantic and Pacific oceans, by sensing the infrared or heat emission of the missiles' exhaust.

An ASAT system effective against such satellites would require ground-based missiles large enough to give their payload the sort of energies necessary for lunar and planetary missions. These would reach target at synchronous altitude in a minimum of about 1½ hours. There could be significant difficulty in finding the targets if they are "uncooperative" and do not radiate or broadcast. Aircraft missile basing offers no advantage for this ASAT mission.

A ground-based laser system against satellites at this altitude is probably not feasible so far as we know now. Such a system based in the USSR could not see all three DSP satellites, in any case. A space-based laser system to attack satellites at that altitude would be extraordinarily expensive if it were feasible at all. In theory it could attack all three satellites within minutes.

Another approach to attacking distant satellites would be to pre-position missiles near them, missiles that could be commanded to attack and explode when required. The cost, though high, might be of the same order as that of the system attacked (a space-based laser system would cost far more).

It is not clear whether such pre-positioning could be done covertly: It would depend on the nature and quality of U.S. counterefforts. Agreed-to rules of the road requiring, for example, verifiable minimum separation distances between satellites could increase the possibility of detecting covert deployments. If violated, they could provide a significant period of warning. Clearly, a warning system will have fulfilled at least much of its mission if attempts to interfere with it can be unambiguously interpreted in a timely way. On receipt of information that such interference is going on, bombers and other aircraft can be launched, other force elements can be put on a high state of alert, and, most importantly, the command structure can be placed in a far more effective and less vulnerable situation than it is normally.

It should be clear from the foregoing brief survey that space systems may be, but need not be, the weakest links in the chain of stable deterrence. Multiplying ground stations and satellites, interlinking them, and raising satellite altitude where feasible can make the space systems as resilient to attack as the weapons systems they are associated with.

Turning now to arms control in space, if space systems have only a few key ground stations and ground communication nodes, which are vulnerable because they are limited in number, a ban against arms in space would not provide protection against attack on the systems. In addition, if the critical satellites themselves are few in number, a small number of attacking ASATs could, in a short time, destroy all of the ones carrying out essential functions. If only a few ASAT launchers are needed, verification of their presence or absence among the much larger number of Soviet launchers would be difficult or impossible. Verification of a test program for ASATs could be ambiguous. The kind of test program necessary to develop a successful ASAT consists essentially in developing the capability to place a payload at a selected point in space close to another satellite. Such a capability is likely to be developed in any case, for reasons having nothing to do with ASAT but rather with the resupply and repair of existing satellites. That kind of capability will increasingly be a necessary and cost-saving part of the utilization of space by all nations.

Thus, in the case of space systems as in the case of strategic weapons, the development of survivable systems is not only an essential requirement for strategic stability, it is probably also a prerequisite to meaningful arms control.

We may ask what sort of outer-space arms control agreements might be envisaged under the assumption that suitable steps are taken toward making our space systems robust against attack. Negotiating a total ASAT ban even then may be difficult. Space systems not only help maintain strategic deterrence, but also have a role in limited warfare, for example for tactical reconnaissance. The Soviet Union already has radar satellites that it can use for the tactical surveillance of naval units. If such systems are used for targeting tactical weapons systems, it will be difficult to argue that one can legitimately attack an aircraft or ship or submarine used for reconnaissance but not a satellite used for the same purpose.

Whether a line can be drawn between the kind of expensive (and probably only partially effective) ASAT capability that would be needed to attack a robust system on the one hand and a much more limited tactical ASAT capability on the other, and whether a level of testing and deployment required for the two would be verifiably different remain to be seen. It is possible, for instance, that strategic and tactical forces might utilize the same satellites and that the space system would be sufficiently robust to make only a very expensive and extensive ASAT capability effective.

One area of negotiation that might be pursued in the near future is that of "rules of the road" to which I alluded before. The development of rules of the road in space might parallel that of rules of the road at sea, making due allowance for the different technical and operational circumstances. Peacetime rules of the road have been accepted for centuries with regard to the use of the oceans by civil and military ships. Such rules, while no guarantor of peace, do fulfill a useful purpose in preventing accidents and needless conflicts. If breached, they can give warning of danger. Possible rules for space that might be negotiable include: minimum separation distance for satellites in orbit, or in transit to orbit, and measures to verify compliance; and the use of cooperative radio beacons (analogous to ships' running lights) on newly launched satellites to permit ready verification of orbit and general function.

Such rules could, if adequately enforceable, provide some assurance that ASAT weapons were not being covertly pre-positioned close to critical satellites. A long-range laser ASAT, if feasible and affordable, would provide a means of circumventing the rules but a space laser would be such a major engineering effort in space that it is unlikely it could be accomplished covertly.

In summary, without adequate built-in system survivability of both space and ground elements, arms control for space is likely to prove unproductive. It may even be counterproductive from the standpoint of enhancing strategic stability if it serves to hinder bureaucratically the programs aimed at improving survivability. Once survivability is reasonably assured, arms control measures in space, while still facing difficult tests, could be a useful adjunct to the other efforts of governments to maintain stable relations. Agreements on such measures as limiting the size and nature of ASAT deployments might help prevent some useless and dangerous undertakings and expenditures if there is a real desire to do so on both sides. Rules of the road might help prevent or minimize the risks of surprise attack. On the whole, however, given the stabilizing influence of improving the survivability of space systems, and the technical inability of arms control agreements in space to provide such stability, I believe the emphasis at present should be on such survivability improvements.

Robert Buchheim
U.S. Commissioner, Standing Consultation Commissioner, 1977–1981;
Former Head of U.S. Delegation to U.S.-USSR Antisatellite Negotiations

I will begin by affirming a fact already well known to you: This talk, as is the case with all parts of the conference, is unclassified. I also offer the opinion that carrying on this discussion at the unclassified level is not a significant limitation—reference to specific classified space programs should not be necessary, and, so far as I can judge, no U.S. policies on arms control in this area are firm at this time, except for U.S. commitment to relevant existing agreements and the exercise of common sense.

My remarks might seem a bit tedious in some places—but the devil really is usually in the details, and much of arms control can stand or fall depending upon how we deal with rather tedious details.

A general question of interest is: Is there a useful role for arms control agreements as applied to space systems and activities? The initial part of an orderly answer to this question is that there already is a body of international obligations, to which the United States is party, applicable to space systems and activities, including but not limited to the following:

- The Outer Space Treaty[1]
- The Agreement on the Rescue of Astronauts, the Return of Astronauts and the Return of Space Objects[2]
- The Space Liability Convention[3]
- The Outer Space Registration Convention[4]
- The Limited Test Ban Treaty[5]
- The International Telecommunications Convention and related agreements (for example, the INTELSAT Agreement)[6]
- Various other agreements concerning items such as communications satellites and the space shuttle
- The "Hot Line" Agreement[7] and the subsequent "Hot Line" Modernization Agreement[8]
- The "Accident Measures" Agreement[9]
- The ABM Treaty,[10] the Interim Agreement,[11] and other arms control agreements containing provisions for behavior toward national technical means of verification[12,13,14]

Taking note of the existing body of international obligations as to space systems and activities, a more practical form of the general question is: Would it be in the interest of the United States to undertake additional or amended obligations as to space systems and activities, particularly in the area of antisatellite systems and activities, and, if so, what kinds of obligations? It is conceivable that this question might be answered usefully in the abstract, but I doubt it. It seems to me that sound progress on the question is much more likely to be realized if we proceed in an essentially experimental fashion—taking it as a hypothesis that we might wish to put into place some kind of further agreement or agreements on antisatellite systems and activities, then trying to explore in detail what kinds of possible agreements we might pursue, what might be involved in implementing each of them, and what they each might offer to the furtherance of U.S. interests. The possibilities, of course, include no new agreement on antisatellite matters; but the body of relevant existing agreements is the platform from which we depart in explorations of other agreement possibilities.

In advocating an experimental approach I am not referring to any process of trying out different propositions in negotiations; in fact, I am not going to deal with negotiating aspects at all today, except to remind you that three negotiating rounds have already been conducted between the United States and USSR on antisatellite matters.[15–21] The experimental process to which I am referring now is the process to be undertaken in our own private councils in which we carry out intellectual experiments as to objectives and questions of implementation. Such experiments will inevitably lead to conclusions that some posited objectives would, if converted into specific agreements, serve U.S. interests well and others would not. Such estimates will, in some cases, flow largely from the objectives themselves and, in other cases, flow largely from the implementation requirements of the agreements. On such topics I will speak as though some such intellectual experiments have already been carried out and brought to definite conclusions. That will save time, and I am sure it will not inhibit discussion in this conference.

An important practical question is: What is an antisatellite system? There is no generally accepted definition of such a system, and it would probably not be desirable to try to create a negotiated definition, at least for the time being. For my purpose today I will assert that an antisatellite system is any kind of system to destroy a satellite, to damage a satellite (for example, by poking a hole in its skin), or to damage a satellite by damaging equipment incorporated in the satellite—in short, any kind of system for doing violence to a satellite. My reason for adopting this view will, I believe, become clear when we discuss the distinction between actions against a satellite and actions to influence the carrying out of a mission using a system in which a satellite is a component.

Another practical question with which to experiment is: Why would anybody want to develop and/or deploy an antisatellite system? Possibilities include the following.

- To actually do violence to spaceborne assets, or to be able to do so quickly
- To retaliate in kind if violence is done to one's own spaceborne assets
- To rectify any substantial asymmetry that might arise from possession by one party of an ASAT capability superior to that of another[22]
- To sustain the notion that space can remain a sanctuary from warfare[22]
- To lure another government into a space game on the basis of a view that net advantage could be gained by doing so
- To make a political point that attacks on satellites, or clear preparedness for such attacks, are acceptable forms of behavior except as limited specifically by agreements in force

- A general R&D interest in understanding and advancing proficiency in space technology and operations as a hedge against possible future contingencies
- A nonspecific interest in being seen as generally ahead in this kind of space capability;[23,24,25]
- As a cover for some other kind of activity

Next, there is need for careful exploration of the question: Why might we want to put agreed limitations on antisatellite operations and/or means for such operations? Some possible reasons follow.

- To save money. A dollar spent on an ASAT system is a dollar spent, period; a dollar to be spent on an ASAT system might be, and probably would be, charged to the "military space" part of the budget, tending to compromise allocation of resources to positive military space programs;
- Recognition of the fact that a U.S. antisatellite system will not provide protection to U.S. spaceborne assets, unless it has a very prompt anti-antisatellite effectiveness against a competing ASAT system and is supported by an adequately agile decision and control arrangement;
- Recognition of the fact that the United States and others rely increasingly on spaceborne assets for military, economic, scientific and other purposes;[26]
- Appeal to the argument that an ASAT-limitation agreement would reinforce other arms control agreements, particularly by adding to assurance of observance of provisions prohibiting interference with national technical means of verification; this argument, however, would be served only by an ASAT agreement that placed effective limitations on means for carrying out violent operations against satellite components of verification systems; prohibitions on the carrying out of such operations already exist in the arms control agreement contemplated in this argument;
- To suppress the likelihood of an arms race in space, or a race in space weapons;[27,28,29]
- To deal confidently with the problem of ambiguity in determining the mission being carried out using a particular satellite.[30]

Then there is the question of agreement coverage as concerns the dynamic classes of spaceborne objects to be dealt with. It is convenient short-hand to talk of satellites and antisatellite systems; however, there are interesting objects on trajectories other than orbits around the earth. Existing agreements—for example, the liability[3] and registration[4] conventions—refer to "space objects" to cover things such as interplanetary probes in addition to earth satellites. There is no evident reason for not contemplating all space objects in explorations of possible new agreements, even though we might refer to them as possible ASAT agreements. A relevant detail: The record associated with the existing agreements[3,4] makes clear that ballistic missiles are not included in the term "space object."

What about coverage as concerns ownership of, control of, or other aspects of, interest in, and responsibility for a space object? We will, almost surely, want any new agreements to cover all space objects in which we have an actual interest; but we will also wish to recognize the fact that there are, or might be, space objects that are none of our business unless they become so by virtue of some appropriate action under prevailing international law or some other aspect of national interest. The Registration Convention[4] provides a partial basis for orderly identification of interest in a space object. The formulation of a complete set of criteria or circumstances that will identify a space object as one covered by an ASAT agreement is another matter to be explored. This is especially important for the United States, in view of our extensive involvement with others in joint space activities, including commercial activities.

Next, there is the question of the possible relationship of any new agreement on ASAT matters to the most general of the existing agreements on space activities, the Outer Space Treaty of 1967.[1] In addition to the basic obligation set forth in that treaty that the parties "shall carry on activities in the exploration and use of outer space—in accordance with international law," the most significant provision from the standpoint of our topic today is the following portion of Article IX: "If a State Party to the Treaty has reason to believe that an activity or experiment planned by it or its nationals in outer space—would cause potentially harmful interference with activities of other States' Parties in the peaceful exploration and use of outer space—it shall undertake appropriate international consultations before proceeding with any such activity or experiment. A State Party to the Treaty which has reason to believe that an activity or experiment planned by another State Party in outer space—would cause potentially harmful interference with activities in the peaceful exploration and use of outer space—may request consultation concerning the activity or experiment." This portion of Article IX of the Outer Space Treaty seems to me to establish an entirely appropriate basis for serious U.S.-USSR discussions concerning ASAT systems and activities. The potential for "harmful interference" is clear on the face of the matter: That is the eventual purpose of any ASAT system or operation. The results, if any, of such consultations (that is, a new agreement) should, of course, be brought to the attention of parties to the Outer Space Treaty; they might, and probably would, wish to consider a multi-lateral agreement in further development of an agreement between the two initial "ASAT powers" consistent with the provisions of the Outer Space Treaty.

It surely would not be appropriate for the United States and the USSR, in a bilateral ASAT agreement, to prescribe terms to be applied to space objects in which neither of them had an interest or with respect to which neither had an acknowledged responsibility; but there is an aspect of third-party circumstances that does require exploration in order to be sure that U.S. interest in joint space programs is dealt with adequately. That is the commitment in the Outer Space Treaty to carry out space activities in accordance with international law. Most governments share approximately the same body of international law, but the body of such law shared by any two specific governments is not exactly the same as the body of such law shared by any two other governments. As a relevant example, international law shared by the United States and the USSR includes the provisions of bilateral arms control agreements, in particular provisions concerning national technical means of verification; no other governments are party to those agreements and they are not included in the bodies of international law to which any other governments have committed themselves. Concerning the Outer Space Treaty itself, its provision are included in the bodies of international law embraced by eighty-nine governments, but the government of the People's Republic of China is not one of the eighty-nine.

Next, we must experiment with possible approaches to the fact that, beyond specific limitations undertaken in existing agreements (more extensive on the part of the United States and the USSR than any other countries), there are no agreed limitations on functions that might be carried out through the use of space objects. A practical ASAT agreement must be crafted in full recognition of this fact and still promote the interests of the parties—not an easy task. We surely would not wish to turn an ASAT agreement inside out and make it, in effect, an agreement on what may or may not be done using space objects. The broad choice with which to begin experimentation is between advocacy of (1) a position that any satellite in which a party has an interest is to be immune from violence no matter what function it might be used to facilitate; or (2) a position that a satellite is a fair target for violence if it is used to facilitate certain kinds of functions that are agreed by the parties to be heinous enough to warrant such violence. Both of these approaches involve some difficult details, which

I will leave to your imagination. This little problem leads naturally to a further, and very important, question.

That question is: Should an ASAT agreement deal strictly with acts of violence against space objects themselves, or should it deal with systems in which space objects are components? Without elaborating, the equivalent of this question is, should an ASAT agreement provide for limitations on what can be done to a space object, or should it also deal with operations to frustrate missions undertaken with systems in which space objects are components? In my view the first alternative is the practical one. Let me try to coax you in this direction with some examples.

• Suppose Party A transmits from a satellite signals of a kind that, when received at TV sets inside the territory of Party B, will enable the viewing of material that the government of Party B deems intolerable, or signals that are not consistent with telecommunications regulations applicable within the territory of Party B.[31,32] Suppose, after trying to persuade Party A to stop, Party B vents its wrath by destroying or damaging the offending satellite. Would that be an ASAT act to be subject to the provisions of an ASAT agreement? I certainly think it would be. Suppose, instead, that Party B acted to suppress the viewing by its citizens of the offending program material by forbidding the watching of it, or sending the police to seize or smash everyone's television set, or putting a tax on TV sets so high that none of its citizens could afford one, or by emitting jamming signals so that the offending program material could not be viewed within its territory. Would these be ASAT acts to be subject to the provisions of an ASAT agreement? I think not; they might represent human rights questions, but they should not be dragged into an ASAT agreement.

• Suppose Party A deploys a satellite containing radio receiving equipment, with the possible purpose of picking up radio signals from military units in the territory of Party B and relaying such signals to ground stations for military analysis. Would it be appropriate to deal in an ASAT agreement with Party B's possible temptation to destroy or damage the satellite? I think it would. Would it make sense to try to include in an ASAT agreement a limitation on Party B's rights to turn off military emitters when they think their signals might be received by Party A to the disadvantage of Party B? I think not. Would it make sense to try to include in an ASAT agreement a limitation on Party B's right to turn on additional emitters to influence analysis of their signals? I think not. There is not now, and probably never will be, any meaningful general international agreement in which a government undertakes to guarantee the uninhibited gathering by others of information about all of its military radio emitters. There would be no sense in trying to include in an ASAT agreement any provisions that would have the effect of such an improbable guarantee.

• This same line of reasoning applies to the distinction between a satellite and a system exploiting the satellite as a component in order to carry out, for example, the mission of targeting ships or the mission of communicating with overseas forces in combat operations.

Advocacy of any ASAT agreement on prohibiting violent acts against satellites, but not dealing with other measures to counter missions, would not be a complete policy and should not be viewed as such. There are already agreements that deal with the countering of certain specific missions and other agreements of this kind could be brought into being in the future; but this is a separate subject that we ought not try to assimilate in an ASAT agreement.

Current agreements that deal with the countering of missions include certain of the bilateral U.S.-USSR arms control agreements[12-16] that prohibit interference with national technical means for verification of compliance with the provisions of those agreements. In these agreements the mission is clearly stated and any interference with the carrying out of the stated mission is prohibited. The prohibition is not confined to the blowing up of satellites and the national technical means referred to might or might not be systems including satellites as components. The International Telecommunications Convention[6] also contains provisions limiting interference with "communications facilities," and the mission of such facilities is described in the convention; the systems used might or might not include satellites.

It is virtually certain that any agreements having to do with counters to missions and systems for carrying out those missions will continue to be case-by-case developments. No single general agreement, ASAT or otherwise, is likely to be a productive vehicle for this class of subjects.

The distinctive nature of agreements directed to missions is further illustrated by another circumstance: There is not, and probably never will be, an international agreement to prohibit interference with a system used to target ships. However, if such a system were used to facilitate a humanitarian rescue operation, the International Telecommunications Convention would prohibit any interference with the system while it is being so used.

One can pose this question: Suppose an ASAT agreement prohibits the damaging of a space object, and suppose some action of a party inadvertently damages a space object? The elements of a sensible answer are:

- Accidents will happen;
- Provisions for consultation should be included in any practical agreement to deal with such contingencies, among other things;
- Note should be taken again of the provisions of Article IX of the Outer Space Treaty. If any party is going to launch a space object that will contain items unusually susceptible to "harmful interference" from activities of any other party, Article IX provides a clear basis for going to other parties, describing the potential problem, and seeking cooperation in avoiding or moderating such a problem. Such consultations might not be easy—most international dealings are not easy—but they should be feasible in most instances of civil functions. As to military functions, the choice for or against such an approach might be more gripping. However, we already have one toe in the water and pointed in this direction: Article 3 of the "Measures Agreement" of 30 September 1971 provides that the Parties undertake to notify each other immediately in the event of signs of interference with missile warning systems or with related communication facilities, if such occurrences could create a risk of outbreak of nuclear war between the two countries, and Article VII provides for consultations.

Let me summarize what I have said here.
- There are reasonable considerations for and against seeking further international agreements as to antisatellite activities and means to facilitate such activities;
- Such agreements, hypothetical at this time, could take a variety of forms, and each recognizable form should be examined by us as to its potential value to the United States; one cannot be for or against an "ASAT agreement" regardless of its scope and terms. Each discernible form should be assigned its pros and cons; and judgments might change with time and circumstances;
- Examination of possible ASAT agreements must take into account relevant existing agreements;
- A particularly important factor is the distinction between a "space object"—the unique artifact present in space—and the system that includes such an object as a component. As a first, and probably rather good, approximation, there is no such thing as a "space system" except in U.S. nomenclature, which has no international standing; there are likely only to be space objects or systems in which space objects figure as components;

• In my opinion, general agreement as to violence against space objects is a practical objective, while agreement as to measures to influence the carrying out of missions can only proceed on a case-by-case basis.

You have, no doubt, noticed that I have not gone very far into several important subjects, including specific limitations on means for antisatellite operations and verification. These are not oversights, nor expressions of lack of interest; rather, it seems to me that the first order of business is to deal with the questions I have chosen to address. Handling ASAT means and verification questions will be hard enough, but might not be possible at all without clarity on the operations of interest.

As to elimination of ASAT means, or prohibitions on their possession, or quantitative or qualitative limitations on them, the central problem, of course, is that of devising practical and effective provisions through which to implement such objectives. This is a difficult task, not made easier by the fact that an ASAT system is quite likely to exploit assets, for example ground-based tracking and communications systems, that support other kinds of activities, and the fact that some other kinds of systems, for example ABM systems, are likely to have some degree of ASAT capability.[27,28]

Notes

1. Treaty on Principles Governing the Activities of States in the Exploration and Use of Outer Space, Including the Moon and Other Celestial Bodies. Signed at Washington, London, and Moscow on 27 January 1967; ratification advised by the U.S. Senate on 25 April 1967; ratified by the President of the United States on 24 May 1967; entered into force on 10 October 1967; signed for eighty-nine governments.

2. Agreement on the Rescue of Astronauts, the Return of Astronauts and the Return of Objects Launched into Outer Space. Done at Washington, London, and Moscow on 22 April 1968; ratification advised by the U.S. Senate on 8 October 1968; ratified by the President of the United States on 18 October 1968; entered into force on 3 December 1968; signed for eighty-one governments.

3. Convention on International Liability for Damage Caused by Space Objects. Done at Washington, London, and Moscow on 29 March 1972; ratification advised by the U.S. Senate on 6 October 1972; ratified by the President of the United States on 18 May 1973; entered into force on 9 October 1973; signed for seventy-three governments.

4. Convention on the Registration of Objects Launched Into Outer Space. Opened for signature at New York on 14 January 1975; ratification advised

by the U.S. Senate on 21 June 1976; ratified by the President of the United States on 24 July 1976; entered into force on 15 September 1976; signed for twenty-seven governments.

5. Treaty Banning Nuclear Weapon Tests in the Atmosphere, in Outer Space and Under Water. Signed at Moscow on 5 August 1963; ratification advised by the U.S. Senate on 24 September 1963; ratified by the President of the United States on 7 October 1963; entered into force on 10 October 1963; signed for 106 governments.

6. A convenient general reference document is *Space Law—Selected Basic Documents, Second Edition,* prepared at the request of Hon. Howard W. Cannon, Chairman, Committee on Commerce, Science, and Transportation. U.S. Senate; 95th Congress, 2nd Session; December 1978; U.S. Government Printing Office (32-231-0).

7. Memorandum of Understanding Between the United States of America and the Union of Soviet Socialist Republics Regarding the Establishment of a Direct Communications Link (With Annex). Signed at Geneva on 20 June 1963; entered into force on 20 June 1963.

8. Agreement Between the United States of America and the Union of Soviet Socialist Republics on Measures to Improve the U.S.A.-U.S.S.R. Direct Communications Link. Signed at Washington on 30 September 1971; entered into force on 30 September 1971.

9. Agreement on Measures to Reduce the Risk of Outbreak of Nuclear War Between the United States of America and the Union of Soviet Socialist Republics. Signed at Washington on 30 September 1971; entered into force on 30 September 1971.

10. Treaty Between the United States of America and the Union of Soviet Socialist Republics on the Limitation of Anti-Ballistic Missile Systems. Signed at Moscow on 26 May 1972; ratification advised by the U.S. Senate on 3 August 1972; ratified by the President of the United States on 30 September 1972; entered into force on 3 October 1972.

11. Interim Agreement Between the United States of America and the Union of Soviet Socialist Republics on certain Measures With Respect to the Limitation of Strategic Offensive Arms. Signed at Moscow on 26 May 1972; approval authorized by the U.S. Congress on 30 September 1972; approved by the President of the United States on 30 September 1972; entered into force on 3 October 1972.

12. Treaty Between the United States of America and the Union of Soviet Socialist Republics on the Limitation of Underground Nuclear Weapon Tests. Signed at Moscow on 3 July 1974.

13. Treaty Between the United States of America and the Union of Soviet Socialist Republics on Underground Nuclear Explosions for Peaceful Purposes. Signed at Washington and Moscow on 28 May 1976.

14. Treaty Between the United States of America and the Union of Soviet Socialist Republics on the Limitation of Strategic Offensive Arms; signed at Vienna on 18 June 1979.

15. *U.S.–U.S.S.R. Talks on Anti-Satellite Systems.* Press Release 78-10, U.S. Arms Control and Disarmament Agency, 8 May 1978.

16. *U.S.-Soviet Negotiations Take Up Anti-Satellite Weapons.* America Center (U.S. Embassy), Helsinki, 7 June 1978 (first round in Helsinki).

17. *Initial Anti-Satellite Talks End in Helsinki.* Press Release 78-14, U.S. Arms Control and Disarmament Agency, 17 June 1978.

18. *Anti-Satellite Discussions Resume.* Press Release 79-2, U.S. Arms Control and Disarmament Agency, 10 January 1979 (second round in Bern).

19. *Anti-Satellite Talks Termed 'Frank, Businesslike'.* Press Release 79-5, U.S. Arms Control and Disarmament Agency, 19 February 1979.

20. *ASAT Talks Resume.* Press Release 79-9, U.S. Arms Control and Disarmament Agency, 14 April 1979.

21. *Arms Control 1979.* Nineteenth annual report, U.S. Arms Control and Disarmament Agency, Publication 104, June 1980, p. 38.

22. "AFA Policy Paper—Force Modernization and R&D." *Air Force Magazine,* November 1980, p. 71.

23. Walter S. Mossberg, "Soviets Could Build Laser Weapon to Kill Satellites in 5 Years, Pentagon Aide Says." *The Wall Street Journal.* 11 February 1981, p. 6.

24. Thomas O'Toole, "Success Puts U.S. Ahead of Russians." *The Washington Post,* 15 April 1981.

25. Edmund G. Brown, Jr., "Space to Grow." *The New York Times,* 15 April 1981.

26. An outstanding example of growth in use of spacecraft is the broad field of communications (see, for example, Robert J. Hermann, "Electronics in Warfare: A Look Ahead." *Air Force Magazine,* July 1980, p. 76). It is interesting to note, against this modern background, a historical circumstance: What has been described as England's first offensive act of World War I, undertaken in the early hours of the first day of that war, was the cutting of Germany's undersea transatlantic communications cables, with very extensive and largely unanticipated consequences. See Barbara W. Tuchman, *The Zimmerman Telegram* (New York: Bantam Books, 1971), p. 8.

27. Malcolm Wallop, "Opportunities and Imperatives of Ballistic Missile Defense." *Strategic Review,* Fall 1979, p. 13.

28. "Military Race in Space." *The Defense Monitor,* I.S.S.N. #0195-6450, 1980.

29. Donald L. Hafner, "Averting a Brobdingnagian Skeet Shoot." *International Security,* Winter 1980/81.

30. Nicholas L. Johnson, "Soviet Satellite Reconnaissance Activities and Trends." *Air Force Magazine,* March 1981, p. 90.

31. *Direct Broadcast Satellite Communications—Proceedings of a Symposium.* Sponsored by the Space Applications Board and the Board on Telecommunications–Computer Applications, Assembly of Engineering; National Academy of Sciences, 8 April 1980.

32. John M. Geddes, "German Government's Antennae Twitch at Possibility of Television via Satellite." *The Wall Street Journal,* 2 March 1981, p. 21.

PANELISTS

Jeffrey Cooper
Jeffrey Cooper Associates, McLean, Virginia

In May's presentation he noted three categories of satellites, two of which are in operation now, a variety of low-altitude satellites and many in synchronous orbit. His middle category, medium-altitude, in particular the Global Positioning System, is not in operation now as an operational system. Depending on Air Force funding profiles and Office of the Secretary of Defense (OSD) decisions, it may or may not come into being. If it comes into being, it will add a highly valuable class of satellites that we do not currently possess. It will also open the possibility of extending the current range of military missions to uses more tied to actual war fighting than support functions. GPS cannot only provide accurate navigation to ships and planes but it could, in fact, be used to provide highly accurate terminal guidance to weapon systems. Therefore, our perceptions of the value of space systems are likely to change as capabilities change, and that is particularly important as we examine the asymmetry between U.S. and Soviet uses of space, particularly with respect to the issue of when they are valuable and critical resources.

We have spent large amounts of money building systems that perform important missions largely during peacetime: a variety of national technical means of verification, a variety of national technical intelligence assets, and high bulk communications assets. The Soviets, on the other hand, have a somewhat different style. While they do some of the same things, they have also put up satellites that will serve operational commanders for actual targeting of U.S. naval vessels during wartime, an area that we may move toward in the future. But at this time, the asymmetry in our postures and uses of space means that we have different functional requirements for protection of our space systems due to differences in when those systems are critically important.

I agree with May on the need for survivability improvements as precursors to negotiated limitations, but I think that the point needs to be made more concrete. He spoke about possible separation distances as one possible set of "rules of the road." Yet depending on the type of ASAT and the relative hardness of our own assets in space, the required separation distance for safety could be anywhere from one-half of a kilometer to several thousand kilometers. This raises a point that neither Buchheim nor May made, that of nuclear weapons in space. This does not necessarily imply the use of nuclear weapons in space directed toward earth targets, which would be in violation of the outer space agreement, but nuclear weapons could be directed against space objects, an ASAT for example. The size of the relative kill volumes capable of being achieved with the nuclear weapon might call for significantly different functional requirements in a space arms control agreement.

There's a general set of questions that Buchheim's paper raised, both explicitly and implicitly, that I would like to lay out but not take a position on. The current space treaty protects peaceful exploration and use of outer space from harmful interference. As a general question, do we wish to extend that provision to military capable systems as well? Particularly, military capable systems that will function during wartime as actual targeting systems for weapons?

I have a slight disagreement, and I think it may be more a semantic difference than anything else, when he talks about protection of objects versus systems as a matter of the basic style of the treaty. He alluded to this latter issue when he spoke about the inherent protection for national technical means of verification in the ABM agreement, which goes well beyond protection of the mere systems as he noted. And yet there really is a danger as one begins to concretize a space arms control agreement about removing some of the protections that already exist. Additions to law can go either way. Not only can they build on extant law and add to it, they can also take away from what already exists; and I would suggest as a note that if, in fact, we wish to protect the same types of systems functions, as well as the objects themselves, we should approach the subject of protection of object versus system with due care and attention.

Last, a conjunct point. Do we wish to define or give sanction explicitly to permitted uses of space systems in an agreement? One can argue both sides of that, but one should recognize the real dangers of each. Often, that which is not explicitly noted is assumed to be permitted. That works both ways. If we specifically note the purposes for which some satellites will be held sacrosanct, there is an implication that purposes other than those, in fact, are subject to exactly the types of measures that we might be seeking to prevent in a space arms control agreement. On the other hand, we should recognize that the ABM agreement, which the Soviets signed, for the first time gives sanction in a real sense in a bilateral agreement to what they have previously regarded as espionage—in the legal sense of that term, espionage being an illegal act.

Not all of our national technical means are used solely for verification of existing arms control agreements; we use them for a variety of other purposes. We might in the future have dedicated satellites that don't have verification functions, which do serve reconnaissance and surveillance purposes. We should keep in mind that how we define what is to be permitted and what is to be protected could in fact remove some of the inherent protections we have built for national technical means.

Donald Vogt
Brig. Gen., USAF, Military Assistant, Office of Under Secretary of Defense

I would like to make four points about space arms control. I believe they have been covered fairly well, but I would like to add my personal views.

First, space arms control is not an easy problem. There are some people who say that if we cannot achieve arms control in space, where we have yet to deploy weapons, we are in big trouble and should proceed at once in the arms control direction. There has been quite a bit of negotiation that has produced a body of space law. There are also operational military-related satellites. As such, where we go from here is not just a simple launch into a void. However, there is a large void in understanding just what we are trying to protect and why we use space.

We have not, in the international arena, explicitly defined an acceptable act in space under our general agreements to support peaceful activities. It is not easy to distinguish among acts that are peaceful, those that are peace-keeping, and those that are war-deterring or warmaking. At some point in that spectrum, we would like to keep some of those activities out of space, if not for our side, at least for the other side. Yet, we really have not come to grips with the problem. Most of our negotiations dealing with space have involved the civilian use of space, such as remote sensing and direct broadcast satellites. If we should want to try to define (as Buchheim would rather not do, and I agree with him) allowable acts in space, we should recognize the complexities. Also, it is not a closed set because we are continually advancing our technologies and it is a difficult problem to define in totality.

Part of the problem one confronts is that these are global systems, and the differing viewpoints among nations during negotiations are very much affected by their social system. We tend to view the availability of information as an obvious good. Other societies tend to view the availability of information as obviously bad. It takes considerable work to negotiate these points. In my opinion, before we can really determine what value ASAT restrictions have for us, we must understand what we are accepting. As an example, Soviet capability to affect sea battles from space has already been highlighted. Are we willing to accept their capability to threaten our fleets using that detection capability from space? Possibly we can now. If they were to increase that capability to locate our submarines, would we still feel the same way? There needs to be quite a bit of investigation and thought along these lines.

So far, we have not talked much about monitoring capability for ASAT agreements. While I agree that it is one of the things you arrive at near the end of deliberations, I believe there is room for a warning on the quantitative difference between the ASAT monitoring problem and the strategic monitoring problem. If you are trying to monitor a thousand strategic launchers and you miss by two or three, it is not a major problem. However, if the other side has only two or three ASAT launchers, he could possibly take out some of your satellite systems fairly rapidly. Thus, we are not talking a large-number problem, we are talking a small-number one.

Another output of the monitoring problem is that it is difficult to distinguish an ASAT capability from other capabilities. An ASAT launcher looks much like a strategic launcher. A ground-based laser may look much like a scientific experiment station. It is difficult to really determine whether the other side has, or does not have, an ASAT system in the total context. So that will be a problem. Similarly, it is very difficult to determine whether testing is actually for ASAT purposes, or in fact for some other system capability, such as an ABM or ICBM test. The distinction can be blurred.

Another problem that has gone unmentioned is breakout potential. This is a significant problem for space systems. If the other side breaks out with a new system and you see that he has one, you have very little time to react, given our present overall weapons system development cycle. Also, many of our satellites are now approaching a five year life, so if the other side breaks out, and it takes a year for them to reach operational capability, they would be in a position to threaten a satellite for four years of its life before we would be ready to put up another one. This then leads to another problem in the space arena. Since we have longer lived satellites, we no longer have the luxury of large numbers of satellites in the pipeline that we can quickly modify and launch.

Donald Hafner

Associate Professor, Political Science Department, Boston College

I would like to start by saying that generally I endorse May's concerns about satellite survivability. I think there is nothing more disheartening than watching the progressive dependency of U.S. military forces upon our satellite systems, coupled with the kind of lethargy that we have shown in ensuring satellite survivability.

But May has argued that we ought to address satellite survivability first, and then move on to arms control matters. I would argue instead that the task of making satellite systems robust against attack will certainly be a lot easier, whatever the survivability measures we can come up with, if we also have an arms control regime covering ASAT weapons. So rather than approach these matters in a sequential fashion, I would advocate addressing survivability and arms control simultaneously.

The arguments against ASAT arms control limits tend to cluster into two sorts. I doubt that these are exhaustive categories, but let me at least address these. One line of argument focuses upon near-term anxieties, particularly that the Soviets already have an ASAT weapon and that therefore the United States also ought to have an ASAT system in order to deter Soviet attacks. Now this is an argument that we really have to think about carefully. We have been reminded in recent debate over strategic nuclear doctrine that we don't necessarily have deterrence simply because we have some weapon that allows us to blast back at the Soviets. What we have to pay attention to instead are the relative U.S. and Soviet positions that emerge after various sorts of exchanges. It is the case, as Cooper has pointed out in his remarks, that the United States has a higher dependency upon satellite systems than the Soviets now, and this will continue. We have a lower replacement capacity and rate for our satellite systems than the Soviets do; the spots on the globe that we are concerned about are geographically closer to the Soviet Union, and therefore the Soviets would enjoy certain advantages in using ground-based alternatives to satellites. In short, the argument that our being able to blast away at Soviet satellites with an ASAT weapon will deter the Soviets from blasting away at ours is not very sound. The Soviets might well expect to emerge from such an exchange in a relatively superior position.

There is another near-term anxiety often expressed, which is that the United States must have an ASAT system in order to kill specific Soviet satellites that threaten U.S. forces. The satellites generally cited are those which allow the Soviets to target U.S. naval vessels at sea. Again, we need to look at this argument in a sophisticated fashion. To begin with, it isn't clear that shooting down these Soviet satellites can be the only way to cope with them. I'll come back to this point in a moment. More important, when weighing the marginal protection that we may gain for our naval forces by shooting down Soviet satellites, we must consider also the enhanced dangers to all of our own satellite systems that would result from unrestrained Soviet competition or

Soviet advancement in ASAT weapons. It is the balance of our gains in protecting our navy, versus the general losses that we might suffer in the effectiveness of all our other strategic forces or military forces as a result of compromising our satellites' survivability that matters here.

I would also point out that even if the United States had an ASAT system to shoot down Soviet satellites, such as those that can be used for targeting, we would still have to develop other modes for dealing with these specific types of Soviet satellites. The reason is that any ASAT system we have is going to have operational limits. It is not going to be instantaneous; it won't be able to sweep the skies at the moment conflict breaks out. As May has pointed out, it may take anywhere from hours to days to get an ASAT interceptor into a proper position for attack. I assume that in the interim, we don't wish our forces to be left unprotected. That is to say, we will have to develop other techniques for coping with Soviet satellites in order to keep our forces hidden, to deceive Soviet satellites, and to thwart Soviet attacks. In short, ASAT isn't going to be the only solution to this problem; clearly it cannot be the only solution to it. Instead, an ASAT system would be a redundancy, an additional countermeasure, with of course the additional costs.

These, as I see it, are the near-term anxieties most often expressed. I mentioned at the outset that there were two lines of argument made against ASAT arms control. The second line focuses not on anxieties, but upon long-term optimism. There appears to be a general confidence among those who press for a U.S. ASAT weapon that, regardless of the problems we can foresee in ASAT arms competition, U.S. technological superiority will always provide a solution and we will be able to maintain an advantage. In short, we have nothing to fear from unrestrained weapons competition in outer space.

In response to this, I would remind you of the remarks by Nitze in response to questions by McDonald. Nitze was skeptical, specifically in the strategic nuclear realm, about our confidence in technological solutions to all our problems. It certainly isn't clear to me why Mother Nature and the genies who guard the secrets of weapons technology inevitably will step in and save us from the messes that we get ourselves in. It's not clear that they always will, nor that they always have. It's not clear that Mother Nature or the genies will yield their favors to the highest bidder; it's not even clear to me that we will always be the highest bidder. Hence, I don't think we can be excessively confident that our technological prowess will always work in our favor.

Second, I would point out that the relevant measure here of technological achievement of the United States versus the Soviet Union is not some aesthetic standard of technological sweetness. What we are concerned about is technological capability relevant to the military mission requirement that each side has before it. For example, the guidance system for the MX is undoubtedly technically sweeter than the guidance system of the Soviet SS-18, and will remain so for a good long while. But the guidance system for the SS-18, whatever its crudities, is nonetheless quite adequate to the mission of hazarding the *Minuteman* system.

Similarly, the issue isn't whether the United States can build a more elegant ASAT system than the Soviet Union. I think that in such competition we probably can. The question is, can we build effective satellite defenses against whatever technology the Soviet Union deploys in its ASATs. Again, perhaps *Minuteman* with its vulnerability problem provides an instructive case. Two solutions were proposed when *Minuteman* vulnerability was anticipated—ABM site defense and mobile ICBMs. Both may be technically feasible, although there is considerable debate on that. But thus far neither of these technical solutions has been feasible at a cost that could be borne by available resources—and I'm referring to both monetary and political resources. Unrestrained ASAT competition promises to be enormously expensive. It promises to complicate our security tasks as we now see them and to drain our resources away from other urgent tasks. In short, abstract technical prowess has not always translated into practical solutions to our problems, and we cannot have blind and unreasoning confidence that it will in the ASAT case.

In surveying the ASAT arms control issue, what I'm asking for is neither terribly novel nor terribly profound. I'm asking only that we apply the lessons we have learned from earlier technical and political problems in developing new weapon systems. We need to review our experience first, carefully, before we rush headlong into an ASAT competition with the Soviets. We need to ask ourselves whether going into unrestrained ASAT competition is truly the most prudent way to address the specific security problems that we are facing in the future in outer space. Such a review, I believe, will yield strong arguments, not for ASAT arms competition, but for ASAT arms control.

DISCUSSION

Harold Rosenbaum: I have a question for May regarding the possible roles for man in space. Both the United States and the Soviet Union have made relatively significant gains in the past few years. The Soviet Union for the endurance of their cosmonauts in space, and the United

States, most notably for the space shuttle. Are there any implications, either from a reconstitution point of view [replacing satellites that have been destroyed] or from an ASAT point of view, for the manned space programs of the United States and the Soviet Union?

Michael May: Man in space brings in intelligence, and that means that man in space provides a better ability to see what the space environment is, to make measurements, to observe opportunities for doing things differently that might not otherwise be clear. I think that's an inestimable advantage for just the general exploration and understanding of space, civilian or military. Beyond that, I haven't identified a mission or specific major mission where introducing a man in space would be useful, but that doesn't mean that other people haven't.

Donald Vogt: I have a brief comment on that. There has been a question over the years as to whether we should put military man in space. There's been a little change with the shuttle now—we will have military man in space. The question is, what can he do to perform military functions better than you can do automatically? And the answer to that question is far from clear. We now have a history of doing things technically, automatically, without the man, and people are comfortable doing it that way. It's even hard to get them to consider what a man might do. If you have the information on the ground you can have a panel of experts consult the information and determine what is the right decision based on that information. It is not clear that you want to delegate that to a man in the air without strictures on his freedom of action. Additionally, there's the support required to keep man in space. It's not clear that we have military missions for man in space at this point outside of the normal shuttle-related ones.

Jeffrey Cooper: Rosenbaum referred to reconstitution and I think the shuttle is a perfect example of going in exactly the wrong direction for thinking about reconstitution. The shuttle is large and vulnerable with, at most, two launching positions—one east coast, one west coast. There is a long, highly intricate checkout system that takes at least a couple of weeks, if NASA is right, before it can be reflown. Unless you really believe that we are going to have a nice, neat, separated space war and nothing is going to be happening to facilities on the ground, the shuttle is unlikely to play any role in reconstitution of space assets at all.

Michael Intriligator: May said that he felt the weakest part of our strategic deterrent systems was the space component in terms of reconnaissance, command and control, surveillance. I had a few questions derived from that.

One, does he believe that this is a more pressing issue than the *Minuteman* reliability or the MX basing question? Next, does he believe that there's evidence that the Soviets have a similar perception in terms of their statements, deployments, or whatever?

Michael May: I said that the weakest spot would be the space system as a whole including its ground components, not just the space components. My answer to your first question, as to whether it's more pressing to fix than the *Minuteman* and the MX, is yes. As to the second question, whether the Soviets have a similar perception, I don't know the Soviet perception but the indication is that they do, from my reading of their published writings on the problems of communication and control systems.

Francis Hoeber: A quarter of a century ago we had a debacle called an Open Skies Conference, and agreed not to agree on open skies. As I recall, this was because we knew how to shoot down airplanes. At that time we knew we were about to have orbiters and we didn't know how to shoot them down. Accordingly, we had a tacit agreement, certainly for peacetime, to ignore for spacecraft all the objections we had to being observed from our own space.

Much of Buchheim's discussion addresses what we would tolerate in peacetime. What I am concerned about is that space might be the place for the opening moves in a real war, a "big war." What I would like, is a little more discussion by Buchheim as to what controls may be feasible that will help us not only in peacetime incidents, but in case there is a war.

Now there have been several references to the difficulties of identifying and counting for verification. ASATs are going to be very hard to separate from other weapons. They are small. They are not necessarily the same size as the vehicle that puts up an orbiter, for they have only to put up a limited amount of material to do their job.

Can we rely then on testing? We have to have something that we can verify or hope to verify before things start happening and not just argue about what is legitimate to interfere with and what is not. Particularly, in view of the comments that we are much more dependent on space assets than are the Soviets, we should really have much more concern than we do about this issue.

Robert Buchheim: There are several parts to your remarks and all of them are important. Concerning the old open skies idea, there were a couple of problems there that led to its nonresult. One is you can do more with an airplane than just look down. At the time, as I recall, we contemplated using B-36s for the open sky job. And you have to admit there is some reason for a fellow to be a little skeptical about what else might be in those airplanes. Second, to move back to my tedious citation of existing international agreements, at that time, as today, virtually all countries shared the view embedded in international law that you can't violate with impunity their air space. Now, there is no real parallel in terms of space activities. That's one of the features that enabled the present relative freedom in operating satellites. There are no prohibitions on overflight with spacecraft in effect. Also, it's one of the arrangements that the United States and the Soviet Union chose to enter into in order to facilitate the SALT agreements. It's one of the things that would clearly be lost without those agreements.

Those undertakings are peculiar to our two countries. There is nothing anywhere that says or implies that the Soviet Union will tolerate without comment satellite reconnaissance undertaken by the Central African Empire, for example. And one of the oddities in this situation that has a bearing on what you asked about, and also on the prospects for an ASAT agreement, is that even the very loose and rudimentary rules of civilized behavior that are embedded in the outer space treaty have not been embraced by the People's Republic of China (PRC). While opinions may differ, I do not think the Soviet Union is about to commit itself to tolerate just any behavior that the PRC may engage in. And I think that's a problem that needs to be attended to.

What are the possibilities? The possibilities for an agreement depend, in part, on curing that little nuance. In terms of the measures that might add to the security of our space operations in other than peacetime, the only thing I know that can be done in drafting an agreement is to be silent on that subject. There is no need to stipulate in an agreement that this applies to only peacetime or anything like that. That's pointless. The chances are that it would come under some prejudice in wartime. The proper way of dealing with that problem has to do with two measures and only two that I know of.

One is the survivability improvement that May alluded to for our satellite systems and the other is to try to get the Soviets to divest themselves of any satellite ASAT capability and that is a difficult task indeed. I don't think we're up to that quite yet, but we should work on it.

Michael May: I want to make one brief comment on the point Buchheim raised, which was also raised at least inferentially by others. Even if we could reliably and verifiably get the Soviet Union to get rid of all ASAT capability, and I don't think that's feasible, we would not have the required survivability and robustness in our systems because the ground stations would not be protected. So if it's important to have survivable communications and reconnaissance, ground stations, in particular, have to be protected. That's more important than whatever we may or may not do in space.

Dalimil Kybal: I agree with you about the high vulnerability of our space systems and particularly the ground stations. Given this, the question arises, how can these systems, which are extremely important, be made to endure in the situation where there is more than a single strike?

Michael May: Briefly, it's entirely feasible to protect the capability embodied in most ground stations. The key to it is to multiply the ground stations and to provide alternative links for communications that don't rely on space. That's actually not protecting them so much as looking for alternatives. It's not hard to proliferate receivers and it's not hard to proliferate transmitters. There is no political or public objection to that. It's cheaper and easier than it is to proliferate missiles or holes in the ground. You can easily present thousands of targets to an attacker, most of which would be in locations unknown to him.

That doesn't solve all problems. There are some capabilities that probably cannot be maintained in wartime. But you can go a long way toward making an attack on those functions unprofitable.

Pierre Lellouche: Although the subject this morning is arms control in space, we have only spoken about American-Soviet problems and ASAT problems. There was a proposal put forward by France in 1978 before the UN, which attracted a great deal of support from a number of countries, that consisted of creating an international agency for satellites—verification satellites, observation satellites. It was dual purpose. One purpose would be to put at the disposal of the international community a means for verifying arms control agreements. The other would be to help prevent conflict and to serve as a warning in crisis situations. These would be transferred to the UN. A very nice and generous idea, which is technically feasible, even by a medium-size power like us. Obviously, this is not very pleasant for you and the Soviets, and both of the two superpowers have stalled on this. The question I want to ask is, do you expect any change of attitude on the part of the United States toward the French proposal?

Robert Buchheim: The U.S. government did not support the French proposal. In order not to just let it go as abruptly as that, I'd like again to return to my tiresome remarks about the outer space treaty. It really is important to deal with these little legal niceties because I'm quite sure that if the United States and the Soviet Union ever did draft an agreement in which they declared they would not blow up each other's satellites, and published that agreement, there would immediately be a great hue and cry from all of the other parties to the outer space treaty saying, "Well, what the hell! Does this mean that you reserve the right to blow up mine?" Clearly the answer to that has got to be "no," or "no but." I've always been convinced that if bilateral negotiations on ASAT matters achieve an agreement, there will be an immediate entry into multi-lateral discussions on that subject, which will quickly widen into a multi-lateral discussion of space activities in general. What that may lead to with respect to the French proposal I haven't the slightest idea, but I would be willing to guess that it would be taken note of.

Jeffrey Cooper: There is a difference between verification and simple intelligence gathering, and in order to have verification, you really do have to have an arms control agreement to verify. And I found the French proposal somewhat disingenuous in that if you look at the number of international arms control agreements, aside from U.S.-Soviet bilateral agreements, there seemed to be precious few for which an optical satellite would aid in verification. That raises the question as to whether the real motive behind the French proposal was not verification of arms control agreements but rather a proposal to sanction a nationally supported program for intelligence gathering through an international agency in terms of helping the French develop their own technology.

William Barletta: This question is addressed to May. In your remarks you seem to suggest that one of the activities we might consider in a first treaty is proscribing certain activities or encouraging certain other activities in relation to your rules of the road to make more difficult the covert emplacement of objects in space. On the other hand one might take the point of view that we would like to retain those capabilities and in fact enhance those capabilities for covert emplacement because that might become the means of ensuring the survivability of extremely valuable assets.

Michael May: That's true, one could, and I don't know where the government or any particular person would come out in trying to balance those two. I think rules of the road like the ones suggested should be explored. I'm not sure they are the right thing. I don't know myself how we would come out after a more careful study. I just made a suggestion as an example of rules of the road that could be explored. It is true there would be some disadvantages along with the advantages.

6
NON-PROLIFERATION POLICIES

SPEAKERS

Joseph Nye
Professor of Government, Harvard University;
Deputy to Under Secretary for Security Assistance,
Science and Technology, Department of State, 1977–1978

Yesterday we concluded that arms control works only when it is an answer, or part of an answer, to a security interest. Arms control measures should be judged in relation to a security issue. And that brings us to the question of the security concern that the United States has in the proliferation of nuclear weapons. There is a very real security concern that leads to a continuity in policy. There is always a tendency for each new administration, particularly in its early stages, to maximize the differences from its predecessor. That is the nature of our political process. Yet, if one looks back over thirty years, one finds a striking degree of continuity in U.S. policy in the area of non-proliferation. The reason for that is the relationship to our underlying security concerns.

What are those security interests? Let us start with a null hypothesis. The issue of what a proliferated world would be like and what the cost would be to us is one that we have to take seriously. Some people believe that further proliferation would generalize the deterrent relationship that has worked relatively well in the U.S.-Soviet relationship. In other words, one of the reasons that we have not had war between the great powers in the period since 1945 has something to do with the existence of nuclear weapons. And the argument is sometimes made that if nuclear deterrence works for the superpowers, it should work for others. Sauce for the goose is sauce for the gander. But such a proposition depends on other things being equal. For many areas, those other things are not equal. Take, for example, the capability to control and command a new weapon system in a region of unstable governments. Statistically, if we look at where governments are overthrown and where countries fission, one finds that few regions are not like the relationship between the superpowers. The danger is that in an area like the Middle East, an overlay of nuclear weaponry on top of the existing passions would create great instability. There is some possibility that the converse is true. But it strikes me that the risks are enormously greater on the pessimistic side. Prudence argues against the proposition that generalizing nuclear deterrence will work for a more stable world.

Another argument by skeptics regarding our security interest in non-proliferation admits that one cannot generalize deterrence to all regions. Some regions are indeed different from the central nuclear relationship. But that's just too bad for them, this argument says. That's their problem, and it need not affect the superpowers. If the Pakistanis choose to follow the Indian example and launch an explosion, too bad for the South Asians, but it's not necessarily a major concern of the United States.

The trouble with that argument is that it implies that there are regions from which we can disengage our interest as a global power. And although there may be some, there are not all that many. If we are going to have forward positions, the stationing of troops, then the spread of nuclear weapons does complicate our defense efforts. In addition, there is the danger that if there is a rapid or wide proliferation of nuclear weaponry, under the unstable conditions, it will break the tradition of non-use. Perhaps equally profoundly, if the spread of nuclear weapons among poor and Third World countries eventually feeds back into the central system, we could see a considerable change in what has been the balance of power since 1945. An interesting feature about the world we live in today is that two of the great powers of the pre-war period, Germany and Japan, the defeated powers, have been reintegrated into the world system as major economic powers, but not major nuclear military powers. And it's led to a strange asymmetrical, but stable, relationship. Before we undo things that have a degree of stability in them, we ought to think very hard and close about it.

So, I think there are some very significant American security interests, which go back thirty or more years, in preventing the proliferation of nuclear weapons. On the other hand, given that security interest, what should be our goal? Because if you look realistically at the situation and ask the question, "Will the bomb spread?"—the answer is clearly "yes." It already has and it will continue to do so. If you are faced with a situation where we have a security interest in having it not spread, but it is also clear that technology spreads, capability spreads, then how do you define the goal for the policy? May has asked, "What should be a long-run goal for an arms control policy?" And that makes a big difference because, if you define an inappropriate goal, you're not going to make any progress. Whereas, if you define a goal that is relevant to the conditions you are likely to face, then you can do something in policy terms.

I'd argue that our long-range goal in the area of non-proliferation should be to slow the rate of proliferation so as to manage the destabilizing effects. That kind of goal is not hostage to the next explosion and it is, I believe, an attainable goal. Why does rate matter? Well, for one thing, three-quarters of the countries that could launch a nuclear explosion have chosen not to. Essentially, the ratios are running in our favor, and if the rate of increase is relatively slow, our prospects for managing the politically destabilizing effects are correspondingly greater. There is a phenomenon in world politics that we've seen in other times, which you might call a scramble in international behavior. A low curve suddenly becomes exponential. Witness the colonization of Africa in the last century. There were enclaves on the coast of Africa right through the middle of the nineteenth century. Then, once it looked like everybody was doing it, you had the division of a whole continent within twenty years. Or look at the extension of national jurisdiction in the law of the sea where a 200-mile resource zone has been extended in the last ten years. Twenty years ago there was a 3-mile limit with some exceptions. But when it looked like everybody was doing it, national extensions suddenly took off. My view is that our goal in non-proliferation policy is to flatten that curve, to prevent it from becoming exponential, so that we can manage the destabilizing effects. And if that is our goal, then, oddly enough, we are not doing that badly in this area of arms control.

Let me remind you of the prediction made in the 1960s that there would be fifteen to twenty nuclear powers by this time. It's interesting that there are not. Not only are there fewer nuclear powers than there technically could be, but the burden of proof is on the would-be nuclear powers. It's sometimes said that one of the great feats in international politics is raising your national interest to the level of a global principle. Oddly enough, in this area we have been able to do that. It is not intuitively obvious, in a world of sovereign states where each has the right of self-defense, that a certain category of weaponry would be prohibited or discouraged or presumed against by the norms of the international system. Here is an example of a productive and useful arms control agreement. That presumption against proliferation doesn't stop all cases, but it does essentially make them more difficult and helps us if our objective is to flatten the curve or to slow a rate. In that sense, the existence of an international regime, the norms and rules and practices of which create a presumption against proliferation, is very much in our security interest. A regime need not work perfectly, any more than domestic laws have to be perfect, to have a restraining effect. There will be some violations, but so long as they are limited, the violations will not vitiate the importance of the regime or its legal structure. The non-proliferation regime is more than just the Non-Proliferation Treaty (NPT). You also have the practices of the International Atomic Energy Agency (IAEA), and regional equivalents like the Treaty of Tlatelolco in Latin America. The regime is based on a philosophy of technology transfer. The Atoms for Peace program has often been criticized as a somewhat poorly implemented venture, perhaps premature in its timing. But, nonetheless, it did provide a basic bargain in which there would be access to nuclear technology for peaceful purposes in return for quite intrusive inspection regarding the use of nuclear energy. And that inspection system again need not be perfect to have a significant deterring effect on misuse. The danger in the syllogism that nuclear proliferation is a function of nuclear energy, therefore we should stop nuclear energy and stop nuclear proliferation, is not only that it is a non sequitur, but that it bears the risk of undermining the foundations of the regime we have. And since international regimes are rare and difficult to construct, when you find one and it's working, even imperfectly, you ought to breathe life into it, not try to work so hard to perfect it that you destroy it.

In the 1970s, there was an erosion of this system. Current problems all have their roots a decade ago. The Indian explosion in 1974, the oil crisis that greatly exaggerated the projections of the use of nuclear energy and the demand for uranium, the transfers of sensitive technology to countries like Korea and Pakistan, which were later disclosed to have had weapons plans, posed a real danger that this regime was going to erode. About ten years ago, the IAEA projected that in the 1980s there would be thirty countries with ordinary use of plutonium in their commercial fuel cycle. Well, whatever else one may think, the institutional framework was not ready to cope with that. So, essentially, what we are trying to do is buy time to develop a better institutional structure and, again, to flatten that curve somewhat.

The answers really start before the Carter administration. In the latter days of the Ford administration, there was Kissinger's establishment of the Nuclear Supplier's Group in London, where suppliers undertook an obligation to exercise restraint in the transfer of sensitive technology. In addition there was the beginning of the deferral of reprocessing that was announced at the end of the Ford administration, and continued in the Carter administration. In my own view, the best thing the Carter administration did was to develop the International Nuclear Fuel Cycle Evaluation (INFCE), which was an extension and generalization of Ford's Reprocessing Evaluation Program. Some people thought this was supposed to be a "technical fix." Some new technology was going to solve the problem. INFCE was never designed to be a technical fix, nor indeed that much of a technical negotiation. But by discussing it in technical terms we were able to draw in countries that were both NPT states and non-NPT states, suppliers and consumers. We got sixty-six countries together discussing our agenda—which was non-proliferation. And to a considerable extent, I think INFCE worked. We did get a sharing of our concerns. We did get final statements reinforcing the norms of non-proliferation by both NPT and non-NPT parties. Specifically, we got more realistic estimates of the uranium reserves. We got a statement saying that thermal recycle for the current reactors is not economically significant. Breeder reactors are important; but they are basically for large countries with large grids and that doesn't include most countries that we are worried about in proliferation terms. So in that sense, I think the INFCE was indeed successful. And part of the proof of that pudding was the NPT Review Conference last year. Many people predicted a break between the less developed countries that were going to focus on Article IV of the NPT, which promised transfer of technology, and the supplier's group that had this restrictive Article VII saying that there'd be restraint on the transfer of certain technologies. By using the results of the fuel cycle evaluation, we were able to say, "Look, by international agreement the kinds of technology that we're not transferring are not significant for your energy needs. We will take a long-run evolutionary view toward your technology needs, but to supply you with this sensitive technology right now when it has no economic function violates Article I of the NPT, which says not to foster proliferation."

Interestingly enough, while there was tension over Article IV at the Review Conference, the greater tension turned out to be over Article VI, which relates to disarmament type issues. So in that sense, I think we have made a degree of progress in maintaining the regime despite the degree of erosion and turmoil that had arisen in the early and mid-1970s. But that leaves open the question of where do we go next? And Malone, who will follow me and is in the Reagan administration, will give a much clearer answer to that in terms of the attitudes of the administration. Let me just flag four problems that are going to be problems for policy, no matter how one decides to resolve them.

One is the problem of the role of the nuclear fuel cycle. It has sometimes been argued that the Carter administration put too much stress on the nuclear fuel cycle. And on that I think there is some justifiable criticism. The uses of nuclear energy for commercial and scientific purposes is not the only, or even perhaps the major, source of proliferation. On the other hand, it was a major source of concern in the mid-1970s because of the projections I have already mentioned, and because of some specific countries using this as a path toward weapons programs. So in that context, my view is that it was useful to have taken steps that discouraged that particular relationship, but it would not be useful to blind ourselves and think that the fuel cycle is the answer to the whole problem, because it's not.

Within the nuclear fuel cycle area, however, there are some useful steps that can be taken in the next stage—for example, developing a system for plutonium management, which is now under discussion in the IAEA, extending full scope safeguards, international spent-fuel storage rather than premature reprocessing, and developing fuel assurances. One need not believe that the fuel cycle is the sole cause of the proliferation problem in order to want to take such steps to reinforce the institutional structure before there is a generational change in technology.

A second kind of problem that policy is going to have to deal with is what kind of priority to give to non-proliferation. The best policy instrument that one has in non-proliferation is the security guarantee. If you can give a clear and credible security guarantee then you can remove a good deal of the incentive for countries to go nuclear. Indeed, that has worked. It's worked in situations like Korea. It's also worked in cases like Taiwan, where even a residual American security guarantee is better than being naked in the presence of your giant next-door neighbor. There are cases, then, where security guarantees will work and should be our first line of defense. But it would be unrealistic to think that we can undertake to provide our nuclear umbrella over all potential proliferators—South Africa is the case in point.

One then has to ask what priorities to give to non-proliferation when other dimensions of security arise. For example, in the case of Pakistan, the current plan to provide massive conventional military aid may be the only remaining device, even though a slender threat, to prevent the Pakistanis from going ahead with their nuclear explosion. But it doesn't answer the hard question of what you do if there is a Pakistani explosion. If the priority of non-proliferation is high, some degree of sanctioning behavior will follow. If, on the other hand, the priority of other questions is much higher, and there is no sanctioning behavior, we may have negative effects on the overall regime. It's a nasty set of tradeoffs.

A third set of problems that policy is going to have to deal with is what I call the rate and degree of proliferation. We have always focused, up until now, very heavily upon the rate of new entrants who have explosions. But one can think of proliferation as a staircase, albeit a staircase in which one landing is broader than others. That's the first explosion, and it is particularly important. Nonetheless, there are many steps a state can take up to the threshold of that landing, and many steps it can take after it. There's a big difference between having had one crude explosion as in India in 1974 and having a fully weaponized program at a thermonuclear level with a sophisticated delivery system. Trying to find diplomatic plateaus after an explosion and deciding how to handle issues of information and technology transfer relating to delivery systems and fusion are problems of advanced proliferation. Yet there is again a difficult dilemma here, because the more we concentrate on advanced proliferation and try to deal with it, the more it seems that we acquiesce in the crossing of the first threshold. That has a negative effect on the rate. And remember that the regime I described is defined legally in terms of rate, not in terms of degree. So the kinds of tools we use to deal with the degree of proliferation will, of necessity, often be kept relatively quiet. Nonetheless, they should be thought about in advance.

Finally, a fourth problem is the relationship among regimes. And here non-proliferation stands intermediate between other arms control issues and energy issues. In the arms control area, we discussed yesterday the relationship of Article VI of the NPT, which commits the superpowers to taking steps to reduce armaments, and the prospects of proliferation. The relationship is nowhere near as tight as the rhetoric at an NPT Review Conference makes it seem. Clearly it is not because of Article VI that countries proliferate. But on the other hand, if we say it makes no difference to us what happens, in other words, if we think that our actions in the arms control area are totally irrelevant to proliferation, or if we stress the usefulness of nuclear weapons in war fighting situations, that is bound, in time, to feed back on the attitudes of other countries. And at the margin, it will have some effect on eroding the kind of regime that is in our security interest. There is a relationship, even though not as tight a relationship as it's often made out to be in the rhetoric.

The other relationship involves energy questions. Clearly if we are trying to keep controls on the peaceful use of nuclear energy, we have to be aware of the larger energy security concerns of other countries. There has been a lot of exaggerated rhetoric in this area about nuclear energy solving energy security problems. I've recently edited a book, *Energy and Security,* which goes into great detail as to why I think that's not the case, and what the real energy security issues are. But again one cannot argue the contrary and pretend indifference to the energy security issues other countries put on the table. So, essentially, how to maintain a reasonable relation between non-proliferation and these other regimes of arms control and energy will be a critical problem for non-proliferation policies.

However these four policy problems are solved by this administration and those that follow it, I think what is worth noting is the degree of continuity in our policy over thirty years, and the degree of success in managing the rate of proliferation. A regime need not be perfect to be a successful arms control regime, but we have to be terribly careful that none of our actions press matters beyond a tipping point where suddenly the curve changes and we cannot cope with the effects. If we set our policy goal as flattening the curve, we have a realistic long-term objective and we have a prospect for a degree of policy success.

James Malone
Assistant Secretary of State for Oceans and International Environmental and Scientific Affairs, Department of State

Cooperation in the international use of nuclear energy and in curbing the spread of nuclear weapons has been for three decades a major element of U.S. foreign policy. The critical importance of these issues is undeniable. The Reagan administration is approaching these critical issues by taking the following factors into account:

- The energy situation of countries, individually and collectively, is an essential context in dealing with nuclear questions;
- Our principal point of departure is the national security context of the United States and other countries; and
- Our policy will build on existing political relationships and commitments.

The main themes of this policy will be realism, commitment, and flexibility. There will be changes of emphasis and substance in U.S. policies. There will also, however, be continuity on long-standing and fundamental elements of our policy. We will move back into the international mainstream. But we are not facing static challenges—we must work creatively with other countries in the development of common mainstream approaches to deal with common concerns.

Against this background, I would like to briefly address our energy, security, and specific policy approaches. The stark facts relating fossil fuel uses, resources, and geographical distribution are generally known to all who care to face them. Also clear are present and generally projected energy demands, and the role of energy in national security and in national development. These all indicate that nuclear energy must play an important role in the world's energy balance. The bulk of that use will clearly be by the United States and by several of our close friends and partners. Further, we must not artificially restrict the time period over which nuclear energy can play that role. A U.S. commitment to effective use of our present nuclear power technology and to expedient development of an option for long-term use of nuclear power is a basic element of our developing policy.

The importance of this commitment is also related to security and non-proliferation considerations—it is not possible to effectively pursue non-proliferation efforts if others suspect an antinuclear motivation behind the effort. Cooperation, trust, and communication on the basis of similar assumptions are indispensable. Our actions must be based on respect and support for the important energy choices and programs of our cooperating partners.

A commitment to the use of nuclear power must be grounded on, not divorced from, a sober view of reality. On one hand, we should forthrightly state the basis for our assessment that nuclear power can and should be an important energy source. For example, the advantage of a major noncombustion power component not contributing to CO_2 levels may soon appear to be of overriding importance. And we should clearly put forward the facts and options related to nuclear waste disposal. The problem is technically soluble, and we should move forward promptly to demonstrate and implement solutions.

At the same time, I do not believe we would do any service to nuclear power programs with less than realistic views of projections and requirements. For example, in dealing with international cooperation, assessments, and technical assistance we should take clearly into account the time, investments, and infrastructures required to pursue or launch sound nuclear power programs. This realism must also apply to fuel cycle questions. It would not be technically or economically appropriate to move forward with large numbers of sensitive fuel cycle facilities that were unrelated to specific needs. Cooperation and realistic approaches are necessary.

Non-proliferation is a component of our overall security efforts. It is in this context that our non-proliferation efforts can be most widely supported, understood, and made effective. Similarly, in dealing with other countries, we must be aware of their political and security contexts. In those few cases where proliferation risks are present, the motivation and perceived incentives or disincentives of the individual countries are critical. We will need to take these into account, strengthen disincentives, and avoid actions that may produce counterproductive results.

The basis of U.S. commitment to non-proliferation is that the world in general, as well as individual states, would be less secure if the number of states possessing nuclear weapons were to increase. To effectively deal with proliferation risks, this fact must be as broadly understood and shared as possible. The probability and consequences of conflict involving nuclear weapons would increase. An important component of security is confidence and predictability of events. Nuclear weapons programs, or fears of such programs, could be seriously destabilizing.

And there is the converse connection: Instability or lack of internal security could be greatly exacerbated by the presence of nuclear weapons. This concern encompasses the possibility of terrorist seizure of such weapons. It also relates to the presence of material from which nuclear weapons might be made. Nuclear weapon states and nonnuclear weapon states have identical problems and challenges in limiting or protecting such material. In that context, the use of highly enriched uranium in research reactors can increasingly be avoided and physical protection standards upgraded.

As I have already mentioned, security includes an energy component. One particular form of this interrelationship can be seen in the negative consequences that would be associated with explosion of nuclear devices by additional countries. International nuclear confidence, cooperation, and commerce would suffer a severe setback from such a development, with further negative consequences for our collective energy security. In short, we may not be able to widely cooperate in nuclear power in a situation of further proliferation.

As in the energy area, realism in security aspects of nuclear policy is necessary. We recognize that there are situations in which ongoing nuclear developments have clear military implications. The international nuclear power community will endanger its credibility if it naively accepts "nuclear power program" labels on developments obviously intended for other purposes. Finally, reflecting a long-standing U.S. view, we must recognize that nuclear explosives, for whatever declared purposes, cannot be distinguished from nuclear weapons.

We can build a stable and durable international structure for future nuclear cooperation and non-proliferation only on the basis of a clear appreciation of the existing political and treaty context. Respect for international commitments is the indispensable basis for nuclear cooperation and non-proliferation. We must fulfill our commitments and must assume others will do likewise.

The foundations for our participation in international nuclear affairs are the Statute of the IAEA and its safeguards agreements with states, the Non-Proliferation Treaty, the Treaty of Tlatelolco, and the set of bilateral U.S. agreements for cooperation.

The IAEA is a unique and remarkably successful international effort. Its success accounts in large measure for the impressive degree of international cooperation in the nuclear area. It is in the interest of all members to respect and strengthen the IAEA.

Our commitment to the NPT is also fundamental. We should collectively be proud of its broad acceptance. There have been a continuing series of new adherents over the last few years, most recently including Egypt. Among its adherents there is unanimous agreement on the importance of the treaty and on the importance of continued implementation of its provisions. There are, of course, serious concerns on the part of many parties to the treaty over the implementation of its provisions on nuclear arms control. Progress has been slow. But this administration, as all of its predecessors since the NPT was negotiated, is committed to real and balanced progress in nuclear arms control. We will continue the effort and, I believe, succeed.

The NPT provides an optimal basis for nuclear cooperation. That basis will continue, and indeed increase in importance, as nuclear power use and our consequent interdependence on nuclear trade increase.

Our dependence on the NPT, our bilateral agreements, and the IAEA's safeguards agreements must, like other elements of our policy, be based on commitment, but must also include realism and flexibility. These agreements are not perfect, are not universally applied, and cannot solve all of the potential future problems. We must continue to consider with the other states evolutionary steps to increase the durability of the international regime. I will mention some of these later.

The United States will be applying these general principles and approaches in a number of concrete ways. I will only touch generally on some of the policy directions we will be taking.

First, an indispensable early step in implementation or formulation of specific policies will be consultation with other countries. We fully recognize that our views, actions, and programs have implications and effects on the programs of other countries and that their situations affect us. This can be seen, for example, in reactor licensing, fuel cycle decisions, and reactor development. Our nuclear program is, of course, defined for our own situation. But international communication and, as appropriate, cooperation can make important contributions to effectiveness and efficiency.

Second, the United States will take the necessary steps to reassert our critical role as a major, reliable, and predictable partner in international nuclear commerce. This will be reflected in administration attitudes and actions. It will also be reflected to the degree necessary in the process of U.S. export licensing and related activities. For example, it is clear that an independent Nuclear Regulatory Commission, seized with critical domestic reactor safety responsibilities, is not an appropriate determinant of foreign policy matters. Reorganization or statutory modification may be required, and we will work closely with Congress in this area.

Third, we will take a practical approach to necessary fuel cycle operations for material subject to our agreements with other countries. We will no longer impose artificial U.S.-defined dates as criteria for judging the validity of agreements for reprocessing and plutonium use. We need to ensure that planned programs can go forward without arbitrary interruption. We are intent on working out practical and predictable arrangements that provide our partners with appropriate long-term planning bases.

Thus, we will be looking at reprocessing and plutonium use without ideological blinders: It is a logical sequential step at a certain point in nuclear programs. This does not mean, however, that the United States and others should be unaware of the need to pursue these steps in a rational sequence under the safest arrangements and best safeguards reasonably achievable.

This leads to a fourth action area: the achievement and maintenance of effective and credible IAEA safeguards. The basis for this must be stability and common purpose within the IAEA. We will be working with other members in continuing to define and support a broadly useful IAEA program and in providing technical assistance through the IAEA. In the safeguards area, we will continue our support efforts. We will constructively contribute to dealing with the key technical challenges, such as those related to reprocessing plants. We will do so without imposing a revisionist definition, which would seek to rule out such fuel cycle facilities on safeguard grounds.

The IAEA safeguards regime covers almost all facilities in nonnuclear weapon states, and three nuclear weapon states have offered to accept safeguards on their civil facilities. It would be a major step forward to universalize this situation. Agreement on full-scope safeguards by all suppliers and by recipients is a key goal. Consensus on such points would greatly help to avoid irritants in relations among nuclear suppliers and with recipients. We will continue to work toward such a consensus. As a final area that should be mentioned, I would like to return to our support for a constructive evolution of international measures and framework. The problems will be growing and revealing new aspects. The potential for subnational and terrorist sabotage or seizure of nuclear material requires serious consideration. It may, in the long term, be the most serious challenge to nuclear programs. International action has led to an upgrading of security systems; this should be continued. A second important measure is successful implementation of technical alternatives to avoid the presence of highly enriched uranium in research reactors. This effort is a good example of successful international collaboration on areas of mutual concern.

A third measure relates to an international plutonium storage system. If such a system could be widely accepted in such a way as to store excess plutonium in a few safe, monitored sites and released only for clearly peaceful uses, it could make a key contribution to confidence and good international nuclear stewardship. The United States will constructively participate in this effort.

Nuclear power, international nuclear cooperation, and non-proliferation are key components of a responsible, stable, and comprehensible U.S. foreign policy. The Reagan administration will deal with these issues in their necessarily broader context as national security and energy security issues. Our efforts will be based on a realistic and flexible approach. We are committed to the continuation of long-standing U.S. contribution to the mainstream of international efforts in these areas. Nuclear energy will no longer be an option of last resort.

PANELISTS

Kathleen Bailey

International Ventures Consultants, San Francisco;
Former Associate Z-Division Leader, Lawrence Livermore National Laboratory

Both of the speakers today stressed that the international non-proliferation regime has comprised a concrete set of institutions and, as Malone has said, is going to continue. He particularly stressed the role of the IAEA and the NPT. Given the importance of the regime, I would like to turn my remarks to three basic questions.

- First, has the regime been successful?
- Second, are the building blocks of the regime solid?
- And third, is there anything that can be done in addition to what Malone said is going to be done?

First of all, several nations appear to have, or to be very near having, nuclear weapons capability. Israel, South Africa, Argentina, Iraq, and Pakistan have or are getting significant nuclear programs and all have the motivation to proliferate. I realize that the question is not whether the non-proliferation regime has prevented proliferation, but whether it has slowed down the rate. But it is important to realize from the outset that nations have been able to get these programs going and do have motivations in spite of our best efforts. Would there have been other nations than those I just listed that would have pursued proliferation or would the pace of proliferation have been faster without the regime? There are some successes we can point to. One of the speakers brought up the case of Korea. Korea wanted a reprocessing facility and the United States took what I would call a personalized policy approach. And this is what I think Malone was talking about when he said the new administration was going to stress looking at individual nations' needs. That is not a new thing. It occurred in the case of Korea. We addressed their needs in terms of defense and security and convinced them not to try to acquire the fuel cycle at that time. There are other examples that are completely independent of the international non-proliferation regime. Take, for example, Japan and the European states. We all know that they have the capability, if they wanted to, but they don't have the motivation. So motivation is a very crucial factor in non-proliferation and it has not been institutionalized by the non-proliferation regime.

Has the regime really slowed proliferation? Almost certainly it has. But what has been the cost? The cost has been rather severe, in my opinion. First of all, the regime has forced the development of indigenous programs. Nations that could not purchase turnkey nuclear facilities and expertise have turned to piecemeal proliferation. That is, they have been importing components, hiring and training scientists, whatever necessary to put together these programs. Let us contrast two countries. Argentina has pursued an indigenous program. They have done very well and may soon have complete control of the fuel cycle. Brazil, on the other hand, purchased from the Federal Republic of Germany an entire fuel cycle, which the United States was not pleased about. As a result of that purchase, there are heavy safeguards and it is a fact that the Brazilians have not moved forward as much as they wished. So, the method for slowing proliferation has been costly in terms of indigenous development of nuclear programs.

Another cost of slowing down proliferation with the regime has been the tarnishing of our image in both Europe and the lesser developed countries. Europe now views us as someone who just wanted to get a hold on the market. The attitude of the lesser developed countries is that we have used the non-proliferation regime to "keep them poor."

My second question asked whether the building blocks of the non-proliferation regime are solid. I'll start with the NPT because that was stressed by both speakers as being a fundamental building block. The NPT can be abrogated with three months' notice. This is a criticism heard very often, but it is an extremely important one. It means that if a nation does get both the capability and the motivation, there is really nothing holding it back. But let's take that as a given, and look at the other problems with the NPT. Articles IV and VI have been under attack and I think will continue to be under attack. As we heard yesterday from Earle, the NPT Review Conference showed that, in particular. Article VI was criticized. I think that as nations increase their desire for having nuclear programs and weapons capability, that the NPT will be less and less important. So, while I agree with leaving it intact, I think that it is not as strong a building block as we would like to assume.

The second building block is control of the fuel cycle. Both speakers have emphasized that. It stresses export controls and technical fixes to control the fuel cycle. I mentioned before that there has been a lot of indigenous development and that the export controls have, essentially, not worked overall; that is, when nations want it enough, they can get it. In terms of the technical fixes, the one most often referred to these days is highly enriched uranium fuel for reactors. The most cogent argument against this technical fix is that using low enriched fuel allows the production of plutonium. Plutonium, of course, requires reprocessing facilities, but just the same there is still the proliferation risk. Overall, technical fixes and export controls have not prevented nations from acquiring fuel cycle technology; thus, the second building block is not very solid. INFCE is another building block. It was unable to develop a resistant fuel cycle. It delayed the U.S. program. It fed the impression of the United States as an obstructionist and it really delayed only one program in terms of use of plutonium, and that was the United States's program.

The Nuclear Non-Proliferation Act (NNPA) is viewed by many people as somewhat tying the hands of the U.S. government in being able to respond to potential proliferants. The way it has been used makes the United States look obstructionist. I think that the Nuclear Non-Proliferation Act, given its history and its severe problems, should be rewritten or sacked.

In the face of this criticism, let me turn to my final question, "What should we do?" I agree with Malone that a more active involvement of the United States in the international arena will certainly have something to do with future success of the non-proliferation regime. The maintenance of the NPT is good, the IAEA is certainly good, but there are other things that we can do as well. Let's go back to the successes, the examples of Korea and the Europeans. Understanding that proliferation is a matter of motivations, we should effect personalized policy and not depend so much on institutions. Helping individual countries with their energy or defense problems is what we should do, not assault them with a blanket institution such as the NNPA.

We should live up to our commitments as a supplier and participate fully in building and using safeguards.

We should seek institutions sponsored or proposed by other states whenever possible rather than always assuming the leadership role ourselves. Involving the Third World countries in formulating institutions, such as the Treaty of Tlatelolco, is a potential solution. Getting them involved will generate a much stronger commitment from them than if we impose our own will.

The last point I'd like to make is that we should prepare for proliferation. At this laboratory, Marv Gustavson has addressed the question of what happens after proliferation occurs. Suppose a less-developed country with very little money, very little expertise overall to devote to its nuclear program, develops nuclear weapons. How do you keep bombs made by that country safe? How do you give them, or assist them in having, technology that will prevent the misuse of such a device, the theft of such a device, or the ill-advised use?

And, finally, in conjunction with the last point, in preparing for proliferation we should emphasize knowledge of who is proliferating and what nuclear programs are being developed. Knowing answers to these questions will be vital in formulating appropriate responses in preventing, postponing, or reacting to proliferation.

Phillip Farley
Senior Research Fellow, Arms Control and Disarmament Program, Stanford University; Deputy Director of the Arms Control and Disarmament Agency, 1969–1973

Since my background is so similar to Nye's and Malone's, you'll not be surprised that I have not too much to add. I don't want to miss this opportunity, however, to get my two cents worth in on what the policy and the posture of the Reagan administration ought to be. This may be my only chance since one of the concrete actions taken after the election was to terminate my consultancy with the Energy Department and the State Department. I've got a captive audience here now.

Unfortunately, after Malone's remarks, I find I have less than I thought to say in the way of advice. I am quite pleased with the general outlines he presented. Indeed, as one thinks of how one would wish the Reagan administration to proceed and how it should put its own personal mark on a policy as central and public as this one, I think one can see two places where it may be anticipated there would be a change in emphasis: in the attitude toward nuclear exports and nuclear cooperation, and in the style with which the administration would deal with other countries.

On the matter of nuclear exports and nuclear cooperation, I think the general line sounds fine. It clearly is something that is going to be tested by the manner of application. A formula that nuclear power is no longer a matter of last resort is fine. I think for most countries, of course, it has not been. On the other hand, a more active nuclear export policy and nuclear cooperation policy is something that is going to have to be subjected to two related regimes. One is the regime of nuclear non-proliferation. It seems to me that that's a point very clearly recognized in the emerging position. Malone used several terms to characterize the approach. The one I had rather looked for was "discrimination." I think probably you included that as part of what you called "flexibility." Personally, I find "discrimination" a clearer term because one of my troubles with the Carter policy was that it did tend to have rigid formulas, often embodied in legislation, which it was then very difficult to accommodate to our differing political or economic relations or security relations with specific countries. And certainly, with regard to nuclear power export, I think a good deal of discrimination is going to be required, not only because of the nuclear proliferation considerations, but also because of energy and energy economic considerations. The picture about the world demand and world usefulness of nuclear power in 1981 is rather different from what it was in the middle 1970s, and certainly an export promotion drive is hardly warranted, either by the state of the market or by the long-term economic interests. So I think a good deal of discrimination is going to have to be applied to nuclear exports, even under a more positive attitude toward nuclear power.

The second area where a new administration might look for its personality is style. Style isn't a trivial thing. Indeed, I really mean by that the kind of thing Malone was talking about when he said that the United States should return to the mainstream of world nuclear activities. Under the Carter administration, we were often in a posture of being someone external to the interests of others, who was lecturing them from a (not very satisfactory) moral position about what they should do about their own nuclear energy programs and about their own security concerns. And if the new style is to rely much more on consultation, cooperation, on action based on consensus, I think that can only be to the advantage of the effectiveness of a non-proliferation regime.

I found only one thing that I would want to take exception with in what Bailey said. As I understood it, she spoke of the withdrawal provision of the Non-Proliferation Treaty as a kind of unfortunate flaw in it. I think we have to recognize that the withdrawal provision is central to the Non-Proliferation Treaty. I've said to many of you before that I believe that the whole essence of the non-proliferation regime is that it's a bargain. It is not international law that rules out the pursuit of nuclear weapons by other countries. It is a regime that recognizes that most countries believe they will be better off if they do not pursue a nuclear weapons program and would like to concert their action because, obviously, countries have to deal with regional and global situations. It's easier not to develop nuclear weapons if your neighbor is not doing so, and you can be more confident of that if he is a party to an agreement where his nuclear activities are under safeguard. But the whole essence of the Non-Proliferation Treaty and of an effective approach to non-proliferation is a cooperative effort where people participate as long as it's in the interest of all.

In the end, I do not see how the United States, with its ongoing nuclear program, can say it is contrary to international law or it is contrary to moral principles for other countries to embark on nuclear weapons programs. It may be against our interests. In which case, on a principle of "discrimination," we do what we can to slow or stop that. But inherent in the Non-Proliferation Treaty is the voluntary act on the other side. So I applaud very much the emphasis on the IAEA, the Non-Proliferation Treaty, the flexible elements of the approach to individual projects with great sensitivity because of their fuel cycle role and the base they could provide for a nuclear weapons capability. At the same time, I hope we will no longer view every step increasing the potential nuclear weapons capability as a step toward a nuclear weapons program. I'm afraid that's a discrimination we will have to make also.

In general, then, I found the program that was outlined a satisfying one. As one small footnote, I would add to the various measures and joint steps to be taken particular attention to international activities to set up standards, to supervise, regulate, and otherwise deal with physical security and safety. If those matters cannot be dealt with satisfactorily, we will have, both nationally and internationally, difficulty in maintaining even a modest degree of nuclear power exploitation and cooperation.

So, in sum, having this great opportunity to give advice, I think basically I would say, "right on." You seem to be proceeding in a good direction. I'm a little more skeptical of the immediate prospects and benefits of nuclear power. But I think when they are clearly there, we have nothing to lose by cooperation in the cases where there is clearly a well-thought-out nuclear program within an overall energy assessment by the country concerned. And I would say as a final comment, I think you have no reason to apologize for delay in developing your policy. I think it's much more important to have worked it out and to have emphasized the continuity of policy over the past decades, an important element of U.S. relationships with the rest of the world that I think needs to be reestablished.

I am glad to see, even in passing, that there is recognition of the importance of consulting with Congress in dealing with matters like export licensing and some of the other provisions of the Non-Proliferation Act. If what is generally a sound policy approach is attended by Executive Branch actions that have not been very carefully prepared with Congress, then we would get into another domestic fight about nuclear policy in this country. I think that would somewhat diminish the effectiveness of this return to the mainstream. One of the problems the other countries have is simply with the predictability of the U.S. government processes and policy. I think a little delay in dealing with some of the problems of the Nuclear Non-Proliferation Act is a small price for getting consensus in the United States, too. There is some flexibility in the act, which I think could carry you quite a while in meeting some of the concerns of other countries. I know from recent first-hand experience that there are some very strong protagonists of that act on Capitol Hill who could be negotiated with to produce perhaps a phased program that would meet the interests of both branches of the government.

Henry Rowen
Graduate School of Business, Stanford University

Let me just pick up three points from the preceding remarks. It has become clear in the last couple of years that the mainstream, as Malone put it, has rejected our initiatives since 1976, and that we had to change, because the consensus against us was so strong. This was particularly true with regard to our major allies with whom we have a lot of things going, most of which, in fact, were thought to be more important than the nuclear fuel cycle. So that's emerged and we need to lower our profile on the subject especially since I don't think we have any good new ideas.

Since we don't have any good new ideas, maybe we should back off. I think we need to be guided by certain principles on non-proliferation, but I'm not sure we should be talking about very much since it's not clear that it's all that productive. I'm not saying we should abandon the NPT and make a 180 degree turn, but we might deal with the concerns expressed this morning in a different way.

The second point has to do with putting nuclear energy in perspective. Some of Malone's remarks exaggerate the role of nuclear energy. I don't doubt that it can and should play a larger role in the United States and in other industrialized countries. But it is important to put it in perspective. Nuclear energy can play a role, but it's not clear that it's all that decisive. Take the Persian Gulf oil interruption problem. That's one we live with right now. We've had three crises in the last eight years. Nuclear energy can make a difference, but not much. Other things are going to have to play a much larger role, such as storing oil.

In the long term, nuclear energy has an important role in the provision of efficient, relatively cheap electricity. If you look at the latest Exxon worldwide forecast to the year 2000, the number one growth fuel is coal. That's by far the largest increment. Tied for second are natural gas and nuclear.

Even if we hadn't had Three Mile Island and if nuclear growth were somewhat more vigorous, we would still see these other fuels playing a very large role, unless, as Malone suggests, the greenhouse effect really does knock off coal. It may be an important uncertainty. This suggests a hedging strategy in which nuclear would play a major role and maybe an absolutely crucial one if the CO_2 problem gets to be dominant.

Turning to the nuclear fuel cycle, while it is true that the mainstream has so far rejected our proposed constraints on various parts of the fuel cycle as a principal strategy, it's also true that the economic analyses that underlay our approach have not been shown to be wrong. The last few years have shown us that those earlier analyses in the mid-1970s were quite sound. On the subject of the breeder, a really good analysis is the one that David Stockman wrote in 1977. It's the Office of Management and Budget that's been out after the Barnwell plant, not wanting to put government money in it, not, as far as I understand, the non-proliferators. The economic arguments are quite sound. This has much to do with the fact that for most of the rest of the world, not including France, the pressure from people wanting to get into separating plutonium from spent fuel or setting up isotope separation isn't all that great. The economics are unattractive. Perhaps we can restore to some extent our earlier position—but never fully restore it.

Finally, as we lower our profile, our focus should be more on problem countries. I have felt for many years that we are making a serious mistake in not using other instruments to affect developments in Pakistan, that is, security assistance. This is now happening. It seemed to me there was no other possible way of hoping to affect developments in that country. Certainly there is no guarantee that we will succeed, but at least we have a better shot at it. There are a number of other countries that have been mentioned, and for each a special treatment is required. The instruments include the full array of political, economic, and military instruments, each tailored to the circumstances of each country. Some, like South Africa, are a lot harder than others. There have been some limited successes, as mentioned. If the United States and others don't succeed in dealing adequately with the problem countries, the consequences could be quite serious because there are spillover effects. If there is a resumption of tests by India, then tests by Pakistan, and something happening in Iraq, it will have a spillover effect. Everyone will be affected by it, so it really is important to try and contain and limit these possible adverse developments.

There have been a few worrisome signs. The fact that there is a reactor in Iraq that is now apparently the target for attack is suggestive of the kinds of actions that we may be seeing more of. If the notion gets around that people's reactors should be subject to air attack, we could have it happening in various parts of the world.

DISCUSSION

James Malone: I would like to comment on the remarks that Farley and Rowen have made. I would like to come down first on the problem-country situation and make it very clear how I think policy is going to develop there. I didn't want to use the pejorative term discriminate, but Farley was quite correct when he said we are going to be flexible in our approach to clear-risk situations. We are going to put a great deal of emphasis upon that. We are going to do everything that we can to increase the motivation not to go nuclear and, recognizing also what Nye said, that inevitably there will be some additional countries that move into the nuclear club, we are going to do everything we can to control that kind of eventuality. We do feel, as I pointed out in my remarks, that there are various tools available. The tools that we are attempting to use in Pakistan on security assistance are good illustrative examples of ways in which we can increase the disincentives or increase the incentives, depending upon how you look at it, and we mean to use the full bag of tricks.

Let me remark also for a moment on the comments with regard to moving back into the mainstream. It's the view of the Reagan administration that unless we are in the mainstream we cannot have a really important effect upon what is happening in proliferation. If we remove ourselves, if we are "nay sayers," if we are ones that say, "Ah-ah, you can't do that because we're telling you not to do that," experience has shown that this is not a particularly productive path to follow. So, we mean to be in the game to the extent that we possibly can, using that as a device to further not only commercial interests, but certainly to further our proliferation interest as well.

An important point that Farley made, which perhaps I did not emphasize to the extent that I should have, is the necessity of working with Congress. It is our intention to work at every phase carefully with Congress in reviewing the Nuclear Non-Proliferation Act. We in the Executive Branch feel that there are a number of things that should be done. It may indeed be that these should be done on an incremental basis as Farley suggested. There's much merit in this suggestion. We intend to consider very carefully each phase with the Congress. I think that even in the case of some people who apparently have expressed opposition, there is more of a reservoir of interest in making appropriate constructive changes than some may think. This is not an easy job. It will take a great deal of effort, but this administration fully intends to make those kinds of efforts.

Finally, I would just like to remark on something that Rowen pointed out, in connection with whether or not it is a good idea to have a non-proliferation policy. At this juncture it is our view that it is, if for no other reason than it is strongly expected by our allies and trading partners. They feel that they have been left at sea, that they haven't known exactly where things are going; and I think there is merit in giving something of a roadmap—this is the way we are going to move on this; let us allay your fears and concerns in that regard. If you have talked to our Japanese friends recently, or some of our other nuclear partners, they have very strongly emphasized these points and I think the points certainly have a good deal of merit. I recognize that there are arguments for not casting the thing too much in concrete, but I think that probably on balance it is desirable to have a stated non-proliferation policy.

And, finally, I can assure you that the Federal Government and David Stockman are not going to put any federal money in Barnwell. Leave that to the private sector.

Phillip Farley: There's been a good deal of talk about the importance of security assurances and security assistance in dealing with some of the problem countries. And I think that is the most immediate and obvious tool. However, the record should not indicate that's all we can think of or that we don't realize that sometimes it doesn't work very well. Pakistan, for example, is not motivated in its nuclear program by looking at the Soviet Union, which is presumably what our security assistance would be oriented toward; it looks at India. And if we are going to influence Pakistan, I believe we have to deal with India. If we are going to influence those countries, we have to work, in some degree, in concert with the Soviet Union, and I would like to suggest a radical thought—that that's the reason why, whenever possible, we should get back in a posture where we can do business with the Soviet Union when it's in our interest.

Next, in the case of a country like South Africa, you cannot, perhaps, solve the problem by classic diplomatic means, but you can do a great deal to ease the excuse of South Africa for a nuclear program, by the sort of efforts made to settle regional problems in Zimbabwe and Namibia, that, I think, were some of the finer achievements of the Carter administration. I hope that such activities will be continued by this administration, as there is some indication, because I think they are more important in defusing the situation in Southern Africa, impossible as it is, than any amount of security assistance.

Samuel Thompson: I'd like to raise a point with respect to remarks made by several of the speakers about preparing for proliferation. I think what we need is a game plan once a given country has developed a nuclear weapon. One of the problems we faced in 1974 when India went nuclear was that we were not prepared and didn't have a clear idea of how we were going to handle the situation. We didn't know how to deal with the Soviets. The Soviets waited for us to do something. We waited for them to do something. The end result was that we did nothing. Don't you believe that we need to have some idea of what to do when a country does go nuclear? That question is for anyone who cares to address it.

Kathleen Bailey: One way that you can prepare is to stress the use of regional specialists who understand the countries and the policies, cultures, and histories of the individual nations in question. Today, mention has been made of Pakistan, and I greatly concur that had we addressed the Pakistani situation in their context, understanding it from their perspective, we could have perhaps brought more to bear. So I think that first, the use of specialists in formulating policy on specific countries and regions should be stressed, and second, that there should be scenario development sponsored by more than one agency, not just by the Department of Energy, not just Defense, but multiple agencies designed to look at what the response would be regionally, and also by the United States and the Soviet Union in the case of actual proliferation.

Peter Zimmerman: Malone identified the subnational group as one of the most important problems. I'd like to know what you think will be effective ways to deal with subnational groups. Are we simply talking about physical safeguards that deny them materials? It's difficult at this point to deny them the knowledge.

James Malone: It is a difficult problem to deal with. I didn't spell it out in my remarks, but Farley brought up the physical protection convention and the transport situation. We are going to emphasize both very strongly. These are partial ways of getting at this problem. But at the moment, the subnational and terrorist problem is not a wholly solvable problem. We think that the reduced enrichment program may be useful, although again not a totally satisfactory solution either. But there are a number of these things, some of which have been pursued in the past, that we will continue. Others we will perhaps re-emphasize. We feel that this is an area that is going to require additional creative thinking and application, because it is an important area, and it's one that this administration must, and intends, to address.

William Potter: My question pertains to the question of the viability of the existing non-proliferation regime. I wonder if it really is very accurate to refer to it as a regime. It may appear to be a superpower regime, for the United States and the Soviet Union and some of the other industrialized states see certain advantages in the existing set of rules and norms. But I wonder if we were to address an audience of Pakistanis, Indians, Brazilians, and representatives from a number of countries in the Third World, whether we would find the same kind of consensus that there is a regime out there.

I'm particularly struck by Nye's comment that the second NPT Review Conference was some indication that a regime still exists and is functioning. It seems to me there would have been at least some document, some statement, in support of the principles of the NPT. Yet my reading of the proceedings of the Second NPT Review Conference suggests that even this basic kind of agreement could not be found. If one looks at the conclusions of INFCE it seems to me that both the critics and the supporters of the Carter administration policies point to the conclusions of INFCE as vindicating their position. So I wonder whether it is really appropriate to talk about a viable regime, and if so what the cornerstone of that regime is? Is it still the NPT Treaty, or is it something else that I may have missed?

Joseph Nye: I would add that if you had a room full of Pakistanis and Indians you'd have bitter criticism, though neither of them, of course, are NPT parties. I think it's worth noticing what states do, as well as what they say, and the difference between the rhetoric and the behavior. And I really think you have to go back to Farley's point, which hits the nail on the head. There's a bargain here. States feel more secure not because they have promised some tradeoff between Article VI and I, or between Article IV and I; that's the stuff you make your speeches about. When you come right down to it, you'd rather know that the country next door has also signed something that allows inspectors onto its territory and gives you at least a three-month warning time, than to have that totally up in the air. In that sense you might think of this as analogous to "confidence building measures," as used in arms control terminology.

One of the problems is that as sensitive technology began to be transferred, it was clear that countries were going to use it. I mentioned some specific instances as a way to use the norms of the regimes to creep up and across the threshold with a fait accompli. The supplier's guidelines were added in 1976. There was an apparent inconsistency between Article VII of the supplier's guidelines, which says that you will not export, or you will exercise restraint in the export of, sensitive technology and Article IV of the NPT. But one of the benefits of the INFCE was to get a general agreement that the type of thing being restricted, particularly reprocessing plants used with the current generation reactors, was not terribly important in energy terms. There is a basic dilemma in non-proliferation—the dilemma of discrimination. And it's rare to get a series of states to sign an international treaty that has discriminatory statements and treatments of states. The important thing is that we had to find some way to soften that degree of tension between the suppliers' guidelines and the Article IV of the NPT. And while there is still much rhetoric against it, there was a degree of softening, because it is now possible for us to say that indeed we will provide technology when it's appropriate, but such technology is not relevant to the needs you have in the current decade, much less the current century. This gives you a way to avoid some of the sharpness of that dilemma. Discrimination is inherent in the regime and will always bring forth rhetoric against it. But the key points are, how states behave and the extent to which we can blur over or soften the discrimination to a point where it doesn't erode an imperfect but nonetheless useful regime.

To go back to Bailey's point on Argentina versus Brazil, Argentina went for an indigenous fuel cycle back in 1950, well before the IAEA or the NPT. I think the example is not very well taken.

James Malone: Nye is quite right with regard to his comments on the NPT bargain, but I would like to point out a couple of other observations in that connection. Although the NPT Review Conference couldn't agree on a consensus document, they did not try to amend the treaty, and nothing has been done to date. And indeed we should recognize that the Committee on Assurances of Supply (CAS) is now developing and functioning. It certainly will be the position of this administration to actively participate in and support that effort. There is a real problem here, but we do have to keep a balance. From our point of view, certainly the safeguards are more important. From the developing countries' point of view, technical assistance is more important. That's why the upcoming election of the new director general of the IAEA is so terribly important. [Hans Blix of Sweden was elected director general.] We need the kind of leadership there that can give balance to these matters in the IAEA, recognizing that appropriate technical assistance is going to have to be undertaken to the extent that the rhetoric at the Review Conference might have called for, while at the same time keeping a solid balance and stability with the safeguard program. But it is something that has to be addressed. I think we recognize that and I think that the CAS work will be very important in this connection.

Charles Wolf: I have a question each for Nye and Malone. Nye made the observation that security guarantees are an important part of the process of creating disincentives to proliferation, which I think is well taken, at least for some of the countries that are potential proliferators, if not for others. Now on the premise that the Soviet Union shares our interest in non-proliferation, one might expect them to engage in similar security guarantees to strengthen the Brezhnev doctrine, for example, with respect to their associated states—perhaps Libya and Iraq would be examples. My question has two parts. Are they doing so and if not, why not? The second part of the question is more conjectural. If the Soviets strengthen the security guarantees that they extend to their associated states, does that run an enhanced risk that those states operating under the guarantee may engage in more truculent behavior? If they do, those states may perhaps be brought into conflict either with the United States or with some of our associated states.

The question for Malone relates to his comment about reorganizing the Nuclear Regulatory Commission on the grounds that it's not an appropriate vehicle for making foreign policy decisions. I agree with that, but in the light of it, I'd like to ask him to consider the hypothetical question of what the Reagan administration would have done with the issue of exporting enriched uranium to India, which the Carter administration agreed to do.

James Malone: The Republican party platform recommended not to do that.

Joseph Nye: The question was about the role of the Russians in security guarantees, and I think it's an important point. The Soviet Union obviously has its sphere of influence, and within that sphere of influence in Eastern Europe, where their security guarantees hold, it's interesting to see that they require return of the spent fuel to the Soviet Union and exercise very tight control. An interesting question is what happens in other areas where they have a weaker influence, but nonetheless some potential influence. Libya and Iraq are the two candidate countries of most interest there. It turns out, I believe, that they have less influence in Iraq than they first thought. For one thing, in the nuclear area, it's really the French and the Italians who are providing most of the materials. The Russian research reactor is really a trivial one compared to the others. In the context of the Iraq-Iran war, they are trying to hedge their bets on both sides and seem to have lost considerable influence in terms of their capabilities in Iraq. Libya is a more interesting case because the Soviets are planning to supply power reactors to Libya. The question is, will they require return of the spent fuel to the Soviet Union, which we have urged them a number of times to do. I remember talking to a Soviet about this in a recent trip to the Soviet Union. I was quite intrigued when he said in an after-dinner conversation over drinks, "We really have a strong common interest in non-proliferation, we ought to take joint actions against new entrants." I said, "That's not very realistic in the current political climate. For example, would you engage in joint political pressure with us against Libya?" and he said, "Certainly yes." This is one Soviet, but the general attitude that they have about the importance of proliferation, particularly since they're the likely target of most of the new entrants, is that it's a very serious security problem for them. Farley's point is particularly important here: While we have a lot of other problems with the Soviets and are going to have a very tension-ridden relationship with them, we shouldn't ignore areas where there is enough common interest that it pays to continue to communicate.

Leonard Ross: I'd like to comment on Nye's question about the relationship between reactors and proliferation. There are two kinds of relationship; one is causal and the other is opportunity cost. Now the causal relationship is admittedly loose, but there's a clear overlap between the technology expertise, bureaucratic power, and sex appeal of civilian nuclear power and the country's military program, and specific cases like Argentina where the Atomic Energy Commission overruled the president on an issue of safeguards. I think the more important relationship is one of opportunity cost. Having a promotional policy toward nuclear power has the opportunity cost of not thinking, as Harry Rowen suggested, of better ways of addressing the oil problem, including conservation, which hasn't been mentioned here. One of the assumptions that I think has crippled policy has been believing that what a country expresses as its policy on energy or nuclear power is going to remain fixed. A country in this context usually means the representative at a nuclear related meeting, who may well come from a nuclear establishment. Even if you make that assumption, countries have been changing very rapidly in their views of nuclear power and of conservation. Finally, I would like to suggest that one way of fulfilling the Article IV bargain of the NPT is to say we promised you something that we and no one else can deliver now. We promised cheap, safe, effective nuclear energy, we can have the most permissive rules possible, but we can't deliver that. And so we will deliver assistance for conservation or exploration or anything else that fulfills the real economics of the bargain as well as permission, but not promotion, for nuclear reactors.

Joseph Nye: It's one thing to be realistic about the economics of nuclear energy, which you might call swimming with the tide, which is a sensible thing to do; part of the efforts in INFCE were to get people to be more realistic before too much steel and concrete was built upon unrealistic estimates of the early 1970s. That I agree with; but I think it would be a mistake to take an antinuclear position because the international regime we have, with all its norms, is based upon that early bargain in terms of transfer of technology. I think, frankly, that the Carter administration often spoke with many voices at the same time, and that some of the voices that tended to come out with an antinuclear view, did, in fact, hurt us in our non-proliferation policy. So there's a difference between being realistic without being overly promotional and having an explicitly antinuclear energy program, which I think is self-defeating because the regime is built upon that transfer of technology.

James Malone: Let me expand on something that Nye just said, and something that was implicit in his remarks. I would certainly agree that we do not want to oversell nuclear, that we want to be realistic, and I was trying to emphasize that in my comments on realism. But it is very important and certainly it will be the view of this administration that a clear nonnuclear bias would be detrimental to us in accomplishing the goals. The implicit aspect was the pursuit of the all-or-nothing philosophy on safeguards. There are a number of situations, two cases have been identified—Brazil and Argentina. At the moment we don't have any real chance of getting full-scope safeguards in either of those countries. But I have just been to both countries, I have talked with Carlos Castro Medero, Chairman of the Atomic Energy Commission of Argentina, and with the people in Brazil, and I think that we can incrementally make improvements and make progress there if we are not absolutely tied up in a knot over getting all-or-nothing. Progress is quite possible on the Angra One fuel supply, which is still languishing in Brazil. If we can get a nonexplosive-use assurance, and if we can get safeguards on all facilities as of the date of export that comply with the NNPA, that would be a real accomplishment. Just because you are seeing the development of a largely indigenous closed fuel cycle in Argentina doesn't mean that progress in terms of a safeguards program can't be made there too. I want to underscore several times that it is not a perfect system, the safeguard system; it has never been a perfect system. We have to look at making incremental improvements in it, and not just casting out those countries that seem to pose difficult problems.

7

ROUND TABLE DISCUSSION

William Beecher of *The Boston Globe* chaired the round table discussion. He posed the following question to the panelists: The President of the United States is on the telephone. "Regardless of your politics," he says, "what is your vision of where we ought to go in strategic arms control over the next five years, and what specific steps would you urge me to take over the next several months to start down that track?" Assumed under that question are such issues as whether crisis stability should become the over-arching objective of SALT; whether the SALT II Treaty should be left in limbo for the next four years while the two sides seek to leap-frog to SALT II-A; and whether TNF should be used as the bridge to SALT II-A as a mutually face-saving way to resume the strategic dialogue.

SPEAKERS

Paul Nitze

I would suggest to the president that his first task be to select a chairman for an interdepartmental group to which he would look for staff work on the SALT issue. The interdepartmental group should include members from State, Defense, the Joint Chiefs of Staff, ACDA, the CIA, and the National Security Council (NSC) staff. It should be made clear, however, that the chairman is not merely to coordinate but, after hearing all the considerations, is to decide on his recommendations to the president.

I would recommend that the president give the chairman guidance as to his initial approach on the major issues. He should make it clear to the chairman that if the evidence suggests to him that the guidance should be changed, he not hesitate to so recommend. I would suggest that the president give the chairman the following initial guidance.

- The SALT II Treaty is too unequal, ambiguous, and of too short a duration to be of use. Therefore, attention should be focused on negotiating a SALT III agreement. In order to preserve negotiating time, it may be wise to take the position that the United States does not intend to exceed the limits of either SALT I or SALT II provided the USSR does not exceed them, during a reasonable period of time for the negotiations to make progress. Whether this is wise or not depends on the specifics of the administration's defense program and budget, which should be worked out prior to the SALT position being finally decided.
- A SALT III treaty should be of indefinite duration with review and escape provisions similar to those in the ABM Treaty.
- The provisions of the treaty should foster a situation of crisis stability, a situation in which neither side could expect to achieve a gain in relative position by initiating a nuclear exchange.
- The provisions should be consistent with rough equivalence in the capabilities of the two sides.
- The agreement should be designed to achieve a balance between the precision and verifiability of those provisions and their significance.
- The agreement should take into account the interrelationship between central systems and gray-area systems.
- Finally, the agreement should foster radical reductions in the destructive capability of the forces of the two sides, in particular of their fixed MIRVed ICBM forces.

I would suggest that the report prepared by the interdepartmental group include, in addition to the main report, the following annexes.

- An annex dealing with negotiating strategy and tactics. This would include an initial U.S. draft text of the SALT III treaty and an analysis, section by section, of the defense of the treaty's provisions the U.S. delegation would expect to use. An analysis of the probable Soviet negotiation objectives and their probable tactics in fostering those objectives, and an analysis of probable Soviet counterarguments and the way in which the U.S. delegation would be expected to respond to them should be included. In developing this annex it might be useful for the interdepartmental group to commission a "red-blue negotiating wargame" to simulate the negotiations.

- An annex reconciling the draft SALT III treaty with the administration's longer-range defense program and budget. In this connection the intelligence community and the Department of Defense should be asked for an analysis of the net strategic balance between the U.S. and Soviet forces to be expected, both under the treaty and without the treaty.
- An annex dealing with the public information program necessary to support the negotiations.
- An annex outlining how best to deal with the international community, including our allies and the UN.
- Finally, an annex dealing with the Congressional relations aspects of the problem.

Ralph Earle II

I'm glad Nitze went first because he said so many things with which I agree that I won't have to repeat them. I think the team and the study are all quite appropriate. In fact, I think Nitze and I talked about that eight years ago, that a "czar" should be set up for SALT. The problem I have with what Nitze said and the difference in the advice I would give to the president really focuses on one point. And that was Nitze's recommendation that we go directly to SALT III, because I think if the annexes that he described were done, the blue-red war game would indicate that you can't go to SALT III from SALT I and what is now SALT II. You have to go through SALT II, in my view.

Of course, the first thing I would say to the president would be, "Why don't you ratify it?" But that advice would not be taken, so I would then amplify what I think ought to be done. I would say that what ought to be done is what is probably going to happen anyway. That is, and the NATO allies are going to demand it, that we go to the TNF table, but it's pretty hard to go to the TNF table except in the context of SALT. If we didn't make that determination ourselves, the Soviets would make it clear, I think, as they did last year before we went to the preliminary discussions in Geneva, that TNF had to be done in the context of SALT, and that any agreement that might be reached in those talks would come into effect only upon ratification of SALT II. So, whether we determined it or whether the Soviets insisted upon it before they went to the TNF table, we would have to do something about SALT II.

I think under the circumstances, the best and most efficient way to handle it would be to act, either expressly or implicitly, as Nitze suggested in a slightly different context. We would agree that neither side would take any step to violate the provisions of the SALT II Agreement. That doesn't mean that there has to be total compliance. Obviously, we cannot, and could not, expect the Soviets to embark on a dismantling program. But it seems to me that in order to get them to the TNF table there would have to be further discussions of the SALT II Agreement. In that context, I would say to the president, "I know you want to change the agreement. There are three possibilities for change." I should interject here there's a question of whether it should be one forum or two fora. My thought is that two would be better. TNF and a revision of the SALT II Treaty would be a little too much for any one table to bear. That, of course, is a technical matter. But I would say to the president that there are three alternatives in terms of getting a different SALT II agreement. One is to have some cosmetic changes and claim it to be your own. These cosmetic changes could embody the kind of understandings that the Foreign Relations Committee raised and that the Carter administration accepted during the markup in the fall of 1979. An example of a cosmetic change would be an agreement that the agreed statements and common understandings are legally binding. They are, but one could have an express agreement to that effect.

Going beyond the cosmetic changes, it seems to me that one might try for some slight substantive changes. It's hard to think of examples, but perhaps one could be, as Nitze suggested, a clearer definition of a mobile ICBM launcher. It would be hard to do but possible.

The third possibility would be to seek to change what has been determined to be the fatal flaws in the treaty. That would result in a truly substantive negotiation and I would simply advise the president that the moment one begins to do that, the Soviets will have under the table with them a rather large briefcase with a very long list of changes that they would like to have made in the treaty. I have the feeling that the Soviet military would not agree that it was fatally flawed in favor of the Soviet Union. Rather I sense that they believe it to be fatally flawed as far as the Soviet Union is concerned.

I think that's the practical way to do it. As I said, I am in accord with all the other suggestions or recommendations that Nitze made in terms of how to go about it, teams, leaders, annexes. But I do think that you cannot get truly into SALT and/or TNF without doing something between the present point and a true SALT III.

Paul Seabury

I cannot come up with any catalogue of prescriptions that would add to what this distinguished group of specialists can offer. I think, though, that if I were in a philosophical mind and the president shared that mood, that one thing is very important to point out to him. The SALT process is more than a process that aims at consummation in an agreement. That agreement with the passage of time will become unstuck. We are really talking about a process that will go on for a very long time, staged in phases as the nature of the strategic relationship changes. Thus a SALT agreement should be constructed with the flexibility to deal with a changing strategic relationship, based upon a realistic view of what that relationship is, and what it could become.

On the suggestion that SALT III-A might be the one to encapsulate the theater nuclear force arrangement, it seems to me that that issue is becoming more and more crucial. I don't know how the evolution of the political perceptions of that are going to go, but unless something happens that knits the European theater problem into the bipolar strategic one, we are going to be in a great deal of trouble with our allies.

Pursuing the philosophical question further, it seems to me that there has been a tendency among some to think that this whole process can somehow be isolated from the general strategic situation that surrounds the process itself, and dealt with, as the Germans say, as a "ding-an-sich." I don't think that is possible. The collapse of the political support of SALT III in the Senate during the late part of the Carter administration has shown this. Not only that, we need to ask ourselves whether the view, shared by many arms controllers, that arms control is an autonomous process, or should be, is really mirrored and recip-rocated in the Soviets' view of the matter. It is not. It seems to me that we have attached an extraordinary amount of importance to this view as a symbol of a relationship that we wish to have with the Soviets without carefully inquiring as to whether the Soviets attach a similar importance to it. It seems to me that the answer to that is very clear; for them the SALT process is lodged within a larger strategic framework of thought and doctrine and does not stand aside from it nor stand above it. Until we can soberly begin to absorb that lesson we are always going to be at a very grave disadvantage in these negotiations.

Walter Slocombe

First, in the wholly unlikely event that the president called me, I would give him Nitze's phone number and urge that he listen carefully. If he has not already called Nitze, I'm sure he will.

But if he did call me, the first thing I would say is that before thinking about the details of SALT, he should set a steady course for strategic programs. Of these programs I believe the first element is an MX in a survivable mode, and I would stress particularly the need for a survivable system. The second most important program issue is making sure that the alliance in fact carries through on the LRTNF program. The failure to succeed on both of those fronts would have a fundamentally bad effect on U.S. diplomacy and security generally and a fortiori on everything we do about SALT. In particular, I would urge the president, before he listens too hard to Senator Paul Laxalt on the subject of MX, to consider very carefully the impact on the LRTNF program in Europe if we abandon the idea of a survivable land-based ICBM force in the United States simply because of local political opposition. I would also urge the president not to let the ABM enthusiasts sell him prematurely a bill of goods on getting out of the ABM Treaty. There are a variety of problems with ABM, both technical and political, and, in particular, ABM is not an alternative to a survivable land-based ICBM force.

I would also urge him, as he is briefed, to pay attention himself, and to try to get his senior colleagues to pay attention, to two basic strategic facts that are not about hardware, but are central to a sound strategic nuclear program. First, the idea that the United States has no alternative to an all-out retaliation against cities is simply false, and second, the regeneration of confidence in the inherent capability of the force that we already have is, I think, a critical part of being able to approach negotiations with seriousness and also with the necessary patience.

With respect to SALT itself, I would say that like Ralph Earle, I think he ought to ratify it. But I would also say, on the assumption that he won't take the advice of either of us, that trying to renegotiate SALT II is probably not a good idea because there is a real danger that renegotiation of minor details will mushroom. As Earle says, the Soviets will have their own minor details (mostly about the protocol, for openers at least) that they would want to renegotiate, and we would end up consuming a great deal of time and effort for very little product. The best course realistically available therefore is probably to keep SALT II (and SALT I) in place tacitly under some such formula as Nitze suggested.

I would add a warning; in my view the principal danger of living with an unratified SALT agreement, while all this is going on, is Soviet pressure on the verification provisions. And I would urge that if President Reagan has any means for getting a message through to the Soviets in this context, it had better be that Soviet adventurism on the subject of verification under the SALT II Agreement is the most likely non-deliberate way to torpedo the process.

With respect to SALT III, I think Nitze's suggestions both procedurally and for general guidelines are the right ones. I would offer some cautions that reductions are critical to public support but are not critical to meeting the crisis stability requirement and that a longer duration for an agreement is important but raises serious problems in relation to how long and exactly how one is going to devise an agreement that can continue to respond to technological and strategic changes. On more specific points, I believe that the problems of heavies and mobiles should be addressed and probably wrapped together to solve both a perceived inequality and a serious stability problem. I would urge his study group to look first at what kinds of legitimate requirements and requests we could make for expanded data exchange; second, to see what could be done, in the SALT context or otherwise, with regard to securing C^3; and third, to work on the very difficult problem of how you expand the range of the SALT agreements to cover air defenses.

I would remind him that he is already committed to TNF discussions by the end of the year. There will be very difficult substantive issues in dealing with those, but they do present an opportunity as a bridge to SALT III, and indeed even as a way to handle some of the difficult SALT issues. He should get either this team or a subgroup of it to agree this year—and it must be pretty soon this year because we will have to consult with the Europeans on it—on a reasonable and serious TNF proposal. In my view, such a proposal should center around the idea of getting an acceptable currency, whether it is warheads on launchers or something else, and proposing the lowest possible equal levels in that currency with a worldwide and a regional sub-ceiling and with an appropriate handling of the reloads problem. I would also say that in the TNF context he will have to face the issue of FBS and that he should seize the opportunity to use FBS as a way to handle the *Backfire* problem, which is a subject he may remember.

I think a plan like this for SALT will fit in with a more vigorous defense program, and it would fit in with the president's stated commitment to an arms control process that corrects what he describes as the fundamental flaws of the SALT II Treaty.

DISCUSSION

Herman Kahn: I'd like to ask Slocombe two questions. Would you just write off the *Minuteman*? And will you go for the racetrack for the MX?

Walter Slocombe: I wouldn't write off the *Minuteman*. I would continue to run them for a while. They obviously are sufficiently vulnerable that they constitute a form of trade goods in the negotiation. As to an MX system at a policy level, rather than an engineering level, I support the idea of having a system that can be moved relatively rapidly among a variety of protective shelters whether it's called multiple aim point, multiple launch system, or multiple protective shelter. I don't think that a truck mobile system is feasible in this country. It should be something that looks like the current MX. The administration can fiddle around with it, write REAGAN all over it instead of CARTER, if they like, and they can announce that they are going to make it verifiable in some totally different way. I think it would be a great mistake to announce they are not going to make it verifiable at all since that's impossible. I think that the basic proposition is that it ought to be land-based, that it ought to use the multiple shelter concept, and I think that it would be a mistake in our long-term interest to proclaim, as a false virtue of it, that it is unverifiable.

Herman Kahn: An ABM system could really solve a lot of those problems.

Walter Slocombe: I don't think an ABM system can deal with a *Minuteman* survivability problem unless it has a multiple shelter system to protect.

Mark Schneider: I agreed with essentially everything Nitze said except for his first instruction to the president. I don't see how you can approach the Russians and tell them you are serious about arms control and realistic balance, verifiable agreement, and at the same time, tell them you are willing to accept for the indefinite future agreements that may be realistic in the sense that they were a product of the balance of power at the time, but now are clearly unbalanced and unverifiable. Another thing, I do not see how the United States can recover its survivable ICBM force under the combination of SALT I and SALT II constraints, particularly the launcher limitation and the so-called new missile limitation with its largely unilateral effect on the United States. In other words, limiting us either to MX or a small ICBM, I simply do not conceive how we, given the domestic political constraints under which we're operating, can ultimately get a survivable ICBM force unless we renegotiate some of the basic provisions of the interim agreement and the SALT II Treaty.

Paul Nitze: I purposely did not say "indefinite"; I said, provided the Soviets do not violate. I grant you it was left open. I have an idea that on a review of this, one might well come to the conclusion that for the five-year term of the SALT II Treaty we would be prepared to abide by the SALT II ceilings. I'm not sure you'd find that you wanted to go beyond five years. This is something that deserves looking at very carefully. I tend to agree with you, that in order to work out systems that will be survivable and will meet the criteria that I've outlined, beyond 1985, you've got to do things that are not necessarily consistent with the SALT I and SALT II treaties. But it seems to me that from now until 1985 is an adequately long period to try the negotiating track along this formula. If you can't get something done by 1985, then you've got to be free to do what's necessary in order to preserve the survivability of various components of your strategic system.

Mark Schneider: The problem as I see it is that if you want to limit the window of vulnerability to the minimum possible time, you're going to have to initiate some programs and do it as rapidly as possible. The new missile provision of SALT II is really the critical one because if you are going to go forward with MX in a basing mode, and a small missile, you're going to hit on that provision. The Russians don't face that problem because of the 5 percent rule. In fact, they have five or six operational types of ICBMs to play around with; we don't. I simply can't conceive of a critical decision being made on the small missile issue without a prior decision on continued U.S. adherence to the interim agreement and SALT II, particularly when you combine that with the ABM Treaty restrictions, which limit the survivability of the ICBM force and the bomber force.

Paul Nitze: So far I haven't seen any indication that the Executive Branch is moving forward with both the MX and the small missile. Now it may be true that they will come to that decision, but I haven't seen that yet as being a likely prospect. If that does occur, then you're quite right that there is a problem.

Walter Slocombe: One reason why I think it's important to settle on a steady course for strategic programs is that while it's critical in a good SALT agreement to keep open the options that need to be kept open, that is very different from keeping open all of the options. If you haven't been able to decide what you want to do, and you try to keep all the options open because you haven't decided, then you won't have a meaningful agreement. You won't have closed off any concerns with the Soviets. I'm not in favor of trying to do two missiles and probably two bombers and hopefully two submarines, so that we can get one out on time. But I agree at least to the extent of saying you ought to decide what you are going to do, stop pulling up the plant by the roots to see how it's coming, and protect that option; but recognize that the purpose of arms control is to close off some Soviet options and the cost of that is closing off some U.S. options.

Frank Hoeber: I would like to address a comment to Ralph Earle. You can't say, "We're not going to reconsider the ABM Treaty in 1982." In the first place, we're going to have discussions of it, hopefully less routine than in 1977. It offers all sorts of options that ought to be at least considered. As you point out, it changes what you might want to do with the MX or whatever you really have as your next missile. You cannot discuss particular SALT negotiations in isolation from all the other topics that ought to be concerning us here very deeply.

Ralph Earle: I'd just like to make a brief comment relating to that. I think there's a misconception about the 1982 Review Conference of the ABM Treaty. The treaty does, in fact, call for a Review Conference every five years, but that in no way constitutes any kind of a deadline. The Standing Consultative Commission (SCC) meets in Geneva twice a year. In effect, they review the ABM Treaty every time they meet. It should not creep into people's minds that if we don't change the ABM Treaty in 1982, we have to wait five more years to change it.

Robert Scheer: I'm wondering whether any members of the panel would be inclined to challenge some of the president's political assumptions about Soviets and their motivations. In particular, I have four in mind. One is that they have been winners on the international situation and that they translated military power into political power successfully. If that is the case, how would they explain the defection of China and Egypt. I would be curious as to whether they would challenge the president's apparent assumption that the Soviets are behind every single problem in the world from terrorism to coups d'etat and whether they would enlighten him to the fact that there are also right-wing terrorists. I wonder whether they would challenge the assumption that the Soviets have to stop being "red" in order not be "dead," the Pipes position, and that it is impossible to do business with them unless they abandon their ideology. If that's the case, how do you explain our being able to do business with the Chinese, who at one time were thought to be rather fervent Marxists. And the fourth and final one is, I wonder whether they would disagree with any of the assumptions about the geopolitical drive behind the Soviets—the one that used to be mentioned most commonly was their overwhelming need for oil, and therefore the inevitable drive by the Soviets into the Middle East. That one has been abandoned but I gather there are still others that are thought to drive them. And so, in short, would you be inclined to challenge any of these assumptions that seem to be basic to why the Reagan administration is not inclined to engage in SALT negotiations or any other kind.

Paul Nitze: I think one always gets into difficulty when one takes simplified absolute propositions. It certainly is obvious to everybody, and I think to everybody in the Reagan administration, that the Soviets are not behind every act of terrorism. The question at issue is, do they tend to be behind the terrorism in the world? Have they acted sympathetically to the training of terrorists in Aden and in various other places? Have they tended to encourage terrorism or have they not? I don't believe anybody in the Reagan administration as a whole seriously takes the view that they are behind everything. Similarly, have they been winners or have they not? I don't believe that anybody, or the Reagan administration as whole, takes the view that they have uniformly been winners. Certainly they have had successes and lack of successes and reverses. I think that many people in the Reagan administration believe that, net on balance, their position today is stronger in the Third World than it was ten years ago. Now, one can debate that, but I believe that is their view and not the extreme view that you suggested.

It's certainly true that not everybody in the Reagan administration supports Richard Pipes's view with respect to the origins and the background of the Soviet position. He tends to put the origin and the particular character of the Soviet regime largely as being derived from Russian history, Russian tradition, Russian background, which clearly does not apply to China. There is quite a different background and tradition in China. So, I don't think your point there is well taken either. Certainly it's debatable as to the degree to which the nature of the Soviet regime springs from the particular history of the development of Marxism-Leninism in Russia and the degree to which it springs from the particular history and background of the USSR.

As to the question whether everything springs from the military, that clearly is not the view of those I know in the Reagan administration. I think they take a much broader view of Soviet thought with regard to the correlation of forces and the components of the correlation of forces in which the military is an essential element, but not necessarily the prime element—certainly not in every situation is it the prime element. In a way, they look upon the psychological and political elements as being even more important than the military element.

I think you didn't make much of a point on the oil matter. I haven't heard that really emphasized in the Reagan administration. I think that the judgment with respect to the coming shortage of oil in the Soviet Union was made by the CIA during the previous administration, not by the Reagan administration.

Joel McKean: I would ask the panel, is there anything, at least in the longer term, that you would advise the president to do in areas other than SALT and TNF?

Ralph Earle: I'll volunteer and raise at least one thing. Arms control in space is an area that, as I mentioned in my prepared remarks, I would urge him to do something about promptly.

William Barletta: Let me address this to Slocombe. You've addressed some of the issues with regard to strategic weapon procurement and the arms control problem. Mention was made of the costs with regard to the degradation of the performance of our strategic system. I want to ask what particular linkage you would make in order to insure that in the event our arms control goals are not fully satisfied, the performance of our systems degrades gracefully. Likewise, if we do accept arms control agreements, such as a comprehensive test ban, what should we do specifically to make sure that systems degrade as gracefully as possible?

Walter Slocombe: With respect to action under CTB, I think the chances of there being a CTB in the near term are very, very low. And I can't improve on York's list of things one would do to deal with the reliability problem if you did have one. With respect to SALT, let me answer your question in a slightly broader way. You can't expect SALT to solve problems you are not prepared to solve unilaterally. The reason, on the whole, for some of the strategic problems the United States has gotten into in the last ten years has not been the SALT I Agreement. No number of people saying it is the SALT I Agreement, or saying that we've let arms control drive our policies, makes it true. It has been an unwillingness to put sufficient resources into the right things at the right time. A SALT agreement itself will not automatically meet the crisis stability condition or the essential equivalence condition. Inevitably you will be forced to make compromises that fall short of your total objectives. U.S. superiority, a return to the period of the 1950s would be nice. It's not obtainable. You have to ask the question, does the agreement allow us to do the things we need to do in the face of the Soviet force that will exist under the agreement, with appropriate allowances for uncertainties about verification, and so on. I completely agree that you cannot responsibly sign an agreement that prevents you from doing the things you need to do to respond to the Soviet programs permitted under the agreement. We could have an argument over whether or not the SALT II Treaty meets that requirement, but it's a perfectly good guideline for a future agreement.

Michael May: I'd like to address this question to Slocombe. You said that you'd like to see the defense community quit examining alternatives again and again and you gave some views regarding the MPS system and MX. Now, the problem of defending against a Soviet attack, of providing a defense for the ICBM against the Soviet attack, is very difficult. And it is entirely likely that there isn't going to be a once-and-for-all solution, not even a single solution for the next few years. There might very well have to be a package of solutions. This is particularly true if we go toward reductions. The ability of technologists to come up with a good permanent solution is usually overrated by the other participants in the SALT process.

Do you see any prospect for reframing SALT agreements in such a way as to put the emphasis on limiting and then reducing such parameters as size of the missile, size of the reentry vehicle, and the like, and yet allow enough flexibility in the parameters to permit survivability to occur under a variety of difficult conditions? And if you do see some sort of a hope for that kind of reframing, do you think that adherence to SALT II meanwhile is a positive or a negative factor on the road to it?

Walter Slocombe: I don't think there is any prospect now of negotiating an agreement with the Soviet Union that will make the *Minuteman* survivable. We are going to have to come up with some answer to the problem ourselves. I do think that even the SALT II Treaty makes some contribution to making the process of responding to the problem easier. For reasons that you are familiar with, I think the SALT II Agreement made some contribution in that direction, particularly by permitting mobiles and by limiting the number of RVs that the Soviets can put on their ICBMs. And we ought to continue to press in the negotiations for more steps that will make the process of survivability easier and the process of attacking systems harder. That is basically the operational consequence of focusing on crisis stability. I'm not criticizing the defense community for coming up with a lot of alternatives, I'm criticizing the political leadership for not picking one. There are a variety of not terribly good, not terribly bad answers. I am criticizing the political leadership for failing to make a choice. I do think that it's important, if you're going to relate arms control to a defense policy, to know which option to defend, so that you don't try to defend everything. My experience in dealing with the negotiations showed that if we could make it clear to the Soviets that the reason we were insisting on a certain provision was that it was essential in order to carry out a program that we were absolutely going to carry out, it was an argument they could understand. The endless defense of options that nobody is really interested in, simply because they are options, is a very difficult negotiating brief for any negotiator because he has no sense of priorities. He has no sense of which options are really important to keep open, and which ones are merely conceivable.

8
ON THE PURSUIT
OF INTERNATIONAL SECURITY

SPEAKER

David Saxon
*President, Systemwide Administration, University of California**

In his 1975 book, *My Country and the World,* Andrei Sakharov expressed with stunning force and clarity the reason for symposia such as this. He wrote: "The unchecked growth of thermonuclear arsenals and the build-up toward confrontation threaten mankind with the death of civilization and physical annihilation. The elimination of that threat takes unquestionable priority over all other problems in international relations. This is why disarmament talks, which offer a ray of hope in the dark world of suicidal nuclear madness, are so important" (translated by Guy Daniels, New York: Alfred A. Knopf, 1975, p. 63).

And yet in many respects we seem further away than ever from realizing that goal. The Carter initiatives have largely come to naught. SALT II was signed, but not ratified; neither a comprehensive test ban nor a chemical and weapons treaty was concluded; other proposals were shelved after early and unpromising discussions. It would be a mistake, of course, to associate these outcomes with just the Carter administration. The whole history of attempts to control weapons proliferation, to limit nuclear testing, to reduce nuclear armaments, doesn't encourage any easy optimism.

Whether distant or close at hand, however, agreement on workable and permanent arms control measures, agreement that promises to maintain some genuine degree of balance and stability among the nuclear powers, is both urgent and indispensable. We seem to be on dead center just now, which is why this conference is especially significant

*This chapter is reprinted with the permission of the *Chronicle of Higher Education.*

and why your efforts to get us moving again are so greatly needed. I congratulate you on both counts, and wish you every success in your endeavors here.

My own interest in arms control issues, while deep and genuine, is that of a citizen, not an expert. Like so many other citizens, I feel a profound unease at the precarious balance of forces that has, so far, permitted us to avert ultimate catastrophe. And I wonder about just how stable—or unstable—that balance actually is. Like so many other citizens, I am deeply worried. And I ask myself, what can be done? Obviously we can't simply let matters take their course. Nor is it enough just to hope that by skillful crisis management we can always contrive to pull back from the brink of nuclear war. In addition to our pursuit of mechanisms for the effective control of armaments, aren't there other avenues we should be pursuing with special vigor? And I ask myself what my own institution, the University of California, should be doing, especially in light of its historical role in managing the laboratories at Los Alamos and here at Livermore.

In his famous letter of 20 October 1980, Sakharov wrote to the president of the Russian Academy of Sciences that, "I am convinced that the prevention of thermonuclear war is our most important problem and must take absolute priority over all other issues. The resolution of that problem involves politics, economics, the creation of international trust among open societies, the unconditional observance of fundamental civil and political rights, and disarmament" (*Chronicle of Human Rights in the USSR* 40, Oct.-Dec. 1980).

In other words, we need to look not only at the terrifying symptom of our problem—the continuing build-up of nuclear arsenals—but at its underlying causes as well. Those causes are painfully reflected in the deep divisions we see among the nations of the world, between East and West, in the free world. To pursue only arms control is to concentrate on the symptoms while the disease rages unchecked.

Any catalogue of the causes of the arms race would have to include such questions as the social, economic, and ideological forces that intensify competition; cultural differences and how they alter the equation; the whole ancient, tangled, discouraging complex of circumstances that work against cooperation among nations. All of these topics demand our attention because they are directly related to our chances for survival into the twenty-first century. They need to be looked at both urgently and carefully, and our knowledge of their implications deepened. It makes no difference that each has been addressed in one way or another in one forum or another. There is very little evidence, as far as I can see, that they have been considered in as interrelated and coherent a way as they need to be.

And, I would argue, it is from this perspective that the University of California, and other universities as well, have something special to offer. Universities are superbly suited to the systematic, thorough, and thoughtful examination of hard problems, particularly those problems that demand study over a span of years. The spectacular successes of academic science during World War II established beyond question the capacity of research universities to serve the national interest in technical fields. And yet I doubt that as a nation we have even begun to take advantage of similar capacities of our research universities in other domains. Four years ago I was one of a group of educators from leading private and public universities who issued a joint report on research universities and the national interest. We concluded, among other things, that international studies were a neglected area of higher education and that problem-centered research on important international issues has never received the attention it deserves.

Now, if universities in general—and the University of California in particular—have a contribution to make to our understanding of the complex and interconnecting causes of the arms race, it will only be by sticking to what they know how to do, only if they undertake work that incorporates the special skills, talents, and characteristics that universities possess.

What this means, in my view, is that universities will make their most important and lasting contributions if they concentrate on the long-term issues and problems. Universities are not the places in which to decide this year's urgent issues—the strategic desirability of the MX missile or whether the government ought to construct such a missile or whether neutron bombs are or are not useful to the defense of the West. Questions like these demand immediate answers. Similarly, there is little universities can contribute to our national response to such flare-ups as those that occurred this year in Poland and Iran and Syria. Crisis management and firefighting, the swift response and counter-response, highly sensitive and classified analyses—these are not tasks universities are cut out to do.

But universities do excel at taking the long view. There is a certain probability—fortunately, quite small—that armed conflict will break out in a given year, statistically speaking. But even if the statistical likelihood of war during a particular twelve month period is small, over time the accumulated probability becomes quite large. The probability per decade or per quarter century, in other words, is far from small.

Anything that can be done to reduce that probability as it accumulates over the decades must be done, for if we find ways to ease international tensions, to reduce whatever forces impel us toward nuclear confrontation, then we have bought the world another ten or twenty-five or fifty years in which to seek a lasting solution. Here I am not talking about technical or political breakthroughs, not about crash programs and spectacular progress; I am talking about the slow, patient, difficult steps that lead to increased understanding, about the possibilities of a gradual evolution in our attitudes, about a slow but steady accumulation of ameliorating elements over these same decades. I certainly don't intend to give the impression that nothing is being done at the University of California right now to strengthen our understanding of the conditions for international harmony and the control of conflict among nations— quite the contrary. Besides the work being done in the social sciences, in public health, in agriculture, to name a few relevant areas, we also have a number of research centers devoted to the study of broad international questions, among them the Center for International Studies at Berkeley. What I have begun to explore with our faculty, however, is the possibility of a continuing and more deliberately organized effort of the sort I have just described within the university. I intend this effort to comprise a very broad set of issues, and an equally broad set of activities. As some of you may know, some months ago I appointed a committee chaired by Professor York to begin thinking and planning for a conference to be held next year on various questions relating to international security and arms control. [The conference was held from 30 March to 1 April 1982.] But my intentions are much more ambitious than just to hold a conference, important as that is. I would like to see more of the talent and knowledge available within this university— in politics, in economics, in geography, in history, in any disciplines that have a contribution to make—devoted to these long-term matters. Therefore, I have asked the committee to look beyond next year's conference and to consider just what those issues should be, and just how we should organize ourselves to pursue them.

There are so many questions that need to be answered that the biggest problem may be deciding where to begin. What are the advantages and disadvantages, for example, of a renewed effort by the United States to foster international, cultural, and intellectual exchange; and to do so, perhaps, on a truly massive scale? Are national policies, ours and others, so different that the differences cannot be bridged? Are attitudes so hardened as to be beyond alteration? In the short term, maybe yes; but in the long term, perhaps no. What is the role of social and geographical and economic factors and to what extent are they mutually reinforcing? Is the polemical level of discussion between us and the Soviets too high, too intense? Or just the reverse? What are the implications for our relationships over the long term?

I don't know whether these, or an entirely different set of questions, should be pursued. I do know that it is important to make a deeply serious effort to do what we can. History provides examples of how different academic communities responded, or failed to respond, to the grave problems and tensions of the day. Some aggravated, intentionally or not, the conflicts implicit in their society. Others withdrew entirely and left society to its fate. Still others helped in the search for solutions. America's research universities, with their tradition of involvement with society, have overwhelmingly followed this last pattern. One example of that tradition of public service is the University of California's management of the laboratories at Los Alamos and here at Livermore, whose technical excellence is indispensable to the security of the United States. I intend that we render another and complementary service at the university by exploring the problems and tensions that threaten harmonious relations not only between the United States and the Soviet Union but among all nations.

The noted economist John Kenneth Galbraith has eloquently summed up our situation: "If we fail in the control of the nuclear arms race, all of the other matters we debate in these days will be without meaning. There will be no question of civil rights, for there will be no one to enjoy them. They will be gone. Let us agree that we will tell all of our countrymen, all of our allies, all human beings, that we will work to have an end to this nuclear horror that now hovers as a cloud over all humankind" (*A Life in Our Times,* Boston: Houghton Mifflin, 1981, p. 537).

I don't believe that ending the arms race and securing international stability are simple problems with simple answers. They are obviously formidable in their difficulty. But, to end, as I began, with the words of Andrei Sakharov, I am convinced, as he is, that "there is a need to create ideals even when you can't see any route by which to achieve them, because if there are no ideals, then there can be no hope, and then one would be completely in the dark . . ." (*Sakharov Speaks,* London: Collins & Harvill, 1974, p. 73).

In seeking the ideal of a peaceful world we have an important ally within our universities—the power of the open and inquiring intelligence to clarify, to interpret, to illuminate. It has served us well in the past and holds out one of our best hopes for the future.

GLOSSARY

ABM	anti-ballistic missile
ACDA	Arms Control and Disarmament Agency
ASAT	antisatellite
B-36	former U.S. bomber
B-52, B-1	U.S. heavy bombers
Backfire	Soviet bomber
Bear	Soviet bomber
Bison	Soviet bomber
BMD	ballistic missile defense
C^3	command, control, and communication
CAS	Committee on Assurances of Supply
CIA	Central Intelligence Agency
CTB	comprehensive test ban
DSP	defense support program, early warning satellite
FBS	forward-based systems
F-15	U.S. fighter aircraft
F-111, FB-111	U.S. fighter bombers
FRG	Federal Republic of Germany
GLCM	ground launched cruise missile
GPS	Satellite Global Positioning System
"Gray-area" systems	intermediate range nuclear delivery systems
IAEA	International Atomic Energy Agency
ICBM	intercontinental ballistic missile
IISS	International Institute of Strategic Studies (London)
INF	intermediate-range nuclear force negotiations
INFCE	International Nuclear Fuel Cycle Evaluation
JCS	Joint Chiefs of Staff
kiloton	nuclear yield measured in chemical TNT kilotons equivalent
LANL	Los Alamos National Laboratory
LBL	Lawrence Berkeley Laboratory
LLNL	Lawrence Livermore National Laboratory
LRTNF	long-range theater nuclear forces

MBFR	mutual balanced force reduction
MIRV	multiple independently targetable re-entry vehicles
MAP	multiple aim point
MC-14/3	NATO document of 1967 outlining nuclear response to Soviet breakthroughs
MLF	multi-lateral nuclear force
MPS	multiple protective structures (shelters)
MX	missile experimental, U.S. ICBM under development
NASA	National Aeronautics and Space Administration
NATO	North Atlantic Treaty Organization
NNPA	Nuclear Non-Proliferation Act, enacted 1978
NPT	Treaty on the Non-Proliferation of Nuclear Weapons
NSC	National Security Council
NTM	national technical means
OSD	Office of the Secretary of Defense
Polaris	U.S. nuclear strategic submarine
PRC	People's Republic of China
R&D	research and development
RV	Re-entry Vehicle
SACEUR	Supreme Allied Commander, Europe
SALT I & II	strategic arms limitation treaties
SCC	Standing Consultative Commission to the ABM Treaty
Situation Q	stable relationship between United States and USSR
SLBM	submarine launched ballistic missile
SPD	Social Democratic Party of Germany (West German)
SSBN	nuclear-powered strategic ballistic missile submarine
SS-11, SS-12	Soviet missiles
SS-16	Soviet land-mobile ICBM (not deployed)
SS-18	Soviet heavy ICBM
SS-20	Soviet intermediate-range ballistic missile (land-mobile)
TTBT	Threshold Test Ban Treaty

ABOUT THE DISCUSSANTS

David Aaron: Oppenheimer & Co., Inc., New York; Deputy Assistant to the President for National Security, 1977–1981.

Kathleen Bailey: International Ventures Consultants, San Francisco; Former Associate Z-Division Leader, Lawrence Livermore National Laboratory.

William Barletta: Staff Physicist, Lawrence Livermore National Laboratory.

William Beecher: *The Boston Globe.*

Barry Blechman: Carnegie Endowment for International Peace; Assistant Director, Arms Control and Disarmament Agency, 1977–1979.

Avis Bohlen: European Bureau, Department of State.

Robert Buchheim: U.S. Commissioner, Standing Consultation Commission, 1977–1981; former head, U.S. Delegation to U.S.-USSR Antisatellite negotiations.

Ludger Buerstedde: Embassy of the Federal Republic of Germany, Washington, D.C.

Robert Coffin: Lt. Gen. (Ret.), Carmel, California.

Tom Comstock: Political Science Department, University of California, Berkeley.

Jeffrey Cooper: Jeffrey Cooper Associates, McLean, Virginia.

Ralph Earle II: Director, Arms Control and Disarmament Agency, 1980–1981; member SALT delegation, 1973–1979.

Phillip Farley: Senior Research Fellow, Arms Control and Disarmament Program, Stanford University; Deputy Director, Arms Control and Disarmament Agency, 1969–1973.

Ralph Goldman: Political Science Department, San Francisco State University.

Donald Hafner: Associate Professor, Political Science Department, Boston College.

Charles Henkin: IBM, Roslynn, Virginia.

Michael Higgins: Science Applications, La Jolla, California.

Francis Hoeber: Hoeber Corp., Arlington, Virginia.

Van Hudson:	Vice-President, Jaycor, San Diego, California.
Michael Intriligator:	Department of Economics and Center for International and Strategic Affairs (CISA), University of California, Los Angeles.
Herman Kahn:	Chairman and Director, Hudson Institute.
Spurgeon Keeny, Jr.:	Scholar in Residence, National Academy of Science; Deputy Director, Arms Control and Disarmament Agency, 1977–1981.
Donald Kerr:	Director, Los Alamos National Laboratory.
Roman Kolkowitz:	Director, Political Science/Center for International and Strategic Affairs, University of California, Los Angeles.
Dalimil Kybal:	Federal Emergency Management Agency.
Pierre Lellouche:	Institut Francais des Relations Internationales.
Charles McDonald:	R&D Associates, Los Angeles.
Joel McKean:	Col., Air Force Strategic Arms Limitation Office, The Pentagon.
James Malone:	Assistant Secretary of State for Oceans and International Environmental and Scientific Affairs, Department of State.
Michael May:	Associate Director, Lawrence Livermore National Laboratory; member SALT Delegation, 1974–1976.
Paul Nitze:	Head, U.S. Delegation to Intermediate-Range Nuclear Force Negotiations; former Policy Chairman, Committee on Present Danger.
Joseph Nye:	Professor of Government, Harvard University; Deputy to Under Secretary for Security Assistance, Science and Technology, Department of State, 1977–1978.
Ray Orbach:	Department of Physics and CISA, University of California, Los Angeles.
William Potter:	Department of Political Science and CISA, University of California, Los Angeles.
Gough Reinhardt:	Staff Physicist, Lawrence Livermore National Laboratory.
Harold Rosenbaum:	Rosenbaum Associates, Burlington, Massachusetts.
Leonard Ross:	Law School, University of California, Berkeley.
Henry Rowen:	Graduate School of Business, Stanford University.
Jack Ruina:	Center for International Studies, Massachusetts Institute of Technology.
Robert Scheer:	*Los Angeles Times.*
Mark Schneider:	Policy Planning Staff, Department of State.
George Schneiter:	Center for Naval Analysis, Washington; former Deputy Director, SALT Task Force, Department of Defense.
Charles Schwartz:	Department of Physics, University of California, Berkeley.
Brent Scowcroft:	International Six, Inc., Washington, D.C.; Assistant to the President for National Security Affairs, 1975–1977.

Paul Seabury:	Department of Political Science, University of California, Berkeley.
Walter Slocombe:	Caplin and Drysdale, Washington, D.C.; Deputy Under Secretary of Defense (Policy Planning), 1977–1981.
Joseph Taylor:	Assistant Associate Director, Arms Control, Lawrence Livermore National Laboratory.
Samuel Thompson:	International Security Affairs, Department of Energy.
Donald Vogt:	Brig. Gen., USAF, Military Assistant, Office of Under Secretary of Defense.
Richard Wagner:	Assistant to the Secretary of Defense for Atomic Energy; former Associate Director for Nuclear Tests, Lawrence Livermore National Laboratory.
Charles Wolf:	Rand Corporation.
John Woodworth:	Office of the Assistant Secretary of Defense (International Security Policy).
Herbert York:	Professor of Physics, University of California at San Diego; U.S. Ambassador to Comprehensive Test Ban Negotiations, 1979–1981.
Peter Zimmerman:	Department of Physics, Louisiana State University.

INDEX